Pictures of Girlhood

Pictures of Girlhood

Modern Female Adolescence on Film

SARAH HENTGES

McFarland & Company, Inc., Publishers
Jefferson, North Carolina, and London

LIBRARY OF CONGRESS CATALOGUING-IN-PUBLICATION DATA

Hentges, Sarah, 1976–
    Pictures of girlhood : modern female adolescence on film /
Sarah Hentges.
        p.   cm.
    Includes bibliographical references and index.

    ISBN 0-7864-2402-8 (softcover : 50# alkaline paper) ∞

    1. Girls in motion pictures.   2. Teenage girls in motion
pictures.   I. Title.
    PN1995.9.G57H36   2006
    791.43'652352—dc22   2005025353

British Library cataloguing data are available

Cover photograph ©2005 PhotoSpin

Manufactured in the United States of America

McFarland & Company, Inc., Publishers
  Box 611, Jefferson, North Carolina 28640
    www.mcfarlandpub.com

ACKNOWLEDGMENTS

As a naive graduate student I began working on a project about sex and sexuality in teen films that has become the subject of this book. This project began as a paper for a teen films class that I took with Jon Lewis at Oregon State University and became the subject of my master's thesis. I have continued to work on this manuscript off and on before and during my Ph.D. work at Washington State University, at times driven by outside interest, and at other times by my own passion and interest in the topic. Thus, it is fitting that this subject has grown and matured as I have. It has taken on new dimensions and new depths, and it has grown in directions I could not have imagined when I began. Through my personal and professional growth, this book has finally found its form.

As a teen I always felt like an adult, and as an adult (so far) I often feel like I am still a teen. This feeling is, perhaps, a result of the shift from thinking I know, or can know, everything to knowing that I'll always have more to learn. Thus, my graduate studies and teaching at Oregon State and Washington State have been key to my development as a writer and scholar and activist and teacher, making this experience key to the evolution and completion of this book. And there have been many people who have helped me to make this work possible. I'd like to thank David Boxer for giving me my first teaching opportunity at Humboldt State University and setting me on the path I'm on today. I'd also like to thank my teachers and advisors at OSU—Jon Lewis, without whom this project would never have been done; Linc Kesler, who inspired some of my first interest in social and cultural revolution; and Sheila Cordray, who encouraged me and kept me realistic. At WSU, my dissertation committee members—Rory Ong, T.V. Reed, David Leonard, and Mary Bloodsworth-Lugo—have been key in the development of my work along with many other wonderful professors. I'd also like to thank my women's studies intern, Kim D'Andrade, who formatted and compiled the filmography, and my brother, Zack Weingartner, who tracked down photos, videos, and DVDs, and did all sorts of other little things to help me finish this book. And thanks also go to Bria Blakey, Alicia Scott, and others whose work helped me to complete this project.

But there are many more people who have helped to make this book a reality from those who fostered and supported my interest in writing to those who have inspired me. Without the interest and persistence of my publisher, this project would be in a box somewhere. My parents have always compelled me to do my best and have fostered my talents from an early age while also pushing me to try a variety of pursuits and activities to make me a more well-rounded person. My late grandmother has always inspired me and, sadly, she did not live to see the fruits of this inspiration, though I continue to think of her often. My high school teachers and mentors Linda Meyer and Theresa Kemper not only encouraged me daily to follow my dreams and ambitions but also instilled in me the belief that these dreams and ambitions are fluid—that they, and I, will change. I still remember the excitement on Mrs. Meyer's face when she pulled me out of history class to tell me that I had won an award for one of my poems. This was only part of the passion she passed on to me and many of her students. And I'd like to thank Mrs. Kemper for her practical critical nature and her patience and friendship, and for teaching me, perhaps inadvertently, that the status quo is not all its cracked up to be—that there is space for negotiation.

And, finally, my thanks to all the women in my life who have been, and continue to be, an inspiration to me—Ruth Angus, Nancy Weingartner, Marge Sevier, Jill Hogue, Stacy Moore, Lauren Cooper, Becca Stone Weingartner, Josie Weingartner, Debbie Hentges Maria Van Dyke, Sasja Hulsmans-Catania, Beth Barnett, Erin Moore, Loren Redwood, Kris Kellijian, Serena Peters, Carmen Lugo-Lugo, Cheris Brewer, Kristal Moore, Jocelyn Pacleb, Mary Bloodsworth-Lugo Ayano Ginoza, Natasha Caldwell, Michelle Bunderson, Yolanda Flores-Niemann and many other friends, colleagues, and (especially) students I haven't named. And, of course, to Lee, who watched more teen films than he ever wanted to, who has grown with me and supported me, and who lets me be whoever I want to be and loves me for who I am, unconditionally.

TABLE OF CONTENTS

Preface

When I was, officially, a girl, in the 1980s and early 1990s, the popular culture I consumed rarely focused on girls. Instead, I found myself automatically identifying with the main character regardless of that character's gender. But even as I found powerful stories through male characters, I was also well aware of the spaces that the girls occupied. I would play characters like Princess Leia in *Star Wars*, or Lynda Carter's Wonder Woman—"strong" but also sexualized female characters. In fact, I would seek out female protagonists, even when they were dumbed down or hypersexualized. Still, as a girl, I came to expect very little of myself because the popular culture where I saw myself reflected, directly or indirectly, expected very little from me, and reflected little of me. If I had a boyfriend or husband, some kids, maybe a job and a house, then I had exactly what any woman should want.

But the desires for these things, and for nothing more, clearly reflect the limited and outdated ideals of the American mainstream. And the mainstream adapts new versions of the same old stories and new versions of desire. It wasn't until I began to discover popular culture at the edge of the mainstream that I was better able to negotiate the lessons that popular culture had taught me. In all these ways, particularly the last, pop culture has been crucial in my "coming of age" at various stages in my life. And it continues to be, not just for me.

For many of us, mainstream U.S. popular culture is the only kind we know. And it very much affects our lives. The films, TV, music, magazines, and other popular culture forms most readily available are all produced by a few corporations that are invested not only in the market, but also in the ideas that get produced and marketed. These ideas limit girls to a narrow range of plot lines, characters, products, and activities. Further, African American, Native American, Asian American, and Latina girls, as well as queer, working-class, and other marginalized girls, have been

1

virtually erased. And when they do appear they are often whitewashed. Further, girls have always been positioned in relationship to the boys, often as objects. And we have always been forced to consume stereotypical versions of ourselves on television, in movies, in advertisements, in magazines, in music, and in our educations. Further, we have always been given the idea that we should settle down and have a family, but most of all that we should keep our mouths shut and be happy with what we have. And again, these expectations are even harsher for girls of color, and girls who are poor or queer. These are things that I began to notice more and more as I have "come of age," as I have made the transition from the space occupied by girls to that occupied by women. Both of these spaces, especially within mainstream culture and popular culture, are ruled by the formal and informal demands of mainstream America. Both of these spaces are dominated by the interests and desires of (rich, white) men. And both of these spaces require girls and women to find their own alternatives within and without the mainstream.

This is, of course, a simplified explanation of my early relationship to popular culture and of the spaces that girls and women occupy. Many other factors influenced me (positively and negatively) as I was growing up, and these factors vary greatly among girls and women within the United States, especially as we converge and diverge along lines of race, class, gender, sexuality, religion, and geographic location, for instance. Nevertheless, the influence of popular culture looms large in most lives, making it a worthy subject of study. And popular culture has power—tapped and untapped—and potential.

Many analyses of popular culture make simplistic assumptions about the ways in which girls and women watch and read it. This is especially true of some early works, like *Reviving Ophelia*. But many women have done work that challenges these simplistic notions of girls' and women's relationships to popular culture as well as our place within U.S. culture more generally. This book adds to a rich and growing body of work surrounding girls, girls' culture, and popular culture including *Growing Up Girls: Popular Culture and the Construction of Identity*, edited by Sharon R. Mazzarella and Norma Odom Pecora; *Girls: Feminine Adolescence in Popular Culture and Cultural Theory*, written by Catherine Driscoll; and a variety of other works in and out of academia, many of which are discussed in these two books (or which can be found in the bibliography section at the end of this book).

But this book is different from previous studies in a variety of ways. First of all, in this book I am looking at a specific genre of films that I am defining as teen coming-of-age films about girls and designating as "girls' film." This definition brings together a body of films that cuts across the teen film genre as well as a number of subgenres like makeover films, horror films, and family films. I designate these films as girls' film in order to empower girls and women by highlighting a specific body of films that speak directly to our experiences of growing up in the U.S. The films in this study are characterized by their focus on a lead female character and her coming of age. I am not looking for "good" or "bad" elements of these films, or "positive" and negative"; instead, I am looking for the ways in which the girls in these films negotiate the narrow expectations that mainstream U.S. culture dictates. But I am also looking at the ways in which this genre speaks to girls' similar and disparate experiences of growing up in the U.S. These expectations and experiences are similar throughout all forms of mainstream popular culture, but I have chosen to look at films as a kind of case study for this phenomenon. These films speak to and about American girls' adolescent experiences.

In looking at this genre I am aiming for breadth as well as depth. Some films are discussed in great detail while others are mentioned in passing. I highlight the themes of sex and romance, sexuality, race and class, power and empowerment, and coming of age, as found in the stories told and retold in films about girls and women (and a few that include us in narratives focused on boys and men).

In exploring the story of girls in the United States as it has been told in girls' film, I also try to look at what is left out of the story. This is the story that provides us with a history and a terrain. But most of all it provides us with a variety of cultural reference points regarding our individual and collective coming of age. Thus, I look at the ways in which mainstream and independent films challenge common ideas about girls and coming of age. This challenge is what attracts me to these films, and the stories within serve as entertainment, guidance, retreat, and strength to many girls and women at various stages in our lives. This book also acts as a resource, bringing together a body of films for contemplation, discussion, and recreation. It is my hope that this book further opens spaces for the negotiation of mainstream popular culture as well as the production of popular culture like films, TV shows, and music that truly empower girls and women.

Ultimately, the enjoyment that these films bring to me, and to other viewers, is part of what makes them a compelling space to consider the issues that emerge again and again—questions about what it means to come of age in the U.S. From these films we can weave together an alternative coming-of-age story, one which makes this process more meaningful and more powerful.

PART I

AMERICAN ADOLESCENCE: GIRLS' MAINSTREAM TERRAIN

ONE

RACE, CLASS, GENDER, SEXUALITY AND CITIZENSHIP
A Possessive Investment in the Mainstream

The distinction between mainstream films and alternative or independent films is not always easy to make, especially in the teen film genre. Unlike TV, whose only "alternative" to the five corporations that own virtually all U.S. TV stations is PBS, film has some room for narratives not totally manufactured by the formal powers of the industry. These films are not always as available as mainstream films because they are advertised less and distributed less widely. Thus, in addition to visibility, one characteristic that defines mainstream films is their profit-making form and function. A film will not be produced by a major corporation unless it is guaranteed to make money. These films rely upon star power and predictable plots, and not only are they aggressively marketed, but they outlive their theatrical release on video, DVD, TV (often highly edited), and sometimes TV spinoffs like *Clueless* and *Buffy the Vampire Slayer*.

Many films are made only for the money they will bring in, but some film productions are far enough removed from the central power that this power is diluted. Films like *Belly Fruit* are made independent from mainstream powers and thus may have limited exposure and distribution, which can make it particularly difficult to put the films in front of an audience, especially an audience of teens. For instance, in a conversation with Northwest independent filmmaker Paul Ahrens, he told me that it was difficult to find an advertising forum to attract local teens to his film since the most available source of advertising—the newspaper—was more likely to

7

reach their parents. If independent films hope to make any money or achieve any fame or exposure on a widespread scale, they have to have a powerful benefactor, a distributor, a popular subject, and a "lucky" break. And the potential monetary returns are always a key factor in a film's production and distribution, which is why, perhaps, we see so many sequels to films that have been successful, such as the *American Pie* series, *Bring It On Again, Cruel Intentions II, The Princess Diaries II*, and *Scream II and III*, though the sequels rarely do as well as the originals. In addition to sequels, many films have the same basic plot line, stars, and jokes. For instance, countless teen films begin with the introduction of the high school cliques, which seem to become more and more narrow, and many characters are made over, going from socially awkward to fashionably hip. Further, stars like Julia Stiles and Kirsten Dunst, themes like romance and love, and characters like "mean girls" and "good girls" appear in several films in this study. I trace these themes in order to help us to see the contours and departures of teen films about girls, a "girls' film" genre that primarily grows out of teen films.

The beginnings of the teen film genre represent a shift from teens playing out the dramas of their particular generation as in *Rebel Without a Cause*, or previous generations as in *Splendor in the Grass*, to teens as consumers and initiators of culture as in *Mean Girls* and *What a Girl Wants*, for instance. And this shift has burgeoned into a genre intimately connected to consumption—consumption of ideas and images, as well as a variety of material products, a reflection of the times as well. Ford and Mitchell, authors of *The Makeover in Movies*, argue that it took a non-teen film, *Titanic*, to show producers the potential of targeting teens, and 1999 was deemed the year of the teen film. The last decade has seen a tremendous output of films directed at general teen audiences, as well as a variety of romantic films, like *Titanic*, aimed at the female teen constituency, though these films reach beyond the teen demographic. Thus, the business world has been more than happy to oblige the "experimentation" of the teen years; after all, "trying on new fashions, music, TV shows and movies, products, ideas and attitudes, is what being a teen is all about" (Palladino), according to one executive quoted in *Business Week*. While the products manufactured for youth have produced more fashions, music, TV shows, movies, and products, they have not created more opportunities and alternatives, especially in the realm of ideas. The experimentation that seems "safe" is really only a superficial and inadequate placebo; it is safe only because this experimentation does not truly challenge the values of adult culture. Instead, this experience sustains the values of a culture that is most concerned with its own perpetuation, second only to its bottom line. This superficial, predictable, invested culture is the culture from which the genre of girls' film emerges. But however superficial, girls' film as a genre, and the girls involved in production and consumption, make girls' film a truly empowering means toward coming of age. Before exploring this genre further, it is important to consider the difference between "girl power" as a function of the mainstream, and girls' empowerment as negotiated in and out of the mainstream.

From Girl Power to Empowerment

In "The Secret Life of Teenage Girls," a 2000 article in *Rolling Stone*, Jancee Dunn describes this "secret life," but what she uncovers is hardly a secret since it is easily supported through a variety of material (and materialistic) evidence. The article includes interviews from several different girls, and Dunn recognizes the same "noncommittal, nonconfrontational" voices that adolescent psychologists and sociologists have recognized as a condition of adolescence. But Dunn claims that girls, "for the first time in American history, wield tangible power in dictating popular culture, and they are confident consumers, secure in their opinions." She describes each of these girls according to what she buys, owns, and eats—all of which reveal what kind of consumer she is. The incongruence between confident consumers and confident girls shows what kind of power is important to mainstream culture. It is not what a girl says that makes her powerful; it is what she buys. And it is the latter that Dunn attributes to "secure opinions." In other words, girls do not have confidence in themselves as much as they have confidence in the products they consume, and in the eyes of mainstream culture, these products, and not the confidence, determine the girl. Girls without consumer power, girls without extra spending money, by default, are not considered at all, unless they are portrayed as the outcast, the loser, or the slut. Does this mean that they are not secure in their opinions? It certainly means that they, and their interests, are not represented positively in popular culture, if they are represented at all.

Thus, what consumer "girl power" fails to take into account is girls' lack of power in other areas of their lives. They may appear to dictate pop culture, but with corporations involved, the pop culture girls dictate is repackaged and sold to them; thus, they cannot dictate the circumstances that surround their coming of age (which is part of what the riot grrrl subculture, for instance, offers) any more than they can truly decide for themselves not what products they want or do not want to consume but not to be consumed themselves. The age of "girlpower" makes girls powerful, but only in a way that legitimates the dominant consumer culture. Culture has left girls searching for these solutions in products and in manufactured role models, as well as the corporate-created myths that surround them. But more importantly, this formula only works for girls with the money, or other cultural capital, to spend. A girl with no money, a girl who is portrayed negatively across popular culture texts, has to turn to other means of survival, let alone the luxury of "girl power."

A girl can, as Dunn suggests, "safely reinvent [her]self with new shoes and lipstick," but she has changed only her surface, not her interior; she has adopted old alternatives, but she has not created new ones. Shoes and lipstick may help girls "safely reinvent," but they do not help girls make sense of themselves or the culture that confines them. When new shoes and lipstick aren't enough, what are girls to do? And when girls become the 40-year-olds with diluted "girl power" that Dunn describes and still lack a sense of self, voice, confidence and identity, where are they to find these things? In another product or another target market? Clearly a new vision of girl power and empowerment is needed. And this attempts to provide an alternative vision of girls' power and empowerment, their and our coming of age, and their and our future potential. What we do with this vision, this handbook, this collective story, this representation of the range of coming-of-age stories available in U.S. film, is what is important.

It is often assumed that popular culture is a shallow substitute for more meaningful rites of passage. However, it is my contention in this book that popular culture absolutely acts as a set of myths and markers for adolescence, that film, when considered as a mass media vehicle of cultural meaning, is, at least potentially, a powerful determinant of social, cultural, and economic realities. Looking at this body of films, and considering its uneven, shifting terrain as well as its trends and tropes, it is clear that adolescence is far more complicated than it appears in the mainstream. But it is also clear that girls have unique spaces for contesting this terrain in life and in film, in and out of the mainstream. It is my hope that in better understanding this terrain we might better understand ourselves, and in better understanding ourselves we might also better understand how we can work to change the structures that define and confine us, not only for ourselves but for others as well. For significant social and cultural change to happen, many kinds of change, on many different levels and in many different forms, must happen, but many of these changes are well within our reaches as individuals and collectively. At the very least, this book is a map of where the girls have been. Where we're going is of much more importance. It is this coming of age, composed of myriad strands, markers, struggles, understandings, and misunderstandings, that this book begins. It is up to the readers and viewers and potentially the producers to continue to write, share, and tell this story.

Girls' Film, an Introduction

While there are many sites from which to consider girls' culture, I focus on film because of its richness—its legacy and its possibility. And because all of these films are tied together by the common theme of coming of age, they are different from other film genres as well as from other girls' cultures. While the division of this genre into mainstream and independent is largely arbitrary, it is also an important dividing line for considering the conventions and paradigms that determine the genre of coming-of-age films. By looking at the independent films, it is easier to see what the mainstream includes and what it often leaves out, revealing a dearth of possibilities in the mainstream; the possibilities portrayed in independent films, by contrast, are many and varied. Thus, the division between mainstream and independent is not simply an economic one, but more often an ideological distinction, particularly as I'll use it here. Further, because all of the films discussed in this book are available in video stores, they are all accessible through mainstream media channels, which means that all of these films have to balance mainstream conventions to some extent. Thus, while it is somewhat easy to outline the differences between mainstream films and independent films, it is more difficult to categorize a film on one side of this divide or the other. Most films fit somewhere in between based on the film's multiple themes, messages, morals, conventions, and negotiations. The categorization itself is not as important as an analysis of the recurring themes in these films and the ways in which they are negotiated similarly and differently in mainstream and independent films. This analysis reveals much not only about girls' film and the more general genre of teen films, but also about what it means to come of age in U.S. culture. While this is ultimately the task of this book, an overview shows some of the variety and complexity in girls' films and illustrates some of the reasons why this genre speaks so well to U.S. girls' and women's experiences.

In general, mainstream films offer roles that are based upon stereotypes and polarizations, even if the characters challenge these conceptualizations. Protagonists are always pretty and likeable even if they have some attitude, like Daphne in *What a Girl Wants*, whose attitude is portrayed as part of what makes her unique. Considering the rather mild protagonists of similar films like *The Princess Diaries*, *A Cinderella Story*, and *Raise Your Voice*, Daphne's attitude, at least for protagonists in the mainstream of girls' film, is unique. Further, roles and relationships among girls are often split between the good girl and the bad girl, or the virgin and the whore. This is taken to an extreme in some films like *Cruel Intentions*, *Jawbreaker*, *Wild Things*, and *Mean Girls*, films with characterizations that are reinforced by recent books like Simmons' *Odd Girl Out: The Hidden Culture of Aggression in Girls* and Wiseman's *Queen Bees and Wannabes: Helping Your Daughter Survive Cliques, Gossip, Boyfriends, and Other Realities of Adolescence*. These books have exposed the cruelty and violence that girls inflict upon one another, making it clear that it isn't only the boys who behave violently. But while neither of these books is meant to be a scientific study, mainstream media seems totally unable to make such a distinction. And so yet another stereotype is born. And this stereotype appears in films about girls as well as films that focus on a male protagonist or protagonists, like *American Pie* or *Saving Silverman*. In some films, like *The Opposite of Sex*, this stereotype is contested, while in others, like *Jawbreaker*, it is cemented. Regardless, a certain stock of roles are available in teen films and girls have a more limited and limiting repertoire across teen films as well as girls' film.

Girls are sometimes allowed more complex characters and characteristics in mainstream teen films that focus around a boy as the protagonist or boys as the protagonists. But they are also almost always portrayed as eye candy, as competition for the guys, as property, as territory to be conquered, or as fantasies. As I will show in my discussion of *American Pie*, even when girls are allowed to be empowered (often sexually) there are other girls present to provide the most mundane male fantasy tropes— the European sexpot, the horny nerd, the Catholic school girl, or the hot lesbians next door who want to be watched. But these stereotypes of girls as eye candy and arm warmers also appear in films about girls. For instance, most of the popular female characters in a variety of films are hell-bent on having not just a boyfriend, but the most popular boy as boyfriend, like Taylor in *She's All That*, Lana in *The Princess Diaries*, or even, to an extent, Cher in *Clueless*, who claims that high school boys are "like dogs." And in films like *Wild Things* the girls play right into male fantasies by sleeping with their teacher—both individually and together. These girls, especially when they are not easily controlled by men, are often portrayed as "bad girls" and are often juxtaposed with a "good girl" role. For instance, in *Jawbreaker* Liz Purr is "the cat's meow" while Courtney is into "kink," and in *Mean Girls*, Cady is innocent and naïve while

Regina George is cruel and manipulative. Not only does Regina steal Cady's love interest, but she cheats on him with another guy, which really makes her the "slut." Some girls' films, like *Sugar and Spice*, try to make bad girls out of one of the archetypal "good girls"—the cheerleader. And the tagline, "Get ready to cheer for the bad girls," invites the audience to participate in this false dichotomy. Even in the mildest of girls' films, the mean girl appears—for instance, in *The Princess Diaries*, *Raise Your Voice*, and *What a Girl Wants*.

In juxtaposition with the "bad girl" or the "slut," romance is a big theme that appears in almost every film to a degree, and in most mainstream teen films as well. This trope reveals the influence of dominant culture since mainstream teen films almost always involve a heterosexual plot line (often without sex). When these plot lines do include sex, it is most often the boy actively pursuing sex, with or without a relationship, and in mainstream girls' film, only the "sluts" like Regina George and Kathryn in *Cruel Intentions* have sex (before their subsequent downfall). Since sex, when it takes place in these films, is almost always off-screen or post-narrative, and sex is almost always romantically portrayed in mainstream teen films about girls, "love conquers all" is often one of the ending morals of the story. These films almost always have happy, norm-enforcing endings, even when some of these norms are also challenged like in the marginally mainstream film *But I'm a Cheerleader*. Films like *Clueless* and *10 Things I Hate About You* always end with a happy couple who will have marriage (and sex is vaguely implied here) in the postnarrative future. These mainstream films are often shown on television, like *Clueless*, *10 Things I Hate About You*, *I Know What You Did Last Summer*, and *She's All That*; and some of the more controversial mainstream films, like *Cruel Intentions*, are also shown, highly edited, of course.

Most of the characters in these films are upper class, white teens and are almost always popular stars. Teens of color, gay teens, and teens of lower socioeconomic or working-class backgrounds rarely appear. When they do appear they are often tokens, stereotypes, bit characters, or background images. Or, these teens are quietly or desperately trying to fit in with the expectations of the dominant class. Or, these issues aren't touched or are barely touched. For instance, in *She's All That*, a film whose protagonist, Laney, is an outsider for a number of reasons, including her social class. Her status in the film has more to do with her appearance (baggy overalls and big glasses) and her interests (art) than the fact that her father is a "pool man." Also in many mainstream films, the teens of color pepper the background, but few actually have any lines. Sometimes a character of a nonwhite racial group appears, but usually this character is "white" in every way but skin color. Such "multicultural" inclusions are found throughout mainstream teen films like Bianca's best friend in *10 Things I Hate About You*, and Cher's best friend, Dionne, and her boyfriend in *Clueless*. Or, sometimes these inclusions provide plot lines for the white characters to follow like in *Bring It On* where the East Compton Clovers, a more talented but less privileged cheerleading squad, provide competition and a chance to showcase respect and equality across racial groups. Or, in *The Craft*, one of the witches is a light-skinned African American and has to deal with the blatant racism of one of the popular (blonde) girls at school who outright says that she "just [doesn't] like Negroids." In this case Rochelle is fighting against the only form of racism ever really dealt with in teen or girls' films: overt, ignorant racism. But most often teens of color are simply absent, and whiteness is reinscribed as the norm, particularly in girls' film, which lacks the mainstream equivalents of films that attempt to shatter stereotypes like *Antwone Fisher*, *Do the Right Thing*, *Drumline* or *Harold and Kumar Go to White Castle*, or even the independent equivalent of films like *Better Luck Tomorrow*, which centers the narrative around Asian teens (and includes only one girl, a cheerleader) and especially *Smoke Signals*, a film that deals with two Native American boys' coming of age.

In mainstream films, girls are sometimes portrayed in powerful or empowering roles, but their power is also often qualified in important ways. Most of the protagonists end up conforming to the dominant culture's expectations in some way, and many often end up sacrificing their individuality for conformity or for love. These protagonists often end up in what appears to be an empowered position, but this empowerment comes at some other cost. For instance, in *Clueless*, Cher grows and changes but does so without having to make any real or hard sacrifices. She takes up charity work and realizes that she's been "clueless," but her father's money and the support network that comes along with this are still firmly in place. And in *But I'm a Cheerleader*, Megan is able to openly embrace her homosexuality, but only within the model of a heterosexual couple. Thus, these films can be a mixture of power and autonomy with conformity and compromise. This doesn't necessarily mean that films that fit these criteria are not useful for this study, or for the girls and women who watch them. Because interpretation is always subjective, the most empowering characters can fall short for some viewers, and the protagonists that fall short for some inspire others. However, the weaknesses of mainstream teen and girls' films can, perhaps, be most recognized when compared to the characteristics that define the independent, or less-well-known girls' films in this study.

Independent girls' films often deal with more complicated issues than mainstream films, or deal with the same issues and themes, like romance and love, pregnancy, or drug abuse, in different ways. Thus, girls often confront stereotypes and victimhood, often in unconventional plots. For instance, while sexual harassment is a joke in *Clueless*, it has much more serious implications in films like *Foxfire* and *Girls Town*. And while girls like Courtney in *Jawbreaker* are considered sluts and can even be ostracized and laughed off the stage, her comic demise is much less to endure than Brenda's daily punishments in *Whatever*. And, finally, while Megan can find true love and a happy ending in *But I'm a Cheerleader*, the same ending is not possible for Victoria and Polly in *Lost and Delirious*, and especially not for Brandon Teena in *Boys Don't Cry*.

The characters and actors in these films are more diverse than they are in mainstream films. The protagonists are more often less-well-known actors and are more diverse in terms of race, class, gender, and sexual orientation. However, largely because of the whitewashed nature of popular culture generally, and teen films specifically, this is not always the case. For instance, two mainstream films that deal with interracial relationships, *Crazy/Beautiful* and *Save the Last Dance*, star two of the biggest (and blondest) teen stars, Kirsten Dunst and Julia Stiles respectively. But few, if any, mainstream films feature a black, Asian, Latina, or American Indian girl as protagonist. One notable exception is a film that is neither U.S. nor mainstream, *Bend It Like Beckham*, a British film that gained popularity in the U.S., perhaps because of the popularity of soccer among U.S. girls, and the empowering messages of the film (despite, or perhaps also because of, its adherence to various conventions like romance amidst this empowerment). But even then, Parminder Nagra shares the lead with her (blonde) costar and finds love despite her parents' initial disapproval, has "her culture" reduced, and follows the typical Western narrative of success and romance. Plus, as the largest ethnic minority population in England, Nagra's role is also a long time coming.

Girls also take more control of their sexuality in independent and less-well-known films. They are more often active, not acted upon. And sometimes they don't even need love or romance, or even a man. For instance, in *Slums of Beverly Hills*, Vivian is introduced to masturbation and has an orgasm before she has sex. And when she has sex, she is in charge of where, with whom, and even the position. Further, sex, in independent films, is often on screen and is rarely romantic. Many girls in films from *Ripe*, to *Whatever*, to *Kids*, to *The Smokers* have awkward, painful sex. This can be seen in the images and experiences on screen, as well as in the discussions about it that often take place later in the film. Further,

In *Crazy/Beautiful*, Carlos (Jay Hernandez) and Nicole (Kirsten Dunst) are posed as a stereotypical interracial couple, but their characters and relationships also present more complicated issues. Nicole's father is the epitome of white liberalism gone awry and Carlos's family is protective and essentialist as they try to achieve the American dream through Carlos's potential success. However, it is Nicole's problems, in the end, that dominate and drive this film.

these films offer more diverse sexualities and many of these films have lesbian characters or themes, and even sometimes confront the narrow constructions of these marginalized positions. For instance, Claude in *All Over Me* may not find love with her best friend, but through the process of heartbreak and through a realization of the larger implications of being different, she learns to look elsewhere, to be brave, and to be herself. And in another non–U.S. film, *Show Me Love*, Agnes and Elin deny the narrow minds of their peers and refuse to live according to the standards that the mainstream imposes.

These films often stand out as being written, directed, or produced by women, though this is not always the case. In fact, it can't be the case because the film industry continues to be dominated by rich, white, powerful men, so women (particularly women of color) cannot always make their films in this climate, and many women who do make mainstream films can push only so hard against the boundaries. Men (and celebrities) sometimes have an advantage to access resources and in some cases can aid in the making of an independent film, like Lili

Few films are written, directed, and produced by women. *All Over Me* **is one of these films. Here we see producer, Dolly Hall (left), and director, Alex Sichel (right). These women offer "the real story," as Alex Sichel and Sylvia Sichel state in the "filmmaker's statement" in the press packet, "Not the version we've been told to believe. The one we have to tell ourselves." This statement echoes the stories in many girls' films both in and out of the mainstream.**

Taylor in *Girls Town* and Holly Hunter in *Thirteen*. As can be expected, these films are often less well known, less advertised, less accessible in video stores and online. And even the films that star well-known celebrities and are produced by mainstream production companies and studios, like *Slums of Beverly Hills*, are often less well-known than other, more popularized films.

Ellen (left, Tara Subkoff) and Claude (Alison Folland) are best friends in *All Over Me*, but Ellen is also Claude's potential undoing. Ellen's self-destructive behavior and selfish attitude are a constant source of pain for Claude until she searches elsewhere to find herself. This search entails both personal introspection and guidance from friends.

* * *

Throughout this book I focus on the ways in which these themes and tropes converge and diverge, the ways in which girls' films construct and reinforce, challenge, and dismantle mainstream conceptualizations of sex and sexuality, race and white supremacy, power and empowerment. The remainder of this chapter further details the ways in which teen films are not simply reflective of mainstream dominant cultural paradigms, but are, to use George Lipsitz's term, possessively invested in these paradigms. This chapter also looks closely at two important vectors for this study: the ways in which race and sexuality are constructed in mainstream teen films about girls. In concluding chapter one I look at some of the unreal images and expectations that rule mainstream films. In chapter two I look more closely at the mainstream limitations of coming-of-age narratives including the recycling of familiar plots and stars, the fantastic spaces that influence the settings and plots of many of these films, and the way in which parental and male authority, and the terms of adult conceptualizations of coming of age, dominate many of these narratives, before turning to briefly consider how some films move beyond the expectations and conditions of the mainstream.

In chapter three I look at some of the ways in which these conventions are negotiated within mainstream cultures and structures and rules and realities, beginning with the tools of voice, attitude, and awareness, before looking more closely at the rules of teen fashion and adult culture more generally. I then turn to look at some of the more violent realities that girls negotiate and the variety of ways in which celluloid girls negotiate these realities and the way in which these films negotiate the mainstream's erasure of these realities. Finally, in chapter four, I turn specifically to the ways in which girls negotiate sexuality, romance, physical development, mainstream definitions, and pregnancy, defining and redefining what sexuality means in coming-of-age struggles, and creating spaces for empowering sexuality. In the conclusion I discuss what it means to come of age in these films, and in U.S. culture more generally, considering the possibility of reenvisioning what coming-of-age means.

Race and White Supremacy in Teen Films

One glaring characteristic of the mainstream is its whitewashed characteristics. Not only are white people most often portrayed in the mainstream, but the mainstream is often a bland mixture of the least offensive media, as well as being "white" in its images and politics. The mainstream allows a skin-deep inclusion of other races, ethnicities, and nationalities; customs, cultural products, and myths; and ideas, beliefs, and preferences. These are included as long as they are easily incorporated and exploited, bought and sold. Everyone is equal, every culture is equal, every idea is equal—as long as someone is willing to pay money for it. And thus, peoples, cultures, and ideas are appropriated and integrated into the mainstream, often under the guise of diversity and equality, ignoring important factors like the ways in which race is not a biological reality, but a socially constructed concept with real, material effects. Further, the ways in which "othered" people are included in the mainstream is often through a compromise of some kind. It is far easier for white characters like Lola (and actors like Lindsay Lohan) in *Confessions of a Teenage Drama Queen* to don the style, attitude, and gestures of "black music" through her spoken word/"rap" segment of her song "That Girl," than it is to include any genuine expressions of "black culture" into a film centered on whiteness. The texture, especially the cultural and visual texture, of the mainstream certainly becomes richer with such superficial inclusions, but the basic flavor, and the underlying ideology, is still the same. This is certainly a simplified and perhaps simplistic view of racial ideology in the mainstream, but it is also an accurate description.

Part of this representation stems from the fact that the teen films of each decade have their core group of stars. With the huge number of teen films in the '90s, there are more stars, and more female stars. The stars of teen films get typed whether they are male or female, and all of these types fall within a middle- to upper-class range of roles and all of the stars are good-looking white kids with American Eagle or Abercrombie fashion tastes. However, the typing of girls is homogenized most by their biggest star quality—their sex appeal. And in the mainstream this sex appeal is largely reserved for white girls and women—the Jennifer Love Hewitts and the Sarah Michelle Gellars, and the Kirsten Dunsts, the Julia Stileses and the Lindsay Lohans. In all of these films race is usually an invisible, or at least subordinated issue. Whiteness is taken as the norm, and whiteness doesn't matter as much as money does. African American and less often Asian American characters are included in whitewashed, stereotyped, purely supportive, or parodic roles. But few of these films problematize or even mention whiteness, with the exception of *Mean Girls* which walks the line between critical and reductive when it comes to dealing with race and stereotypes.

Mean Girls falls into many of the same traps of mainstream films. Its star is Lindsay Lohan and her character, Cady, is similar to those in other mainstream girls' films in many ways. Despite the unusual spelling of her name, Cady, pronounced like Katy, is not that much different from other protagonists. She has money and out-of-touch but progressive parents, and she is a "regulation hottie." However, Cady is different from other white protagonists in mainstream films because she has been home-schooled in Africa all of her life by her research scientist parents. This plot is, perhaps, a good way of introducing a character who has no concept of the politics of high school, particularly an attractive, educated, white, middle-class, 16-year-old girl who has not (yet) been corrupted by the status this role affords her. As the queen bee of the Plastics clique quips, "I just love her. She's like a Martian." Further, since Cady has been raised in Africa, the audience can assume that she is "multicultural" and definitely not racist. After all, she likes math "because it is the same in every country." And when she arrives at her "multicultural" school, she should fit right in with the rainbow of students. But like the typical new student, she does not fit in and she finds her friends among the (white) outcasts.

Despite some of the strengths of this film (which will be discussed in other chapters). The problem with this plot is the way in which Cady's whiteness is centered as the norm, and even as Africa itself, when she is repeatedly called "Africa" by Kevin G, the East Asian math nerd and DJ (who claims he dates only women of color), throughout the film. But the most problematic aspect of this film is the way in which "Africa" is evoked throughout this film to show both Cady's social ineptitude as well as her violent and "primitive" (comedic) fantasies. For example, when Cady imagines the teens around the water fountain in the mall as a primitive bunch of animals, we see them acting out these typical stereotypes of people and animals in Africa. Further, as is typical of first-world invocations of Africa, "Africa" is always referred to in the general continental sense, increasing its exoticism. "Africa" only becomes a specific place when Cady's mother is referring to her tribal fertility vase from a specific tribe. But stereotypes of "Africa" are used throughout the film, such as when Regina tells Aaron, the boy Cady has a crush on, that she's obsessed with him and kept a tissue he used, saying she was going to "do some kind of African voodoo on it" to get him to like her.

Further, Cady's parents' work in Africa glosses over the role of the first-world "researcher" in Africa and the past (and present) violence that the indigenous peoples around the world continue to endure. Indigenous scholar Linda Tuhiwai Smith describes some of this impact by researchers on the indigenous peoples, culture and customs, of the Maori in New Zealand. But in *Mean Girls*, this situation of the researcher is uncritically introduced as Cady lives a dream-like life in Africa with her parents who bring home "artifacts." And through Cady's mom we see "Africa" as the ancient vases that decorate her house and the prestigious tenured position she lands at Northwestern University, which is the reason why Cady is introduced into the public school system. Cady's position as the daughter of two white research scientists working in Africa for 15 years is briefly (if ignorantly) problematized when Karen, one of the Plastics, asks her, "So if you're from Africa, why are you white?" But Cady can't answer as Gretchen, another Plastic, says, "Oh my God, Karen, you can't just ask people why they're white." It's rude. Gretchen is correct in that in the world of the Plastics, what Cady calls "girl world," you can't just ask people why they're white. But this is also a rule in the regular world as well. Whiteness is assumed to be the norm, so it is something that cannot be talked about. But Cady, in a classic example of "color-blindness," does not see color. At one point she describes the one other crush she had, as a five-year-old in Africa, on a boy named Nafume. We see her, as a young girl, hug a young (dark) black boy who tells her to go away. Should we assume that he was uninterested in the little white girl, daughter of the research scientists who invaded his village? Or should we assume that a five-year-old boy isn't interested in girls, period? The film leaves this point open for interpretation.

Cady's African origin also provides plenty of comedic moments in the film, such as when the principal comes into her class to introduce her. When he says, "We have a new student from Africa," the teacher (Tina Fey) looks at the one black girl in the classroom and greets her. This girl gives her a funny look and says, "I'm from Michigan." Ms. Norbury's racism is subtly brushed off. And since the teacher begins to date the (black) principal (Tim Meadows), perhaps we are to assume that she is also "color blind." Cady's upbringing in Africa also becomes an issue as she tries to make friends. She greets a table of black kids with an African greeting, "Jambo." This embarrassing moment is her only contact with any of the girls of color in the film, despite the fact that they appear all around her and even have a few speaking roles. Instead, these characters provide more stereotypes like the "unfriendly black hotties." And the "Asian nerds" and "cool Asians" are two more of the narrow cliques at Cady's school. But these cliques have little role in the film. The black hotties are never mentioned again and the hot Asian girls, who don't speak English (and whose words are subtitled, often with !#@%*!), are portrayed as "sluts" as both Trang Pak and her friend are caught making out with the PE coach and fight over him, verbally and physically, several times. Later, at the junior girls' assembly, when some of the Asian girls are working out the differences within their clique, these girls evoke blackness as one girl holds her hand up and says (in subtitles), "Nigga please!" At the end of the film, when the Plastics have been dismantled, Gretchen serves the new queen bee, Trang Pak, but this queen bee does not have the same power as the former regime since it is implied that Cady has, almost single-handedly, brought peace and equality to her formerly clique-ridden school. The competition and cruelty among the girls is portrayed as if it were normal, natural adolescent behavior, rather than the product of a corrupt social order. This corrupt social order is, however, contested by Cady whose privileges play no small part in her ability to dismantle the Plastics and to bring a feel-good quality to their Spring Fling dance. But, Cady's privilege is not challenged even as she has the power to change the power structure at her school without claiming it, and without appointing a new leader. This would seem to be a kinder, gentler version of girl world, but it's clear that Cady still clings to the vestiges of her power, and still sees power struggles in violent terms, as she imagines that the younger Plastics are hit by a bus.

Mean Girls also challenges and reinforces stereotypes about home-schooled kids when Cady narrates about how she is not like those things that the audience may have heard about homeschooled kids. She visually evokes these stereotypes of disfunctional spelling bee nerds and "white trash" kids from the hicks who only learn about God and guns and the wrongs of homosexuality, while proclaiming herself perfectly normal in relation to these stereotypes. While she critically evokes these stereotypes, she then reinforces them. This pattern repeats itself throughout the film as stereotypes are evoked and only sometimes critically dismantled.

As in *Mean Girls*, white supremacy in mainstream teen films and girls' films is a complicated mixture that reflects the culture that produces these films. The absence of nonwhite races, and especially the lack of non-white ethnicities and nationalities, is the most telling factor and most obvious evidence of white supremacy in teen and girls' film. Since most often "inclusive" films include only (often light-skinned) blacks, and are particularly light-skinned when these characters are black females, white supremacy is often hidden behind shallow attempts at "multicultural" inclusion. For instance, of the few African American female actors in teen films, Gabrielle Union plays one of Taylor Vaughn's best friends in *She's All That*, Bianca's best friend in *10 Things I Hate About You*, and the cheerleading competition in *Bring It On*. The talented violin player, Denise, in *Raise Your Voice* provides a similar function to Isis in *Bring It On*. For instance, Denise's attitude is attributed not to her blackness as it is in other films, but to her desire and desperation to land the $10,000 scholarship that will be awarded to one student. However, she is the only black character, the only one who really seems to need the scholarship, and the only one with "attitude." Eventually she befriends her roommate, Terri (star, Hilary Duff), largely because she is so nice and innocent. As Denise points out, Terri is "some kind of retro Brady Buncher." And like Torrence's claim that second "feels like first," Terri does not need to win the scholarship. She has won something far more valuable—belief in herself. Thus, Denise wins because, next to Terri, she is obviously the most talented and the most deserving. Despite these attempts at equity, black characters are often removed to nonspeaking roles, like the professor in the Pygmalion play in *Confessions of a Teenage Drama Queen*, or underdeveloped characters, like Preston in *She's All That*, who is like a third wheel to Zach and Dean. At one point he even backs away from their scheming, saying that "this is between the two of you." Thus, his role is not far from his parodic counterpart in *Not Another Teen Movie*, whose primary function is to perform stereotyped blackness.

Clearly, the white supremacy that is deeply embedded in teen and girls' film is evident even in attempts at "multiculturalism." Because whiteness is taken as the norm, not only are nonwhite characters marginalized in and from films, and not only are they whitewashed or used as "flavor" when they are included, but racism is also used lightly and flippantly as well as in its most bigoted forms. For instance, in the teen film *The Girl Next Door*, racism is portrayed through stereotypes that are only somewhat contested as well as through racist characterization, but also through paternalism. Matthew, the sensitive and misunderstood protagonist, has raised $25,000 to bring Samnang, "the next Einstein," to study at his prestigious high school. This character's function resembles that of Long Duk Dong, the foreign exchange student in *Sixteen Candles*. Samnang is used as the butt of countless sexual innuendoes by the jocks, the "dirty dozen," mostly making predictable puns from his name. When the smarmy porn-producer villain calls him "some Chinese guy," Matthew corrects him, saying that he is Cambodian, only to get the response of whatever, "those little people sure do like their numbers." This response obviously shows the ignorance of this character, but his ignorant stereotypes are a form of the kind of ignorance that people, and popular culture, in the U.S. practice daily, if more covertly. (And this is only reinforced when, for instance, reviewers refer to the stars of *Harold and Kumar Go to White Castle* as "that Asian guy from *American Pie*" and "that Indian guy.") His racism is outdone only by that of the bank teller who, when she gets backed into a corner by her own stupid mistake, lashes out at Matthew, telling him that she doesn't care about him or his "little rice boy." But all of these examples are obvious and are used for effect within the narrative—to make these characters look bad and to make Matthew look better. But Matthew's form of racism is, perhaps, more severe, even as it is cloaked in liberalism and paternalism. Samnang is, possibly, the next genius, and this is the very reason why Matthew wants to bring him to the U.S. When Hunter steals Samnang's money, Matthew is determined to make that money back, if only to stay true to his word. He imagines a scene in Cambodia where Samnang and his mother curse him. Though this scene is presented as if it were a real glimpse at this Cambodian peasant-genius and the squalor he lives in, he and his mother speak English and use colloquial American profanity, making these outsiders better fit in with the themes of the film. And when Samnang arrives, Matthew, in a gesture worthy of a politician, leans over and tells him, "Dude, you better cure cancer." But, of course, Samnang, the "foreigner," is not in on this joke; this one is between Matthew and his audience.

While *The Girl Next Door* shows a range of ways that racism can function in a teen film, more often racism almost seems like "common sense," especially when it is used lightly, or as a joke like in *Confessions of a Teenage Drama Queen*. This film, like most other mainstream films centered on a white character, includes token minorities, mostly through visual representation, though in this film a (nameless) black teen plays the professor role in an updated version of Shaw's *Pygmalion*. But underneath this token inclusion, two statements stand out. First, when Lola is trying to convince Ella that they should lie, that they are supposed to "fly away from the nest" and do things like sneak away to concerts, she argues that "the 15-year-olds in other cultures are grandmothers and no one gave them permission to do that." Besides being irrelevant and not funny, this comment is based upon ignorant assumptions about "other" cultures. And while it is unclear what "other cultures" Lola is referring to, and even Lola wouldn't know which culture she might be referring to, what is clear is that comments like this often slip by unnoticed not only in teen films, but also in popular culture more generally, even as they reinforce notions of cultural superiority. What is more difficult to miss in this film is Lola's embodiment of Gandhi, portrayed through her dress and a sparkly jewel — her trendy bendhi — in between her eyes, and her adoption of his tactic of the hunger strike. In order to protest not her mother's refusal to let her go to the concert, but her mother's insistence that her father drop her off and pick her up, Lola mocks a history of resistance that she, and probably most of her viewers, are unaware, or only partially, aware of. It is this ignorance and assumed cultural superiority that finds its way, in various forms, into many teen and girls' films, and U.S. popular culture more generally.

This cultural superiority also plays outside of U.S. borders. Very few U.S. teen films deal with issues on a scale larger than high school, let alone issues that cross national borders. One of the mainstream films that does is *What a Girl Wants*, a story about a 17-year-old girl who has never met her father, who just happens to be a member of the House of Lords, Lord Henry Dashwood. In this film, England serves not so much as a foreign country as it does a stuffier version of the U.S. Daphne doesn't fit in with the "codes of behavior" passed down to her through her Dashwood heritage, but she is willing to change, at least temporarily, to be what her dad (thinks he) wants. She becomes a politician's daughter, sacrificing individuality in the process, as her boyfriend says, "just call me when Daphne reinhabits your body." But this political strain has very little importance to the world of politics, and has everything to do with Henry's disavowal of his royal position, and his refusal to sacrifice his heart to England as so many of his ancestors have sacrificed their body parts to England. But one subplot to this film is that Henry met Daphne's mother, Libby (who had decided to go out and see the world), in the deserts of Morocco. They were married by a Bedouin tribe, a story that is told and retold to Daphne as if it were a fairy tale. Thus, England takes on a more exotic texture without taking on the legacies of its colonial past. And the Bedouin tribe is not only available for phone calls from Henry's (evil) fianceé, but the Bedouins remarry Henry and Libby, reinforcing their service and subservience to England, if only subtly. International politics are also not important in *The Princess Diaries* despite the fact that her grandmother tells Mia that being a princess is a job. And the fictional Genovia is imagined as a tiny European country that is, in its represen-tation within the film, all white and "Old Europe." Thus, these interna-tional films only superficially represent the rest of the world.

A more marginal mainstream film, *Brokedown Palace*, does deal with international issues, and it must do so centered on two (white) American girls and their problems with the Thai legal system. This film is relatively unique in the girls' film genre in that its protagonists are pulled into the Thai justice system when they unknowingly attempt, under the influence of a smooth-talking guy, to smuggle drugs on a side trip to Hong Kong. With their lack of knowledge of Thai law, the girls are quickly found guilty and are sent to a Thai prison where they have to adapt not only to jail, but to jail in another country. While this film is not set in the U.S., and is not typical of teen films in several ways, it also carries with it many of the premises of teen films. For instance, the girls decide to go to Thai-land because it is more exciting than Hawaii or the Bahamas. The trip is their last time together since Darlene is heading to college, while Alice is left in the same place despite high school graduation. Alice is imme-diately set up as the "bad girl." She is working class, sexually active, and "wild"—all characteristics of a "bad" girl. Further, through flashbacks, the film portrays this "badness" as innate. She has been bad since she was a little girl, and Darlene's father refuses to help Alice, and even yells at her and blames her for getting his daughter into trouble. Darlene is naïve and sheltered, a good student, and a good daughter. But Alice's badness also gives her more "street smarts." While Alice refuses to sign the confession statement prepared for her, Darlene signs easily when kindly coerced.

While this film sets up Thailand, and countries like it, as dangerous places for American tourists, especially young women, it is also a sound critique of the assumptions of the upper-class and other mainstreamed folk about foreign travel. The upper classes can take vacations anywhere they please, and when they get bored with exotic, tourist-filled locations, they can go wherever else they might want to go, to see whatever they might like to see. Often what they see is the pain and suffering of peo-ple who live a life of lack, largely because of their relationship in and to the globalized economy. Many have been displaced or disposed. These people become the scenery, and sometimes the souvenirs, for vacationers who, usually, can escape back to their comparative riches in the U.S. Further, this film was filmed in the Philippines because of its negative portrayal of Thailand. So, not only is *Brokedown Palace* an example of when ignorance can create a situation that dampers, or even removes, the first-world status and privilege that many travelers (and nontravelers) assume, but it is also a product of such first-world privilege. Thailand has more power to deny an American film crew, while the Philippines, a former U.S. holding and a slave to the globalized economy, does not have the same power for this very reason—it is a victim of U.S. imperialism, colonialism, and postcolonialism. But this victimhood is not the subject of this or any other girls' film.

In order to escape their situation, the girls try several methods—some by legal means and others through inside deals that portray Thailand's legal system as corrupt. But none of these tactics work, despite the help of their lawyer, Hank, an American lawyer married to, and partners with, a Thai lawyer, an interesting subplot that gives this film a richer texture. Despite his respect for the Thai culture and law, his fluency in the language, and an understanding of the way in which the law works, "Yankee Hank" is unable to secure the girls' freedom. Instead, the burden is taken upon Alice when she uses the skills she has learned in prison—knowledge of the language and the culture—to confess and negotiate freedom for Darlene. Thus, this "bad girl" sacrifices her own life and freedom for this "good girl" friend who has turned her back on her and has learned little about respect for herself, let alone other peoples or other cultures. While this is the conventional end to the bad-girl–good-girl dichotomy discussed throughout this book, it is also a challenge to the role of the bad girl since Alice's actions make her more honorable, mature, and secure than her friend, with the implication that Alice has come of age, has accepted her place and her fate, while Darlene has a lot more growing to do. Perhaps because of these circumstances, Darlene will become less selfish, as the final narration ensures that she takes up Alice's fight. Despite the fact that Alice remains in prison, she serves as a warning to tourists who assume that their power and privilege could rescue them from any situation. It takes this "bad girl" to illustrate respect and reverence for "'others'" cultures, a characteristic that few "bad girls" have, and a theme few teen or girls' films take up.

The dynamic of the lower-class "bad girl" is a trope across many films and will be discussed in more depth later. What is interesting to note about mainstream films, however, is that black girls are not used to juxtapose, for instance, good and evil, prude and slut. This does not mean that blondes (light) aren't posed against brunettes (dark) in this binary. The whiteness I've describe previously means that the black-white, primary-other binaries are contained within white images, further cementing whiteness as the norm. It is also important to note that in the mainstream this "bad girl" can be transformed, through status, if not economic class. While Alice is one example of a working-class protagonist, the majority of films set in rich or upper-class white homes far outnumber the films about or including teens of color or teens from lower income families. As previously mentioned, even films that do focus on a teen from a lower socioeconomic class, like *She's All That*, include other "others" only marginally. Whiteness is centered in this film as illustrated by a group of African American teens who have nothing better to do than perform a rap about the competition over prom queen, proclaiming that Laney is "all that." This is one kind of investment in whiteness—the focus on white protagonists with the inclusion of a few teens who visibly represent minority ethnic and racial groups even if their actions and ideologies mirror those of the white characters. They often share the same upper-class economic status and the politics and ideology that match this upper echelon, like Bianca's best friend in *10 Things I Hate About You*. Since there are few roles in teen films or girls' films for nonwhite actors, the way in which race is portrayed in the mainstream speaks to the fact that girls' film is "politically correct" in its representations; it plays safely with issues of race and ethnicity (among issues like power, pleasure, love, etc.). Teen films, and to a somewhat lesser extent, girls' films, strictly adhere to the demands of the mainstream, particularly when it comes to dealing with difference.

Even in the few films that deal with issues surrounding race, like *Bring It On*, *Save the Last Dance*, and *Crazy/Beautiful*, the narrative is still focused on whiteness. In the two latter films, both center around a white girl's struggles with the death of her mother and a boyfriend (of color) who rescues her. And while *Bring It On* offers a more equitable representation of the opposing cheerleading squad, the Compton Clovers, who are more talented and end up winning the competition, the focus is still on the white squad and the white protagonist, the rich school and the rich cheerleaders. However, this film introduces many contradictions into what could be a seamless narrative. For instance, when Torrance finds out that the Clovers can't compete in the finals because they don't have the money, she convinces her father that he should ask his company for the money, telling him that he should follow through on the liberal politics he believes in. But Torrance's good will goes only so far as the Compton Clovers see it as an act of charity and refuse the money. Instead, they get money

In *Bring It On*, Torrance (Kirsten Dunst) and Isis (Gabrielle Union) face off at national championships not as enemies, but as competitors. They respect each other as fellow captains and prove it when they "bring it." This film attempts to expose some of the structural problems that keep worthy cheerleaders like the Compton Clovers from being allowed an equal chance at mainstream success. In doing so, it also attempts to legitimize cheerleading as the serious sport that it is.

through the Oprahesque character, a black woman who has achieved success and fame in the white world, but continues to give money and support to those who have not been so lucky or fortunate.

The irony of this film is that the successful Torro cheerleaders, under the previous captain, Red, have been stealing routines from the Compton Clovers for years. When Torrance, as the new captain, discovers this fact via her new friend from L.A., she is mortified. She refuses to steal any more routines and the team flounders when they have to come up with a new routine. They use their money (their legacy of privilege), the one advantage they have over the Compton Clovers, to purchase a new routine, but this backfires on them as they find that several schools have been sold the same routine. They are humiliated at the competition, but because they are last year's champions, they have a second chance to compete at the finals, through their privilege of legacy. Now the Torros have to scramble. They have to figure out what they're made of. And luckily they have the resources to pull from various types of movement—from dance to martial arts—to create a truly original routine worthy of the competition. Their privilege, once again, gives them an advantage over the Clovers who have legitimately made the finals, but lack the money they need to compete.

In the process of cheerleading, a rivalry develops between captains Torrance and Isis. But this rivalry isn't based on race. If anything, it is partially based on Torrance's "white guilt," her desire to make things right for the Clovers. But Torrance isn't their savior, she is their competitor. And while some of the Clover squad don't want to associate with the competition, the captains, Isis assures her teammates, have an understanding. The Compton Clovers are allowed to keep their dignity and the competitive relationship between the two captains is one of respect, if not mutual understanding, based on the one thing they share—cheerleading. Thus, cheerleading, though it is often denied status as a sport, is also the marginalized space that both teams occupy regardless of race. The Torros may have put together a routine worthy of their past glory, but the Clovers win the championship, celebrating their first appearance with their first victory despite the fact that their routines had won the same competition for the past few years. And in the end, when Torrance remarks that second place "feels like first," it is clear that once again, Torrance is a winner. This is yet one more "lucky" day in a series of such days. She even ends up with a new, sensitive boyfriend to add to her rewards.

In both *Save the Last Dance* and *Crazy/Beautiful*, a sensitive boyfriend is a key to the protagonist's survival, and in *Save the Last Dance*, her success. While both of these films provide strong roles for the boys, in doing so they also take away from the strength of the female characters. For instance, in *Save the Last Dance*, Sara cannot complete her audition until Derek appears. However, it is not simply his mere presence that ignites her inner strength and compels her to succeed. He has to actively come up on the stage and give her a pep talk while the judges wait with only mild impatience. In this film, Sara has needed Derek's help in order to survive her mom's death, and in order to compete for a spot at her dream school, Juilliard. She is able to succeed through his help alone, but at least in this process she learns a little bit about the challenges of an interracial relationship. In *Crazy/Beautiful* Carlos has to drag Nicole out of a hot tub where she is drunk and surrounded by predatory boys. He also has to defend her to her father and convince her to talk to him about the problems that she has had since the death of her mother. Thus, in both of these films, the focus of the film is not the secure, supportive, if somewhat confused black or Latino boyfriend; it is the pain and emptiness in

In *Save the Last Dance*, Derek (Sean Patrick Thomas) teaches Sara (Julia Stiles) how to be "hip hop" and she infuses this new dimension of herself into her passion—ballet. Derek becomes her teacher, her friend, her lover, her coach, and her confidant. Here they make use of public school space for lessons. This is one of the few films to at least attempt to deal with issues of race, class and interracial relationships.

the life of the white (blonde) protagonist. By making the minority boys in these films the strong character, the character fighting to achieve success according to the rules set forth by the mainstream, only the path of conformity and integration is available to these characters, and their minority group by extension. Thus, both of these characters' families have expectations for them to represent their race positively to mainstream America. Derek's family expects him to be a doctor and Carlos's mom and brother keep a close eye on him. This sends a very specific message about the place carved out for minorities in the mainstream, and these two boys challenge their families' hopes for them to marry or date within their race, rather than outside of it. This expectation is made clear by Derek's sister who, in the midst of frustration with her baby's father and the larger (stereotypical, but also realistic) situation she is in, she lashes out at Sara about how girls like her come and take away all the good black men, and convinces her to back off, creating a rift between Sara and Derek. When Derek confronts his sister, the issue is passed off as her selfishness and

One of the problematic aspects of *Save the Last Dance* is exemplified in this picture as Sara is literally the center of attention as she demonstrates her skills and the "others" don't simply sit back and watch, but cheer her on. In her fusion of hip hop dance and ballet, black and white, or at least essentialized versions of such, the problems between black and white are romanticized and resolved on a personal level.

frustration, rather than as an expression of a larger cultural concern. These concerns are also made clear to Nicole when she doesn't fit in at Carlos's cousin's quinceanera. She's seen as spoiled and wild, and an outsider. But mostly she is just not really seen. She leaves and sits in her car crying before she calls Carlos to drive her home. In the end, both boys hold tight to their girls and there is hope that racial tensions will resolve themselves. But only the girls in films outside of the mainstream have the opportunity to challenge these proscribed roles, as I'll discuss further in chapter three. In the mainstream, it seems to be, once again, the boys versus the girls.

The similarities and differences between these two female characters and their relationships are telling of this facet of girls' film. Julia Stiles plays a white girl whose mom dies as she is on her way to her daughter's audition at the prestigious Juilliard. As a result of her mother's death, Sara is sent to live with her father, a musician she hardly knows. This move takes her from her comfortable, though lower middle class, life to a much poorer existence in the Bronx, living in a small, run-down, apart-ment where she doesn't even have her own room. She doesn't fully real-ize how hard her mother worked to get her whatever she wanted, in this case, a career in ballet. However, she does realize (or she thinks) that without her mother, she has no career in ballet. This move also takes her from her mostly white high school (where she's a loner) to a mostly black high school where she exhibits just enough attitude to get by and refuses to segregate herself with the other white students. For instance, when looking for a spot to sit in the cafeteria, the segregation at the school, and the white students' low percentage, is apparent. But Sara doesn't choose to sit with the white kids. Instead, she finds one familiar face—Derek's sister.

On the almost opposite end of the spectrum, Kirsten Dunst plays a liberal politician's daughter. Nicole is totally absorbed in her rebellious and vapid existence when she meets Carlos, a conscientious, ambitious student. The two are from totally different worlds, worlds that only inter-sect when people like Nicole's politician dad make them intersect, offering help, a "leg up," to the less fortunate. He is so busy fighting for equality that not only does he fail to be there for his daughter, but he also fails to realize the hypocrisy of his political position. While Sara's father doesn't know how to talk to her and doesn't exactly approve of her boyfriend, he mostly stays out of her way. He doesn't know how to broach the subject of her mother's death, so he leaves her to work things out on her own. Nor does he know how to help her grieve over the loss of her mother, but he is absorbed by his political career and his new young, blonde wife, and their infant daughter, so he just leaves it alone. Nicole's stepmother hardly likes or respects her, let alone has any compassion for her. Thus, before Carlos, Nicole has only her best friend, a party girl like herself (and like characters such as Brenda in *Whatever* or Ellen in *All Over Me*).

Both of these girls have lost their mothers, a situation not unusual in teen films. But what is interesting about these two films is that both of these girls who have lost their mothers, and whose fathers are out of touch with their needs, turn to boys of a different race or ethnicity for love and support, and the boys give this unconditionally because they can. In *Save the Last Dance*, the narrative is so focused on Sara that it is only her future and her audition that matter. Derek's path is clear and steady, and he becomes her rock. Plus, Sara is mostly naive about the social and cultural implications of her relationship. But in *Crazy/Beautiful* Nicole recognizes the cultural capital that her boyfriend could be to her liberal, do-good, politician father, even if this realization only comes through the pain of her father's lack of attention and real concern. She is able to use this cultural capital to help Carlos achieve his dreams, but when this backfires on her and her father tells him that she's only trouble, Carlos takes the easy way out at first. However, his love and honor drive him to sacrifice his chance at success for her. In doing so he not only proves his love, but also his character, morally outshining her father. Thus, this girls' film comes to center its moral more on him than on her. And, in the end, he is achieving his dreams of becoming a pilot while she is in the supportive role.

When mainstream teen films deal with interracial relationships, it is almost always a white girl with some kind of problems and a token boy who is struggling to achieve success according to the standards of the mainstream. This is probably mainly due to the fact that few mainstream films focus on girls of color, period, and especially not in interracial relationships. (An alternative to this scenario is offered with *2 Girls in Love*, to be discussed later. It does not fall victim to this plot because it can't.) Further, films that focus on a female protagonist of color rarely deal with

In *Girls Town* (from left to right) Patti (Lili Taylor), Emma (Anna Grace), and Angela (Bruklin Harris) mean business. They are sick of dealing with oppression, racism, sexism, and adolescence itself. They are forced to take matters into their own hands; they are forced to fight violence with violence. In the process they are empowered, largely through their mutual support of each other.

interracial relationships. They often center their stories on the black community, like in *Love and Basketball* and *Nikita Blues*, which will be discussed later. Both of these films provide a different kind of black female protagonist. For instance, in *Nikita Blues*, an "urban comedy," Nikita has lost her father and aggressively stalks her "fine" African American teacher because, she later confesses, she just wanted some attention. But once this ploy doesn't work, she finds a more appropriate love interest, a youth leader at church — someone her own age, and someone her mother would be proud of. But this film, unlike others in the mainstream, provides a rare space for a black, girl protagonist to come of age, let alone succeed in the mainstream, as Monica does in *Love and Basketball*. For these reasons, narratives focused on black characters and related issues are important alternative spaces. However, these spaces can also be stereotypical, particularly when they are hijacked from their communities, like in *Mi Vida Loca*, which will be discussed more in chapter three.

Since the list of mainstream girls' films that deal with race or white supremacy is a short list, it is no surprise that films outside of the mainstream treat race differently than mainstream films do; however, these films are marginalized in the genre, as well as in the general body of U.S. film. Further, independent films are still largely whitewashed, and don't deal overtly with white supremacy. One of these films, discussed in chapter three, is *Shake, Rattle, and Rock!* This film, more than most, directly (and indirectly) confronts racism. Despite these few exceptions, few mainstream films deal with issues that cross a racial or ethnic spectrum like independent films such as *Girls Town* or *Belly Fruit*, which include white, black, and Latina characters without tokenization. The few independent films that actually deal with issues related to race usually focus on a black female protagonist, and no films in this study feature Asian American protagonists or Native American girls. Since so few mainstream films about girls offer an alternative to mainstream constructions and expectations, many independent films must strive to offer such alternatives, and many more must be funded. These alternatives, including *Nikita Blues* and *Stranger Inside*, will be discussed further in chapter three. For now I turn to the way in which sexuality, like race and ethnicity, is portrayed according to mainstream prescriptions.

Sexuality in Mainstream Girls' Films

The terrain of teen films offers a variety of representations of sex education (from school and parents), as well as its own form of sex education about issues surrounding sex and sexuality. While this variety offers far more than the limited and limiting narratives that most critics, parents, psychologists, and other "authorities" are willing to contend with, the variety of discussions concerning sexuality in mainstream teen films is still limited. While sex appears regularly in mainstream teen films, and less often in mainstream girls' films, in both of these related genres sexuality is still very much limited to what the mainstream considers to be the norm—(romanticized) heterosexuality. In teen films about boys, sex appears often in a variety of forms, but sexuality is less often a (serious) topic of discussion. And in mainstream girls' films, both sex and sexuality are often limited to narratives concerning love or romance, and less often, pregnancy (or fear of pregnancy). To confuse matters of sexuality more, nudity can push a film to an R rating while violence is more accepted at the PG-13 level. Thus, many films that treat sex and sexuality as a serious subject are rated R, for no one under 17 without their parent. This rating system limits such a film's usefulness even as it provides an opportunity for parents and teens to discuss issues surrounding sex and sexuality. Also, because of taboos surrounding nudity, particularly on TV, sex scenes like those in *Fast Times at Ridgemont High*, which portray Stacy as vulnerable and awkward, are cut out along with the nudity in Linda's infamous pool scene, leaving only the red bathing suit and the imagination, and a very particular picture of girls' sexuality. The latter becomes the stuff of legend while the former is conveniently forgotten. Thus, heterosexual objectification is reified while discussions of sexuality are stifled, a pattern that defines the mainstream.

Despite the schizophrenia of American sexuality generally, and teen films specifically, portrayals of sex and sexuality in girls' films have steadily evolved from the rebellion against repression in the films of the 1960s to the open jokes and discussions found in the teen films of the '90s, to the empowering narratives about sex and sexuality found in independent girls' films (discussed in chapter four). Two early teen films, *Where the Boys Are* and *Splendor in the Grass*, offer an interesting look at sex and sexuality in the teen films of the early 1960s. Susan Douglas, in her book *Where the Girls Are: Growing Up Female with the Mass Media*, recognizes that "a film like *Where the Boys Are* offered viewers the opportunity to try on a range of attitudes toward premarital sex by presenting a variety of stock female archetypes, from the confirmed virgin to the fallen angel to the tomboy type who didn't have such worries because no man found her sexually attractive" (79). This is one empowering attribute of the movies; these stock females allow girls the chance to remake themselves not physically with makeup and clothes, but mentally, by trying on several different ideologies and images. But Douglas also recognizes the contradictions that this film presents. "Throughout this film, which is also supposed to be a comedy and a musical, there are so many contradictions about girls and sex that the final message is, according to Douglas, "Every girl must decide for herself." While such contradiction seems a source of unrest for Douglas, there is no truer way to present girls with a representation of their own sexuality than through contradiction. Nothing represents a girl's life better, and perhaps this is why "the main heroine, Merritt, the one we're really supposed to identify with, is a bundle of contradictions" (80). Of course she is. How else is an intelligent girl supposed to feel when she is taking "Courtship and Marriage" class, studying Russian vocabulary, and hiding her high IQ. At the end of the movie, "despite what happened to Melanie, it's simply not clear that premarital sex in all cases is bad, especially if you're smart and sensible like Merritt" (80). What is clear, however, is that Merritt has found a man that loves her, the lack of which was the major downfall of Melanie. So the independent, sensible Merritt will settle down and eventually become the woman Melanie dreamed of being.

While *Where the Boys Are* presents (amid the stock female archetypes) the message of "the horrible costs for girls going all the way," this does not represent all narratives from the early '60s. In *Splendor in the Grass* (1961), it is almost the opposite. "In this film, *not* going all the way completely ruins the young couple's lives," Douglas argues. "Deanie goes crazy as a result of her abstinence and has to be institutionalized, and Bud, after collapsing on a basketball court from sexual frustration, ends up pathetic and defeated, a barefoot dirt farmer in overalls with snot-nosed kids and an ever-pregnant, slatternly wife" (Douglas 78). Douglas' interpretation of the ending of this film is one that undercuts its impact. It is easy to see the ending this way as Deanie appears dressed impeccably in a white dress, hat, and gloves and contrasts sharply with the brown dirt all around her and the small, dingy house where Bud's wife cooks and tends to their child. Deanie is clearly not a part of this world. But is Bud really pathetic and defeated? He has exactly what he wanted, exactly what his father wouldn't let him have. He wanted to be a farmer. It is not the life of the farmer that leaves him pathetic and defeated, but the detour he had to travel to get there. As a man, Bud has the option to drop out of the society that drove his sister and father to their deaths, even if the status quo sees him as pathetic and defeated.

Deanie, on the other hand, is still living out her mother's dream. She has grown beyond the confining and frivolous expectations of her mother, but society offers her no space outside of the mental institution where she can hide from such expectations. She is to be married, of course; there is no other way around it for a girl in 1961, let alone in 1929 (the setting of the film). But she has lost all of her passion. She is mature and thoughtful instead of passionate and confused. The process of coming of age has calmed her down. Douglas writes, "Like most girls in the audience in 1961, Deanie has no place to stand. Torn between her overwhelming physical desires and a moral code that pretends they don't—and shouldn't—exist, Deanie is divided against herself, her mind and body pitted against each other, wanting to succumb to her passion and not daring to do so" (78). But Bud dares, and isn't it this act, and not simply Deanie's abstinence, that sends her over the edge? While Deanie may have provided "a powerful point of identification for the girl in the audience reacting against the moral strictures of the 1950s" (78), she only offers the ideology (and doesn't act upon it). And this ideology seems squelched at the end of the movie. I can't imagine that Deanie leaves Bud's farm, still crisp and white, only to don her red flapper dress and go out on her own sexual escapades. She will more than likely end up in a marriage not unlike her mother's. She may not subscribe exactly to her mother's early advice, allowing her husband near her only to have babies. But she certainly won't be carried away by her passion. We all know what happens to the sexually liberated girl (represented by Bud's sister)—she becomes uncontrollable, embarrassing, and eventually killed, literally or figuratively, by her own reckless behavior. Deanie's fate is much less dramatic.

In both of these films coming of age requires a squelching, or at least a reigning in of passion. Early in *Where the Boys Are*, Merritt challenges her "post-menopausal female professor" (80) by asserting her own beliefs about whether or not a girl should "play house before marriage." Her opinion (yes) gets her thrown out of class. While Merritt presents her rational opinion quite easily, it's not so easy to follow through in the real world and she has the same struggles between body and mind that Deanie has. But while Merritt has a mind that challenges what is expected of her, Deanie doesn't have the same option. The only alternative for Deanie is to be like Juanita (the "slut" that Bud finally uses to relieve his frustrations, an option that isn't open to sweet Deanie) or to be like Bud's sister. She imitates Bud's sister to a certain extent, but she cannot truly be like her. She doesn't know how. Instead she goes mad, mumbling in a hospital, not unlike Melanie after she was raped. Douglas refers to Melanie's rape as a "date rape," a qualification that undermines what happened to her. Melanie had a date with someone else, and the minute Dale comes into the room she is saying "no" in a defeated, helpless tone. She was not overcome with passion, saying "no" a little too late. She was raped by a premeditated manipulation, not by some supposed "fault" of her own, at least not immediately. Together these two films show some of the inherent contradictions in a girl's life and coming of age, especially in terms of sexuality. These contradictions can be seen in a variety of other ways, particularly in the form of advice.

In the midst of these girls' struggles with sex and sexuality, parents are just as contradictory as adolescence itself and mainstream portrayals of adolescent sexuality. In *Rebel Without a Cause* both Jim and Judy are looking for love, guidance, and authority. Jim's father is impotent and spineless and Judy's father pushes her away because he cannot deal with her budding sexuality. In *Splendor in the Grass*, Deanie's mother is hardly helpful as her advice is exactly the opposite of what Deanie is looking for. Bud's father is even worse as he promotes the underbelly of the double standard, telling Bud that there are two kinds of girls, and that he needs to find himself one of those other girls.

The parental advice in these films pales in comparison to films of the '70s and '80s, like *Little Darlings* and *Old Enough*, two films that are difficult to come by today. They offer girls some new, safer spaces for discussions of female, teenage sexuality, a space between the films of the '90s and those of the '60s. Like the parents in the films of the '60s, parents' advice in teen films of the '90s also reflects the nature of sexuality in our culture. Parents are cruel, helpless, absent, controlling, awkward, hilarious, and often hypocritical. But when parents in the movies do talk to their kids about sex, they are often also performing the function of a joke. For instance, in *10 Things I Hate About You*, Kat and Bianca's father is an uptight obstetrician who uses his profession as an occasion for lectures about sex. Of course, neither one of his daughters is having sex, and they consider his advice to be irrelevant mostly because he is assuming that neither of his daughters has any sense. But the ultimate joke of a parent is in *American Pie*. Jim's father strikes up several conversations with his son after encountering some strange sexual situations—the sock and the pie, for instance. He pushes topics that few movie parents (or real parents) tackle—masturbation, the clitoris, foreplay. He buys his son porn and encourages and embarrasses him when his "study date" arrives. He begins to use euphemisms and metaphors like playing tennis and putting on the corsage. The movie even ends with a reawakening of his father's sexuality as he imitates Jim's dance down the hall, away from Jim's door, and back into his own life.

While these contradictions are not resolved through parental advice, nor are they resolved through sex education programs which are also mocked in a variety of films like *Saved!* where the coach tells students,

"Just don't have sex or you'll die," or in *Mean Girls* where the coach not only gives bad advice, but is also caught "practicing" on students more than once. More often these contradictions surface in girls' films both critically and uncritically, consciously and unconsciously. For instance, girls who are active in their sexuality—the "sluts"—usually "get what they deserve." There are countless films, like *Wicked* or *The Crush*, about teenage girls who become obsessed with their teacher, a friend, the man they babysit for, the guy they can't get, and the list goes on. Sometimes these films provide a means of empowerment and growth for the girl, but more often the neurotic girl ends up being the scapegoat of the plot. And this doesn't happen only in girls' films, but films about women as well, such as *The Hand That Rocks the Cradle*.

Not only are sex and sexuality skewed in many mainstream films, the consequences of sex, like violence, pregnancy, and sexually transmitted infections, are often either nonexistent or romanticized, like in *Sugar & Spice*, when the perfect couple—the captain of the football team and the captain of the cheerleading squad—decide to get married after she gets pregnant. This solution seems perfectly logical to them, but their parents are less than pleased. Their financial problems (the only problems they seem to have) are easily solved when Diane and her cheerleader friends rob a bank together and everyone lives happily ever after, at the end of the film, and in the film's future. This film illustrates the mixture of submission and subversion in mainstream films. While *Sugar & Spice* attempts to shatter the preconceived stereotypes of both cheerleaders and pregnant teens, it does so by relying upon the very same stereotypes of girls, as well as the romantic convention. Thus, this film doesn't treat sex or sexuality as a serious subject. This also happens in "family films" like *The Princess Diaries, Confessions of a Teenage Drama Queen*, and *Whatever It Takes*; all three girls end the films with "in love" relationships with boys despite the lack of discussion of sexuality. The closest these films get is Mia's idea about a "foot-popping kiss" (derived from her experience watching romantic movies) and Daphne's father's embarrassed attempts to describe the purpose of a coming-out ball (a heterosexual display of young women who are announcing their eligibility for marriage). This trend of "coming out" parties has been recently resurrected through MTV's series, *My Sweetest Sixteen*, which features teens from across racial, ethnic, and class backgrounds (but particularly spoiled rich kids), as they plan and carryout their sweet 16 parties. With a few exceptions, this show cements ideas of class as well as ideas of adolescence as some teens' parents spend up to a quarter of a million dollars on their child's party. Thus, it is not the sexual aspects of coming of age that are emphasized, but the values of the market and the mainstream.

Because mainstream films rarely deal with sexuality, they also rarely deal with sexuality outside of the heterosexual norm. In *Saved!*, Mary's boyfriend is banished because of his homosexual desires, found by his father in the form of a gay porn magazine. When he returns at the end of the film he has accepted his sexuality, has a boyfriend, and confronts the culture that put him, and others like him, away to be "cured," or saved. But like Megan in *But I'm a Cheerleader*, sending Dean away only opens space for him to come out. And Mary and the other "good" Christians accept him for who he is and he becomes part of Mary's new, extended, family. *Bend It Like Beckham* plays with other stereotypes about homosexuality, even if it tries a little too hard to do so within the context of opposing cultures. Jules's mother assumes that since her daughter is spending so much time alone with her friend, and since she overhears what she thinks is Jules talking about Jess, that her daughter must be a lesbian. On the other hand, Jess's parents assume that she is seeing a man because she is seen standing close to Jules, who has short hair, and hugging her at a bus stop. These films play lightly with issues that are rarely present at all in mainstream films. But sometimes, films like *Mean Girls*, *Bend It Like Beckham* and *Saved!* deal with homosexuality as a plot device and provide some space for discussions of sexuality. In *Mean Girls*, for instance, Cady's friend Damien is "almost too gay to function," a phrase that is only funny when Janis says it, not when Cady uses it to fit in with the Plastics (as Cady realizes later, leading to her decision to bring down the Plastics). When this quip is exposed in the "burn book," Damien is hurt, but eventually forgives Cady. Damien is a good example of the way in which sexuality is glossed over in mainstream film. He is stereotypically gay in his behavior, his interests, his dress, and his mannerisms, but is never in a sexual situation. The closest he comes is when he kisses his best friend, Janis, at the spring fling dance, at which point they both get grossed out and he runs away. Janis is also an example of a stereotype surrounding homosexuality that is not true. The Plastics, particularly Regina, have terrorized Janis throughout her school years, spreading rumors about her being a dyke or a "lesbo," and driving her to act, dress, and look like an outsider. She gets even by exposing Regina's destruction, and in the end she hooks up with the math nerd, Kevin Gnapoor, whom she's kissing in the final scene. In this way, her heterosexuality is reinforced and she is able to escape the confines of her previous identity. However, the fact that she has been victimized in this way by Regina is not problematized and her victimization may end with Cady's help, but her help is not enough. She needs the typical solution—a man—to complete her reentry into the norm. Further, this man complicates factors surrounding race as he earlier claims that he only dates women of color, but "settles" for Janis, who is an outsider of a different "stripe."

Since few mainstream films tackle sexuality, let alone sex, on the margins, sexuality is the focus of many independent films, such as those that will be discussed in greater detail in chapter four, "Empowering Sexuality." But as confused as sexuality is in film, most mainstream teen films and girls' films miss the opportunity for genuine or complicated portrayals of sex and sexuality, or even fun and playful portrayals like those found in boys' films like *American Pie* (which are only sometimes fun and playful for the girls). Most often sex and sexuality are caught up in the convention of romance, which often removes both the sex and the sexuality from their conversations and contexts.

Romance Without Sex

While everything can be romanticized in film—people, life, love, sex, the city, the country, the future, the past—and while love is a "universal" theme, the mainstream market is saturated by a particular version of love: romantic. In the mainstream, sex and romance are so intricately intertwined that sex rarely appears unless it is romantic and if it does, then sexuality outside the expectations of the dominant is punished, sometimes severely. Even films that depict sexuality outside of dominant norms, like *Secretary* and *Splendor*, also represent these "deviant" sexualities within the frame of romance, making it more palatable, if not more accepted. Sometimes, like in *Coyote Ugly*, sex is a part of the romance, though the sex scenes are most often limited to romanticized portrayals (and the actual sex is off screen). However, romance can also appear with only the slightest hint at sex, like in *10 Things I Hate About You* when Bianca finds Kat's black underwear and interprets them as meaning that she wants to have sex "someday." But most often, romance, in mainstream girls' films, is presented without any reference to a sexual relationship or a developed or developing sexuality, like in *Whatever It Takes, Drive Me Crazy, Confessions of a Teenage Drama Queen, Raise Your Voice*, and *What a Girl Wants*. The forces that dictate this relationship between sex and romance (especially as they are separated from sexuality) are the same as those that dictate the uncomplicated and uncritical "multicultural" representations of race and ethnicity discussed in chapter one. Thus, romance is offered as an "empowering narrative," despite its reliance upon mainstream conventions.

In the '80s, most of the plots of teen films relied upon romance. For instance, in *Sixteen Candles* and *Pretty in Pink*, Molly Ringwald's characters are not looking for sex, they are looking for a really cute (and, coincidentally, really rich) boyfriend, a relationship. If any sex does take place, it takes place postnarrative. *Fast Times at Ridgemont High* has a similar narrative, but it breaks most of the rules because writer-director Amy Heckerling wanted it that way. The main character, Stacy (urged by her older friend, Linda) is not looking for a boyfriend as much as she is looking to have sex. In most romantic teen films of the '80s as well as the '90s, sex is pushed off-screen or postnarrative, but in *Fast Times*, Stacy has sex on screen twice. Both times she is disappointed, and the second time she ends up pregnant. After experiencing physical and emotional disappointment, and dealing with other consequences of sex (like abortion), Stacy says: "I finally figured it out. I don't want sex, anyone can have sex. I want a relationship. I want romance." And despite Linda's skepticism ("we can't even get cable TV here, Stacy, and you want romance?"), at the end of the narrative Stacy, and her boyfriend, Rat (neither rich, nor traditionally good-looking), are "having a passionate love affair ... but still haven't gone all the way."

This film, despite being a romance, takes the romance out of sex because sex is not a part of the romantic plot. Sex is used both as comedy and as realism, and as such, sex more closely resembles the reality of teenage life. Teenage sex is not often romantic (or perfect, like Vicky in *American Pie* wants it to be—although she wants to have sex, the time never seems to be right), it is more often painful, disappointing, embarrassing, or frightening, and, thus, not a good choice for romantic subject matter. In *Fast Times* Amy Heckerling keeps the romance and retains sex as a rite of passage and a part of coming of age, but does not romanticize the rites that allow a girl to "settle" for romance. Stacy chooses romance because she has had sex and it was not romantic at all. But Stacy's choice of romance (especially without sex) is unusual, but not unheard of, for a sexually experienced protagonist.

In most romantic, mainstream Hollywood teen films, sex is not a part of the plot. If it is, then the sex is off-screen or a part of the backstory, or glossed over, or romanticized. For instance, in *Confessions of a Teenage Drama Queen*, Lola has an intellectual rather than a sexual or romantic crush on her rock star idol. This relationship can be compared to that of Darcy in *Girl* (a more marginal mainstream movie) who becomes a groupie because of her crush on her rock star idol. Like Lola, Darcy does everything she can to try to meet him, but unlike Lola, Darcy has the goal of having sex with her idol. She becomes the groupie that Lola, the innocent teen, the star on the rise, can never be. Instead, Lola wakes her idol up when she tells him that he's a "total drunk." She has such an impact on him and his life that he appears at the cast party after Lola's play to personally thank her and return her necklace. Thus, Lola's relationship with her idol walks the line between child and adult. When she and Ella find themselves in his clothes, and in his room, they do childish things like jump on his bed and play with his guitars. But when Lola is confronted with his lack of ability to discuss his poetry, she wakes him up and changes his life. Darcy also changes her idol, but she also outgrows him. She conquered him and comforted him but realizes that she doesn't want to be simply a groupie. Thus, she becomes more than most groupies—she lives the fantasy. The similarities and differences between these two relationships show the ways in which romantic themes differ in their treatment of sex, in and out of the mainstream. For Lola it's not on the radar, and for Darcy, it's part of making him love or need her. Further, in many of these "family films," the latest trend in the teen film explosion (seen in films like *Confessions of a Teenage Drama Queen* and *Raise Your Voice*, which are situated in the children's or "family" section of video stores) strange sexual undertones infiltrate narratives that surround fathers and daughters or brothers and sisters. I will discuss one such phenomenon later as I compare *What a Girl Wants* with *American Beauty*, but one example is the relationship between Terri and her brother in *Raise Your Voice*. Shortly before the two get into a car accident, which she survives and he doesn't, Terri's brother films her singing and being silly, which he sends to the summer music institute that she applies for. His voyeuristic filming, while framed innocently, has some creepy undertones that, perhaps, only strike some viewers. Perhaps the subtle undertones of Christianity counter this.

Romantic themes are stock conventions for teen films though many girls' films subvert this convention as well and will be discussed more fully in chapter four. For instance, *The Opposite of Sex* is a diatribe against romance, and Dedee learns to love in nonromantic ways as she scoffs the romantic love that works for others. And in *Virtual Sexuality*, despite all of Justine's romantic expectations, she ends up with a much more practical outlook on sex and love at the end of the film. Some films, like *But I'm a Cheerleader*, challenge romance and heterosexuality by making a love relationship available and viable in the end. While this film offers a new definition of coupledom, its lovers are forced to withdraw from the societies they have known in order to be a couple. And some films, like *Whatever*, offer no form of romance—only harsh realities, like a failed attempt at oral sex and a drug-induced make-out session that could have turned tragic in different circumstances. These films, and others which will be discussed in more detail in part four, offer more complicated, more realistic, and more promising endings than those like *Clueless* where all three girls are perfectly coupled and chattering on about their future weddings.

In *Clueless*, Cher can afford (literally and figuratively) to have a romantic view of sex; she is in control of her life and of the narrative that relates this life to us. When the narrative begins, she is the most popular girl in school; she is a model for fashion and taste. When Cher is unhappy with her grades, she decides that her teacher is unhappy and she and her best friend, Dionne (both named after singing stars), plot to fix up two lonely teachers. Cher uses her talent—makeovers (which "give her a sense of control in a world full of chaos")—as well as her cunning, and not only wins good grades for herself, but adoration and applause from the entire student body. Thus, Cher's best solution for feeling "impotent and out of control, which [she] really hates," is to go to the mall, where her father's credit card puts her life back in perspective. At home, Cher is Daddy's little girl and she plays this part as well as she plays the part of little sister to her "brother" Josh, the son of her ex-stepmother. She makes sure her father remembers to eat and she makes fun of Josh (mostly for his lack of style).

Since Cher is so powerful in high school, this isn't the place where she searches for men because "searching for a boy in high school is as pointless as searching for meaning in a Pauly Shore movie." Her romantic vision, which Dionne jokes about, is "saving herself for Luke Perry." Such a vision cannot be fulfilled by high school boys who are, the girls decide, "like dogs." And Cher's experiences with high school boys do nothing to convince her otherwise. When one boy, Elton, insists on giving her a ride home, he forces himself on her and when she won't cooperate he forces her out of the car in the middle of LA. Cher survives not only what she terms "sexual harassment," but also abandonment and a robbery that strips her of only her cell phone and her purse, and causes her to "ruin" her designer dress. While this representation undermines the seriousness of both date rape and sexual harassment, it is representative of the conditions that rule teenage girls' sexuality—even the most popular and the most perfect girls are targets for boys' "uncontrollable" passions.

In another failed attempt with a high school boy, Cher successfully catches Christian's attention by "showing a little skin," sending herself flowers, and other little ploys meant to make him ask her out. When Cher decides that Christian is "the one," she tries a sure-fire plan to lose her virginity. Di helps her pick out an outfit for the big night and arrange her pillows just right. Cher even attempts (and fails) to bake cookies. But with all of Cher's preparation, it is clear that Christian is not interested in having sex with Cher, not because of any failure on her part, but because he's gay. (Later, the two become friends because he likes to shop as much as she does.)

Although Cher has so much trouble with high school boys, Di and Tai do not have the same problems. Tai becomes more and more popular (after Cher sets her in motion), and Di finally goes all the way with her boyfriend and leaves Cher in the dust. Cher's control continues to dwindle out of control as she finds herself in a situation she can't argue her way out of—she fails her driver's test—and her friend, Tai (who Cher helped to make popular with her make-over talent) takes a stab at her, calling her "a virgin who can't drive." Suddenly the other power that Cher thought she had, defining the criteria necessary to lose her virginity, becomes something that makes her powerless. She realizes that what she thought was taste ("You see how picky I am about my shoes and they only go on my feet"), has really left her clueless.

But in a sweep of romance Cher realizes that she's in love with her nonbrother, Josh (something she was clueless to before) and of course the feeling is mutual. Until Cher realizes she is in love with Josh, she teases him and argues with him. She comes across as being a silly airhead, but every once in a while, Cher surprises him with something intelligent, sensitive, or funny. In some ways Cher "grows up" when she realizes that she was clueless, but this rite of passage is hand-in-hand with sex since she has found a guy that meets her sexual criteria—someone she "really cares about." Even in this romantic coming of age, sex, if not the deciding factor, is the prize, and Cher is hardly powerless in claiming this prize (since she does so postnarrative). But the movie also ends with a wedding scene, not for any of the girls in the film, but for the teacher the girls make over. When the bride throws the bouquet, Cher emerges from the pile of struggling girls and women with the bouquet, a clue that there will, of course, be marriage (and sex) in her future. She'll fight for it. And as the three couples close the film joking about marriage, it is clear that there is an ideal ending to all of their affairs.

While Cher defies many stereotypes and *Clueless* exposes many myths, neither the character, nor the film, do much to subvert these myths. For instance, rather than take issue with the myth of virginity, Cher strives to experience this landmark because she feels left out when Di finally goes all the way. The romantic ending of the film, not only for Cher, but also for Di and Tai, is the only way this film can end. The girls fight over the bouquet as the boys joke about them planning their weddings and this reinforces the idea that women want marriage and men want to do anything they can to avoid it. But during her coming of age, Cher also goes from being a selfish princess to being a selfish princess who takes interest in charitable causes and global issues. Perhaps postnarrative, when she completely grows out of adolescence, Cher will be a more developed version of this person, with the help of Josh, of course, since he is the catalyst for the change in Cher during the narrative. Then again, perhaps Cher's interest in charitable causes and global issues will simply make her feel less guilty as she continuously fills her shopping bags at the mall. After all, she has the cultural and economic capital to do so.

Like *Clueless, 10 Things I Hate About You* is a narrative that relies upon romance without sex through both Kat and Bianca, though this romance takes different forms. In this romantic film, Kat is a "bitchy" feminist who reads Sylvia Plath and applies to Sarah Lawrence College. She wears black and refuses to submit to the pressures of popularity and she is also a strong, empowered character. She does what she wants to without worrying how her actions will look to everyone who is watching. But to her sister, Bianca, and the rest of the student body, Kat is a loser, a mutant, and a bitch. She is even called a "heinous bitch" in class by Joey, a popular model who we later find out was Kat's boyfriend when she was a freshman. Bianca doesn't realize that Joey is responsible for the change in her sister. She doesn't know her sister went out with Joey (and doesn't even believe Kat when she first tells Bianca this). Bianca also doesn't know that Kat didn't get sick of being popular, Joey made her sick of it.

Bianca is concerned only with convincing their father to let them date and Kat is the obstacle that stands in the way, according to their father's rule (no dating until you graduate). What Bianca doesn't know is what a jerk Joey is and that Joey is interested in her because she is a guaranteed virgin. Kat knows this and tries to dissuade Bianca without telling her why she's interfering. But this hardly matters since Bianca finds this out for herself on their first date and quickly dumps Joey for Cameron, a new boy at school who fell in love with Bianca upon first sight. But Kat and her father are still obstacles to Bianca's qualified autonomy (Cameron is such a nice guy) and Cameron and his friend take it upon themselves (with the help of Joey's money) to find someone who will date the undateable Kat so that they can offer to help him "tame the wild beast," as Patrick lightly phrases it, and Cameron will be able to take Bianca out. They choose Patrick because he's mysterious and the wild rumors about him seem to qualify him as the only person equipped to take on Kat.

Thus, the narrative of *10 Things* is focused on Kat and her "taming" while Bianca's shallow pursuits are part of the subplot. While Kat keeps her attitude and her politics, she also falls in love and surrenders to the plotting of her sister. But she also works through a lot of the baggage that made her want to be an outcast. Parts of this working out come from a conversation with Bianca where Kat admits that she had sex with Joey because "everyone was doing it." She says, "after that I swore I would never do anything just because everyone else was doing it." Bianca listens with amazement, but when Kat tries to lecture her, she lashes back. Kat tells her, "not all experiences are good, Bianca. You can't always trust the people you want to." Of course Kat is speaking about Joey and her own experiences. But Bianca doesn't have the same maturing processes as her sister and she replies, "Well, I guess I'll never know, will I?" Bianca's words are like a slap in the face to Kat. Kat was so worried about protecting Bianca that she didn't think about letting her figure all of these things out for herself, and this conversation makes Kat swallow her pride and go to the prom so that Bianca, according to the rules, can also go. Kat is surprised and pleased to see that Bianca did not go to the prom with Joey, but with Cameron. She has been so worried about watching Bianca repeat her past mistakes, that she forgets to let her make her own choices and her own mistakes. However, in this narrative, Bianca doesn't make any mistakes.

Although Kat seems to be the empowered character (at least in a feminist sense), the one who is not afraid to be herself, to be something different from the crowds around her, it is Bianca who comes across as powerful and "empowered" in the course of the narrative. Bianca has all the right answers. She talks back to her father, avoids Joey, sweetly manipulates Cameron, puts her sister in her place, and remains the good girl everyone loves. She even punches Joey several times—once for "making my date bleed," once for her sister, and a final one "for me." But while Bianca exhibits all of this power, she is not empowered. As Patrick describes her to Kat, "she's without." The hero of the movie, in many ways, is also a bland conformist. She doesn't make any hard choices in the course of the narrative—Cameron is clearly the best choice. He's perfect (a sweet, little follower) and Joey is slime. She doesn't even take an active role in the plot to get her sister (and thus herself) a date. Instead, she sits back and whines as the boys do all of the plotting. She is there to be looked at while the boys have the active roles.

Kat, on the other hand, goes through many rites of passage in the span of a few weeks' time which include getting over her preconceptions about people (and boys in particular), working through her past (which Bianca helps her do), talking to her father about her future (and he tells her that he sent the check to Sarah Lawrence despite the fact that he will miss her), letting down some of her defenses, and letting Patrick into her life. All of these rites make Kat less of a "bitch" and more of a person; however, like Cher, this change for the better could not happen without the romance that develops between her and Patrick. Despite the fact that he was paid to take Kat out, Patrick actually turns out to be just perfect for Kat; he's even interested in the indie feminist bands that she likes. He's not afraid or embarrassed to make a romantic gesture for her, and he uses the money he made from the other boys to buy his way into her heart. They still have disagreements, but at the end of the film, they stop arguing to make out while Kat's favorite (nameless) band plays the recognizable tune: "I Want You to Want Me."

In terms of sexuality, convention seems to dominate this film. At the end of the film Bianca is in a perfectly romantic relationship; and while her father was frightened about her "getting jiggy with some boy," she does not show any interest in anything more than kissing (though her father has a comeback for that scenario as well: "kissing isn't what keeps me up to my elbows in placenta all day long"). Bianca won't be doing anything just because everyone else is doing it, but she also won't be doing anything because the narrative will not allow this possibility. It keeps her frozen at this point in her life, and in her personal and sexual development. What the future holds is inconsequential. But while Bianca is confined, the parameters of this romantic narrative are most confining for Kat. Her status as "bitch" when the film begins is a result of her making an autonomous decision about her sexuality and herself. She doesn't want to follow the crowd, especially when it comes to sex. Her decision is not community-sanctioned or supported, but her status as an outcast certainly is. Once Kat is with a boy who is not like Joey, a boy who cares about her and has her best interests in mind throughout the film, she is not allowed to continue her development on screen because the narrative ends before she has to make such choices. The film makes it seem like sex is not even an issue because romance prevails and the two cannot be on screen together in such a film. The subtext, however, is that Kat is, by now, ready to pursue her sexuality in a sexual relationship (but only as an outcome of the romantic narrative). At the end of the film, Kat is no longer identified as a feminist, most likely because popular perceptions of feminism are virtually absent in film. This, perhaps, implies that she is no longer a (man) hater, but a (man) lover.

Many of these romantic films like *10 Things I Hate About You* feature love interests who are not the typical meathead jock. Instead, these boys are everything the typical protagonist in these films could want even if he's a "bad boy" since the "bad boy" often turns out to be much more intellectual and sophisticated than anyone imagined. For instance, in *10*

Things, Patrick is persistent, at first, because he is paid to be so, but in the end his persistence is what she really needs. Another such "bad boy" in *Crossroads* is also misunderstood and the subject of rumors. He, like Patrick, turns out to be, truly, a knight in shining armor. In *What a Girl Wants*, Ian is also persistent in trying to see Daphne again, as many love interests are in girls' films like *Coyote Ugly* and *Saved!* For instance, in *Coyote Ugly*, the love interest is not only persistent in getting Violet to go out with him, but he is also persistent in trying to convince her to get over her stage fright. And in *Saved!*, Patrick gives Mary a ride home, and when she turns him down for a date, he asks if she'll be available the day after, or the day after that. This persistence is a plot device that reoccurs often and is disturbingly similar to the reoccurring theme in mainstream popular culture that when a girl or woman says no, she really means yes. While these girls sometimes say no, the "right" boys and men are persistent regardless. And eventually the girls say yes because, as we all know, even if they don't immediately know, yes is the right answer, at least according to the mainstream myth.

Another romantic trope reoccurs when these enlightened beaus get to a girl's heart through music. For instance, when Ian plays in the band at one of the aristocratic functions Daphne has to attend, he sings a song for her about how "love's been a long time coming." And in *Bring It On*, Cliff, who is more punk than Ian, is also sensitive and supportive. He gives Torrance a tape with a song he wrote and recorded for her and inspires her to find the inspiration to overcome all setbacks. These boys also have all the right lines. For instance, the line that leads Ian and Daphne's first kiss is: "Why are you trying so hard to fit in when you were born to stand out?" And Patrick tells Mary that "God gave us all free will," and that Mary inspires him and amazes him. In fact, there are many such sensitive, supportive boys with all the right lines in girls' film, and even in boys' films like *The Girl Next Door*. However, while the central protagonists in films like *American Pie* and *The Girl Next Door* are allowed to be more sensitive than other boys in teen films, like the stereotypical jocks, these sensitive guys are still pulled in by mainstream expectations and they still remain superior to their love interest. For instance, in *The Girl Next Door*, Matthew is student body president, but rather than being a popular guy like Zach in *She's All That*, Matthew is a brain and his friends provide stock *Revenge of the Nerds*–type characters. Matthew's life is deeply impacted by Danielle, a hot, young woman-girl who wants to get out of the porn business and start over. And Danielle impacts Matthew's life without having sex with him (at least not immediately), helping Matthew discover that "moral fiber" is not what he thought it was. Despite the lures

of the stereotypical porn world, Matthew remains a gentleman throughout the film. However, as a protagonist in a boys' film, the meaning of
gentleman takes on more sinister characteristics, detectable only to some.
As a gentleman Matthew automatically relocates his earth-shattering,
life-changing girl to the margins of his world and his achievements. And
when it comes time for the happy endings, despite Danielle's central role
in the narrative and in Matthew's life, Danielle fades into the background
and becomes the supportive girl on Matthew's arm. Danielle's ambitions
to start over and maybe go to college fade into the background, not simply overshadowed by Matthew's success, but forgotten as he tells the audience about all the money he's made so that he's able to pay for his
education at Georgetown. And Danielle's role continues to be smiling
from the sidelines.

While this perfect boyfriend character in mainstream girls' film is
juxtaposed with unsavory boys like Stiffler in *American Pie*, Joey in *10
Things I Hate About You*, Elton in *Clueless*, and many other boys in independent girls' films, this perfect boy is revealed as just another device of
the romantic plot convention. Since he is too perfect, too uncomplicated,
he also fails to be an agent of change, and he takes on a role similar to
Danielle's function in *The Girl Next Door*—a trophy, something pretty to
look at, and a security blanket. And rarely is this boy portrayed as a temporary love interest as he is in *Virtual Sexuality* or, more subtly in *Raise
Your Voice*, where no mention of the future is made except, perhaps, next
summer. More often his permanence is unspoken, especially when these
films fall into the myth and traps of fate and of one true love for each person. Finally, while this character may help to level the playing field, so to
speak, for girls' sexual power, if we look to this as an example of equality
or empowerment, we are forgetting that we are still playing a man's game,
on a man's turf, according to the dominant culture's rules.

Unrealistic Images and Expectations

While romance can create unrealistic expectations, there are many
ways that we can consider the role of unrealistic images and expectations
in girls' film. In fact, several mainstream films provide physical and other
unrealistic images and expectations within their coming-of-age narratives. These unrealistic images and expectations aren't necessarily "good"
or "bad"; instead, especially together, they provide expectations that don't
fit with their messages. For instance, since many teen characters are
portrayed by adult women, there is an unrealistic standard of physical

development set for younger teens. Such representations, in the visual images they present, can be potentially harmful to understandings of sex and sexuality. For instance, censorship regulations required that Nabakov's Lolita be portrayed by (at least) an 18-year-old body, and ensure that no actor having sex on screen is under 18. Thus, much of the awkwardness of teenage appearance that is seen in films like *Kids* is gone. The bodies of children look like the bodies of adults (because they really are). Unreal images and expectations are flaunted in front of flat chests, acne, and braces. What is made desirable on screen is unattainable physically and realistically until after the awkward stages of adolescence, if ever. Interestingly, however, many of the girls' films that feature teens playing teens (even if not playing their own teen age like Lohan at 17 playing Lola as 15) are marketed as "family films," and offer romantic plots that include kissing and boyfriends, but not sex or marriage. Further, some of these teens, like Lohan, are publicly scrutinized for their physical development through, for instance, rumors about breast augmentation and plastic surgery. While many of these narratives will be discussed in more detail in the following chapter, it is important to note a few of these unrealistic images and expectations here since they largely determine the parameters of mainstream girls' film, and establish patterns for coming of age.

One unreal image and expectation appears in the film *13 Going on 30*, a recycled plot from the film *Big* that is used to accelerate the coming-of-age process, so that the protagonist can learn and grow, but also so that she can try to win back her lost friend, who also happens to be her lost love. In this process, not only is there an unreal expectation, but there is also the unreal image presented in the leap from 13 to 30—a span that takes Jenna from girl to woman physically, but not mentally. And this is exactly what happens to Jenna. She is miserable as a 13-year-old and longs to be one of "the six," the nickname for the queen bees in this film. Jenna doesn't want to be pretty in her own way, and she doesn't want to be original, she wants to be cool. She doesn't want to be awkward and unpopular, she wants to be "30, flirty, and thriving," an idea she gets from her favorite magazine cover. This is the teen mentality she still has when she gets her wish and finds herself in her own body and her own life, 17 years later. But this mentality begins to change as Jenna comes to realize that not only is she a mean, conniving person, but she also let this meanness get in the way of the only true friend she had when she was 13. And, of course, this youthful innocence not only enables her to realize that she doesn't want all of the superficial things that she thought she wanted, but it also gives her a fresh new idea of how to put fun and laughter back into *Poise* magazine (where she is an editor), since she is still close enough to "remember what used to be good." All of these coming-of-age elements are empowering as Jenna realizes that popularity and coolness come at too high a price. However, what is disturbing about this film is the way in which her 13-year-old best friend also becomes her love interest in this film. It's not enough for her to realize that she was really mean to him, and to mend this rift, but, because of the romantic conventions of mainstream films, she also discovers she loves him. So, when 13-year-old Jenna returns to her body and has her whole life to live over, she grabs Matt's hand and tells him to follow her, saying "you'll see" when he asks where they're going. And just like the leap that took Jenna from 13 to 30 earlier in this film, another leap takes the viewer from Jenna at 13 to Jenna back at 30, marrying Matt, and living happily ever after. Thus, it is implied, Jenna doesn't relive her adolescence and early adulthood for herself, and she doesn't find new dreams to pursue as a better, more conscious, person. Those 17 years are inconsequential as she and Matt sit on a couch in their new front yard, eat Razzles, and look at snapshots of the past.

This unreal leap is also used in *Freaky Friday*, a film that reminds women that they should be more like girls and lets girls know it's hard to be a woman. The *Freaky Friday* of 1978 offers a different version of the story than the 2003 version which updates the story to make it more modern and relevant. Thus, the mother becomes a single mother who is getting remarried rather than being a housewife preparing for an important dinner for her husband's client, and the daughter is in a band and wants to be a rock star instead of being a member of a water skiing team. And it's the mother's career that is threatened by the switch, not the father's. But in this revision, rather than switching places simply through whatever strange forces are at work, Anna and her mother switch places when the family goes out for Chinese food, with the help of Pei-Pei's meddling mother. Not only does this plot device portray the Chinese as butting into other people's business, but they are also portrayed as a mystical people with "magical" powers. This orientalist portrayal exoticizes the "other" while also keeping this other on the margins of the narrative, and, thus, reinforces white supremacy. This is further cemented when mother and daughter discuss what happened and Anna (as her mother) says that they must have performed "some strange Asian voodoo." Also in this revision, Anna the tomboy becomes Anna the "punk" rocker who dresses and pierces like a "bad girl" and plays songs with lyrics that express her desire to not grow up, but to get out. But at least in this revision, the "bad girl" is revealed as not being "bad" so much as she is misunderstood by her mother. She may dress like a bad girl, and front some attitude, but this bad girl is really a sharp honors student. But, in another romantic convention, Anna is reunited with the boy of her dreams, the boy that Mom now approves of. Thus, this bad girl is tamed in more than one way.

While these films show unrealistic images and expectations, some unreal expectations can be caused by the marketing and packaging of a film. Taglines, quotes, and images all work to set up these unreal expectations, which, again, aren't necessarily bad. For instance, the box for *Slums of Beverly Hills* claims it is a '70s *Clueless*. And while this film is far from *Clueless* in a variety of ways, this box quote might attract someone to this film who wouldn't otherwise watch it. Because *Clueless* is one of the most recognizable teen and girls' film, many films use it as a point of comparison, like *The Craft*, whose box-cover claims "It's *Carrie* meets *Clueless!*" Sometimes, like in the case of *What a Girl Wants*, the packaging may be changed because of cultural circumstances. The original poster and advertisements for this film showed Amanda Bynes in an American flag tank top, sandwiched between two English guards, flashing a peace sign. But because this film was released during times of war, this peace sign was interpreted as being too controversial. Someone might mistake it as anti–American. Thus, this "girl-power fairy tale" stays apolitical, like most teen films. While previews and packaging can be misleading, sometimes, like in the case of *Splendor*, the packaging is revealing. The box for this film claims it's "an ultra-hip and stylish romantic comedy," and it is. Despite the fact that Veronica has two boyfriends, and this trio finds a way to make their unconventional relationship work, this film is still romantic and has a romantic conclusion. It doesn't really "explore the possibilities" as the box urges. Instead, it shows one possibility, and cements it within mainstream expectations when this trio becomes a family.

Still other unreal expectations are caused by the use of girls' spaces, stereotypes, tools, and talents. For instance, cheerleading is one of these girls' spaces. However, even though 97 percent of all cheerleaders are female, and 81 percent of the nation's cheerleaders are between the ages of 14 and 18, 50 percent of all collegiate cheerleaders are male and colleges give out full cheerleading scholarships to men for stunting (according to promotional materials for *Bring It On*). Thus, while cheerleading is seen as a girls' space, and male and female cheerleaders are stereotyped according to these assumptions, men still enjoy power and prestige in the sport, especially when cheerleading is competitive. Thus, cheerleading, in girls' films, is the only space where this competitive sport may include some boys, but does not value their strength above that of the girls. For instance, in *Sugar and Spice*, this space acts as a support network for Diane when she gets pregnant. And in *But I'm a Cheerleader*, Megan first uses her identity as a cheerleader to deny her sexuality, but then she uses her cheer skills not for a reinforcement of the status quo, but to prove her love for Graham. Finally, in *Bring It On*, the boys in cheerleading are portrayed in ways that make them unsavory or stereotypical characters—one is seemingly unaware that he is gay, one likes to put his fingers in inappropriate places, and one, Torrance's soon to be ex-boyfriend, is a cheating womanizer. In all of these films, cheerleading is not only a girls' space, but it is sometimes used to push the boundaries of this space.

Another stereotype that emerges in a variety of places, including teen and girls' film, is that girls are bad at math and science, but are good at the arts. Thus, we see several characters that are artists: Laney in *She's All That*, Anna in *Whatever*, and the mothers of the girls in several films like *Confessions of a Teenage Drama Queen* and *The Princess Diaries*. Still other girls are musicians, actors, or aspiring musicians and actors, like the girls in *Josie and the Pussycats*, Anna in *Freaky Friday*, Teri in *Raise Your Voice*, Mimi in *Crossroads*, Susan in *Shake, Rattle, and Rock*, Claude in *All Over Me*, and Daphne's mom in *What a Girl Wants*. But just as often, girls idolize (usually male) artists rather than pursue the art themselves, like in *Girl* and *Welcome to the Dollhouse*. And in *Confessions of a Teenage Drama Queen* Lola idolizes Stu Wolf for his amazing poetry, claiming him to be akin to Shakespeare; but she doesn't pursue the creative end of music. She wants to perform, and she sings one of his songs, but never writes her own. Further, girls are rarely into politics, like in *All I Wanna Do*, and even more rarely are they interested in math, like Cady in *Mean Girls*. Since she was not raised in the U.S. public school system, it makes sense that Cady would be a character who likes and excels at something that most girls are encouraged, formally and informally, overtly and covertly, not to pursue.

Another unrealistic expectation of teen films is presented in the fairy-tale revision films like *The Princess Diaries* and *What a Girl Wants* where a young woman does not go from rags to riches, but from her comfortable existence to royalty, the highest rung on the ladder. While these two films are different in many ways, both set up a fairy-tale story that is marketed as a family film. Both of these films have the message that a girl should just be herself, and both of these films present "good" role models for young girls. But both of these films, like *A Cinderella Story*, also play upon the myth that new clothes and new makeup can make a new girl, or, rather, that they can make a girl realize who she truly is. All three of these films are presented as stories of self-discovery more than as coming-of-age films, though there are also important coming-of-age elements that will be discussed in the next chapter. However, here it is important to point out that when it comes down to it, all three of these protagonists have the money to back them up, though not having money is only an issue in *A Cinderella Story*. Sam begins as the victim of her evil stepmother, working at what used to be her father's diner. But she ends up the victor when she finds her father's lost will and gets everything back—the house, the car, the diner—and also gets a ticket to her future. Thus, this film is a rags-to-riches story while *The Princess Diaries* is about the making of a princess.

All of these films with unreal expectations also have another important element of the mainstream—the power of being or becoming a star (whatever form this stardom might take). For instance, in *The Princess Diaries* Mia becomes a princess and adopts the star power that comes with this title as she tries to escape from the prying paparazzi cameras. And even if she doesn't want this attention, she learns to live with it. Likewise, in *Confessions of a Teenage Drama Queen*, *Raise Your Voice* and *A Cinderella Story*, the protagonists are also singing stars, and the DVDs include their music videos for the songs they sing that are featured in the film. Even films where the protagonist is not also a singing star, she may sing, like in *Ella Enchanted*, and music is so important to this genre that many of the newer films also include music videos in their DVD extras, like Kari Kimmel's "It's Not Just Make-Believe" from *Ella Enchanted*. Further, even when a singing star is not the main character, she often sings as part of the narrative. For instance, in both *The Princess Diaries* and *Saved*, Mandy Moore performs as a part of an all-girl singing group, and in both of these films her singing group is slightly satirical.

Perhaps it is cliché to say that all young girls dream of being stars in music, dance, or drama; I certainly bought right into this dream for a while. It's hard not to when it is so ingrained within our entertainment and our coming-of-age stories. The entertainment industry feeds on such dreams because these dreams not only rarely create new stars, but, more frequently, create new consumers. This is largely the function of music in mainstream teen and girls' films, though some girls, like Lohan, make use of this space in order to attempt, for instance, to dispel rumors, which she does in her song "Rumors" from her album *Speak*. However, outside the mainstream, music opens many avenues that it can't open in the mainstream, from the triumphant groupie in *Girl*, to the aspiring musician in *All Over Me* and *Shake, Rattle, and Rock!*, to the engaged listener in *The Smokers*. Further, many of these films provide feminist music throughout the film and on the soundtrack like in *Just Another Girl on the I.R.T.*, *Girls Town*, *Foxfire*, and *All Over Me*.

In the next chapter I deal more specifically with these fantastic spaces as a kind of coming-of-age narrative, but it is important here to point out this fantastic space as a kind of unreal expectation, especially when this dream is set up as a way to "just believe in yourself," like it is in *Confessions of a Teenage Drama Queen* (and in *Raise Your Voice*). In this film, Lindsay Lohan stars as a 15-year-old girl who is forced to move with her mother and sisters to New Jersey, leaving behind New York, the "center of the universe," according to this young teenage drama queen. While Lola may be a good role model for kids because she shows them that they shouldn't be afraid and that they shouldn't let anyone get in their way, as Lohan argues in the behind-the-scenes featurette "Confessions from the Set," Lola achieves these things for herself in a fantasy world, telling kids that they can make life anything they want and they don't have to play by any rules. If anything, this is certainly a mixed message since these messages sound good on film, and only work out so easily in the "real life" of film. The message is that until you "make it," you're "nobody," but that everyone has the chance to be "somebody." However, many girls realize this sad truth through failure, which can be a coming of age just as much as the success stories found in film.

These kind of leaps from adolescence to adulthood, from squalor to wealth, from nobody to somebody, are embodied in another unreal expectation often used in teen films—the expectation that high school graduation is the marker of adulthood and maturity. High school graduation, and the associated markers of prom, sex, drinking, etc. are used in a variety of films to symbolize the passage from teenager to adult, and this makes sense since these events are commonly held up as the markers of adolescence, even if they are considered to be a bad substitute for something more meaningful. Further, many of these films that have stock rites often inflate these rites so that they have an almost mythical importance. This is particularly true in narratives that focus on boys; the big game (football, lacrosse, soccer), the big night (prom, party), the big day (graduation) are all reasons to score. Often these markers are presented uncritically or in exaggerated forms. For instance, in *10 Things I Hate About You*, Kat, who is responsible and doesn't drink or smoke, decides to get wasted at a party, supposedly because of her teenage angst, her anger toward her sister for making what Kat thinks are stupid mistakes, and her annoyance that Patrick has accompanied her to the party. However, Kat's shallow and irrational response is really just an excuse to make her more vulnerable and to give Patrick a chance to save her.

There are also many coming-of-age narratives that leave out, water down, or rewrite these stock rites, and even some that challenge their status as stock. For instance, when Kat attends prom, this event is hardly a stock rite of passage for Kat—in fact, she leaves and this is Bianca's moment to shine. She doesn't gain prestige because she is the only soph-omore at prom, but she gains power because she (violently) puts the sleazy Joey in his place. In the following chapter I look more closely at some of these mainstream coming-of-age narratives and the ways in which these films reinforce mainstream ideology through stock rites of passage and other conventions, and the ways in which these films also sometimes chal-lenge these mainstream conventions. Then, in chapter three, I discuss the ways in which girls in more marginalized roles and films negotiate the structures of culture and society, particularly power, violence, sexuality, and hypocrisy. This discussion reveals some of the ways that sanctioned, predetermined rites of passage are not as powerful or empowering, as deep or as meaningful, as the rites and markers that girls make for themselves as they negotiate coming of age in a variety of circumstances—sometimes stock, but more often not. These circumstances, and the ways in which girl in film negotiate them, are the subject of the following chapters.

TWO

COMING-OF-AGE NARRATIVES
Some Mainstream Contours

In an interview almost 30 years ago, published in *Generation Rap: An Anthology About Youth and the Establishment*, world-famous psychoanalyst Rollo May identified a lack of myths and symbols in American culture. Without myths, he argues, youth lack that which gives them "identity, a sense of being, a style of life." This same argument is now made by this generation about today's youth. For instance, in her book *A Tribe Apart: A Journey into the Heart of American Adolescence*, Patricia Hersch argues that "there are few community-sanctioned moments or formalized thresholds that mark steps on the road toward adulthood." Both of these authors, and plenty of others, argue that this lack of formalized thresholds and lack of myths and symbols means that youth are lost. They are left looking inside themselves in order to "undertake the lonely, confusing task of finding new myths on which to base identity" (Stanford 169). This analysis, and the assumptions based on it, is not totally off-base, but it also doesn't account for the social and cultural changes that the youth of America continue to navigate as they come of age in the U.S. Nor does it consider that pop culture provides a variety of such myths and symbols, and that teens and adults are capable of utilizing these myths and symbols for a variety of needs, desires, and conscious transformations.

Today coming of age is not so much about incorporating the myths and symbols of culture as it is about making sense of ourselves as individuals and as members of local and global societies in the midst of these often contradictory myths and symbols. Myths and symbols, moments and markers, do exist, but in manufactured, predetermined, or empty forms, or in unsanctioned, underexposed, or inaccessible forms. Many fail to "come of age" because we fail to live up to the (often ambiguous) standards our culture has set for this transition. For some this is a position of empowerment in itself, a position from which an individual has some autonomy. For others it is disheartening and can be devastating emotionally, financially, or otherwise. For this individual, autonomy is frightening; the standards society has set are the only standards they know. For still others, this becomes a position of deviance—a reason for violence or other inarticulate acts. (Dick Hebdige and others have written about teens' expression as inarticulate.) While this is certainly a dynamic of some teen cultures, there are plenty of examples that will be discussed throughout this book that are not inarticulate at all, but misunderstood by the forces they oppose. What is inarticulate to the mainstream may be, potentially, more powerful for oppositional narratives. This is particularly true since many mainstream protagonists are inarticulate not because they are misunderstood, but because they fail to say or do anything of real substance. And girls at the margins of the mainstream are inarticulate for different reasons. Their voices often don't count and few bother to listen.

Before looking more closely at the inarticulate acts of adolescents in girls' film, it is important to examine those acts of coming of age, and even of rebellion, in teen and girls' film that are considered articulate, often because they are community-sanctioned. These mainstream coming-of-age narratives may challenge certain characteristics of adult and teen culture, but they do not fundamentally challenge these structures. Instead, they reinforce structures of power and privilege. Thus, coming of age can mean finding oneself or overcoming adversity, but most often in the mainstream it means conforming to adult standards or dominant mainstream expectations. It's important to understand this mainstream terrain in order to appreciate not only where our assumptions about adolescence are formed, and how much room for play there is in the mainstream, but also to appreciate the multiple ways in which independent films challenge these assumptions, which I will turn to in chapters three and four.

Parental Authority in Coming-of-age Narratives, 1960–2004

Like many mainstream films, alternative narratives are couched within what are often highly moralistic and traditional plots. In many films, particularly those of the 1960s, parents represent their parental authority, but they also represent a larger cultural authority that girls have had to fight especially hard against. The girls in 1960s films are all fighting for a transition into the adult world on their own terms and each face a different form of social control. In *Rebel Without a Cause* Judy wants affection from her father despite his discomfort with the sexual development of his daughter, but she also wants to be a woman on her own terms. In *Splendor in the Grass*, Deanie wants to know about sex, and she wants to know why things are the way they are. In *West Side Story*, Maria wants to know why she is not supposed to love Tony. In *Where the Boys Are*, Merritt wants sexual, intellectual freedom, a freedom that her friends (for various reasons) are not ready for. All of these girls are challenging the social controls (formal and informal) that bind girls, but none of them can come to a satisfactory answer. Maria watches Tony die. Merritt finds her intellectualism contributes to Melanie's destruction. Deanie finds herself waiting to be married to a man she loves, but is not passionately in love with. And Judy watches her surrogate son shot down by the police like a deer in their headlights. But what is important to note is that these girls were not just fighting for a rite of passage, they were fighting to be let into the ranks of adult culture, even as they questioned this culture. Through time and across films, this fight is not the same. Thus, the parent-child relationships in film are representative of how a teen may feel about his or her parents at any random point of adolescence, but this relationship is also representative of the ways in which youth view authority more generally and symbolically.

Compared to the recent popularity of teen films, the '70s and '80s did not produce a wide variety of teen films; nor did they produce a number of notable films that revolved around girls. During this period, the teen genre was still largely defined by boys' films like *Porky's* and *Revenge of the Nerds*, since the teen market was also mostly undiscovered. In teen film and girls' film in the '80s, John Hughes ruled the market with his teen films like *The Breakfast Club*, *Say Anything*, and *Ferris Bueller's Day Off*, and his girls' films like *Pretty in Pink* and *Sixteen Candles*. While the teen films like *Porky's* concentrated on boys and their pursuits of sex, the girls' films of this period were focused on romance. What's notable about all of these films, however, is that they focus on teens' dramas, with smaller roles for the parents, signaling a shift in parental authority. A few exceptions to these categories are *Fast Times at Ridgemont High*, *Little Darlings* and *Smooth Talk*. In *Fast Times*, parents are completely absent, though they are referred to at times, and in *Little Darlings*, the girls are at summer camp, so direct parental authority is absent, even if different arms of authority are present. However, in *Smooth Talk*, Connie's mother is not only present, but she is frustrated and has no clue how to deal with her leggy teenage daughter. Part of her mother's cruelty may stem from her own feelings of helplessness, but in some cases this helplessness transforms into the need to exert control over her burgeoning daughter, which she does without much patience or understanding.

In the late '80s the classic teen film *Heathers* offered a different kind of teen film narrative than the other more romantic narratives of the '80s. This film, unlike other girls' films of the time, explored the power relationships in youth culture and challenged the status quo through parody, a device rarely used in girls' films (as will be further discussed in chapter three). Veronica is autonomous, the only Heather not named Heather. And while she fits in with her friends, the Plastics of the '80s, she keeps a bit of her own style and personality, her intellect, and her introspection (diary entries). She meets JD and is interested in him despite Heather's disapproval. They end up playing strip croquet (his first time) and having sex off-camera. In these ways, JD acts as a catalyst of change in Veronica's life. And while this catalyst is corrupt, Veronica's resulting break from the Heathers is not.

Veronica has clear control of the narrative, even if she can't control her relationship with Heather number one (at least not until JD puts an end to Heather). It is only when JD's violence begins to write the narrative that Veronica begins to see her narrative power dwindle. JD has a clear trajectory in mind and Veronica unwittingly goes along with it until she realizes that JD is not as innocent as he pretended to be, which happens shortly after he gave Heather the Drano as a hangover remedy (all the while manipulating the situation to make Veronica think it is her fault). JD's narrative takes on a power of its own and it spirals far out of Veronica's control, as she gets caught up in his game, his rules, his power play. She stays one step ahead of him as she fakes her own suicide, knowing the only way to stop JD is to beat him at his own game. In doing so, she changes the rules of the game. Thus, by the end of the film Veronica no longer needs her narration. She has become empowered. She has come of age by realizing a more egalitarian form of power, not the cruel power of the Heathers. She is "the new sheriff in town," as she tells the current Heather, and Veronica no longer needs a gun. Not only is parental authority not an issue, but the adult world barely intrudes on this teen narrative. However, Jon Lewis notes that, like other films of the '80s, this one still reinforces the teens' need for authority. In the '90s, this authority is far more complex—more and less visible.

The parents of the teen films and girls' films of the '90s and beyond play a variety of roles, but are mostly absent, particularly when it comes to discussions of sex, as discussed in the previous chapter. In a variety of films like *Fast Times at Ridgemont High* the parents never appear. For instance, in *Cruel Intentions* (a movie that could never happen with parents around) we never see the parents, and they are referred to as "parental units" at one point. The teens clearly do not respect their parents, and yet their sexual behavior seems, in some ways, to be an attempt at imitation of what they perceive to be adult behavior. As often as parents are absent or mocked, parents are absent, invisible, dead, or consumed with their own lives. For instance, many parents are barely there like in *The River's Edge*, where Clarissa's mother is only a voice and a glowing light that asks, "Is that you?" This absence is especially telling in *The Smokers*, when Karen gushes over all of the pictures of Jefferson's mom with famous people. Jefferson remarks that she recognizes the clothes, but she can't quite place the face. But Jefferson's little sister Lincoln, an elaborately costumed junior high school student who recites a poem about their keg party, smokes pot, and plays with guns, is, perhaps, the biggest evidence of an absent, and out-of-touch parent. At the end of the film, Jefferson's mom doesn't show up to her graduation, but Lincoln does. And Jefferson takes her under her wing—at least as much as she can.

In *Girls Town*, on the other hand, Angela's mother is there on her way out to do her community duty, and we see Nikki's mother—cold and rigid—only after her suicide. We see Telly's mom in *Kids* just long enough to understand that she has no clue about what her son is doing. And as she stands bouncing a baby on her hip and making half an attempt to force Telly to get a job, it is clear she has no influence over his behavior. Many of the teens in films where parents are not around are the teens who meet tragic ends like the teens in *Cruel Intentions* who suffer both a literal and figurative death or in *The River's Edge*, where the parents' lack of involvement reflects their kids' detachment. In this case, they take up with a parental figure who is a disturbed murderer—not the most subtle of messages. Thus, parents' absence in movies reflects not only teens' desire to not be around their parents, but also reflects the parents' inaccessibility and ghostly role in their teens' lives.

But parents try, or don't try, to be in their kids' lives in a variety of ways. For instance, in *Saved!* Pastor Skip is torn between the life he is living and the life he thinks he should live as a good Christian. And when his son, Patrick, tries to talk to him, Pastor Skip can't relate to his son on a fatherly level, or even on a pastoral level; instead, he lashes out at Patrick. Pastor Skip is so involved with the kids at American Eagle Christian High School, and so involved in his own guilt and perceived hypocrisy, that he is unable and unwilling to listen to his son's more enlightened views of Christianity. Like Pastor Skip's inability to deal with his own baggage, and opposite from invisible parents, Terri's father, in *Raise Your Voice*, is controlling to the point that everyone is afraid of him, as Terri bravely tells him later when she finally stands up for herself. He is juxtaposed by Terri's supportive, but subordinate, mother and her unconventional aunt who both help her lie to her father so that she can pursue her dreams. Terri's father's patriarchal role is only subtly enforced by the Christian undertones of this film, as opposed to the overt Christian elements in *Saved!* But while *Saved!* challenges these Christian dogmas, *Raise Your Voice* subtly reinforces them through things like Terri's father's control of his family, her brother's cross, and her graduation gift to her brother—tickets to what is obviously a Christian rock band. Thus, Terri's controlling father is portrayed as a good man who is just trying to do the right thing in protecting his daughter from anything and everything he sees as dangerous. This is portrayed as the "normal" Christian family while the families in *Saved!* are unconventional. And in *Saved!* a new breed of Christian family and parents are born.

As often as parents command control, sometimes parents are unneeded or ineffectual, despite a strong parental figure, like Libby in *What a Girl Wants* who reminds Daphne that she needs to find herself, or, like Mel in *Thirteen*, who is not only open, helpful, and supportive for her daughter, but also for a community of friends. In both of these cases, the teen girl still struggles with the absence of her father. In the former this absence leads to a romantic tale of travel and self-discovery, security and independence, and a renewed relationship with the father she never knew. In the latter, it leads to a downward spiral at 13, a repeated pattern of an absent, ineffectual father, and a long struggle ahead. Juxtaposing these absent, and often excused, fathers with fathers like Terri's shows two extremes that appear in teen and girls' films. But while parents can be absent or ineffectual, sometimes one or more parent is dead, often adding more (and sometimes less) complexity to the narrative. In films like *Clueless*, *Crazy/Beautiful*, *Save the Last Dance*, and *Coyote Ugly*, the girls' mothers are dead, leaving only their (often out-of-touch) fathers to raise them. For instance, in *Clueless*, Cher's father is helpless; he's there and imposes rules, but hardly enforces those rules. She has a curfew, but she also has a credit card. And in *Save the Last Dance*, Sara's father can hardly find anything to talk to his daughter about, let alone the recent, painful death of her mother. Even more extreme, Nicole's father in *Crazy/Beautiful* transfers his wife's mental problems, and his connected pain, onto his daughter. And when she attempts suicide and acts out of control he blames her instead of considering his role in both the mother and daughter's lives. *Coyote Ugly* differs from these other films because Violet's relationship with her father is closer, and more complex, than any of the other characters. Violet takes care of her father and when she moves out on her own to pursue her dream of being a songwriter, not only does she leave her father to fend for himself, but she also finds herself struggling. When she finds herself in dire need of money, she becomes a coyote girl, dancing on a bar for a lot of money. And when her father finds out, he refuses to talk to her until a car accident helps to force him to come to terms with his daughter's independence. In other films, like *The Princess Diaries,* it's the father who is dead and mother and daughter are close friends. And in some films, like in *Manny and Lo* and *Ripe,* both the parents are dead before the narrative begins. Manny misses her mother so much that she sprays the sheets with her mother's deodorant before going to sleep, just so she can smell her while she sleeps. And in *Ripe,* Rosie's first few words of narration sum up the parents they leave behind: "Our dad was a real motherfucker. So when he bashed that deer, I dragged Violet from the burning car and watched mom and dad explode." In both these cases, the parents' absence compels the elements of the story.

But even in several highly conventional films, like *The Princess Diaries, What a Girl Wants,* and *A Cinderella Story* (discussed in more detail in the next section and others), the death of a parent, or a father—an authority figure in all three of these examples—makes more space, perhaps, for the girl to find herself. In both *The Princess Diaries* and *What a Girl Wants* (and in *Confessions of a Teenage Drama Queen*), Mia and Daphne's (and Lola's) moms are free-spirited, artistic women (painter, singer, potter) who were not princess material, so they've tried to shelter their daughters from their royal fathers. However, both girls, particularly Daphne, feel compelled to get to know their fathers in order to better know themselves. In both of these films, perhaps because they are categorized as "family films," family is a big focus, and in the end, family, in whatever form it takes, is reinforced. This is also true for *Confessions of a Teenage Drama Queen* where Lola initially lies about her father being dead in order to make herself more interesting and defends her single mother as a "victim of circumstance." But in the end, both her parents are supportive, and her father even becomes friends with Lola's singer-songwriter idol. The family element is even further reinforced when Lola and Ella decide to ask their parents for permission rather than sneak out, and, of course, permission is granted. These parents like Pastor Skip, Libby, and Mel are foils to the overly involved and helplessly out-of-touch parents mocked in mainstream films like *American Pie* and *10 Things I Hate About You.* These parents are involved to a comic extreme, and their involvement does not serve as real fatherly or motherly advice, but as comic relief. For instance, the girls' father, an obstetrician, is adamantly against dating because he knows what happens to girls who date. (They have sex, get pregnant, and wind up on his examining table.) Because of his professional experience, he doesn't trust his daughters to make their own choices or mistakes, but he also doesn't realize that his daughters are smarter than he thinks. Kat and Bianca's father is comically portrayed as the out-of-touch parent saying things like, "what's normal? Those damn Dawson's River kids sleeping in each other's beds and what not. I'm down. I've got the 411. And you are not going out and getting jiggy with some boy. I don't care how dope his ride is." In this short burst of passion he confuses all of the lingo of popular teen culture. His assumptions are absurd and this absurdity is reflected by his words. But the true absurdity comes from the contrast between his daughters' and his expectations. His character may be portrayed in ridiculous proportions, but his daughters' reactions to him make it clear that they are not going to live up to his fears. When he lectures the two on the latest teenage girl to visit his delivery room and asks Bianca what she thinks this 15-year-old delivering twins said, Bianca replies: "I'm a crack whore who should have made my skeezy boyfriend wear a condom." He has no reply to these words that simultaneously show common sense about contraception, but also a classist (and mainstream) view about pregnant teens that independent films subvert. He doesn't need to make Bianca wear "the belly" (a weighted contraption meant to simulate the experience of being pregnant); she has learned this lesson. But someone could teach her a bit of compassion.

While parents can be comic relief, supportive friends, or invisible or inaccessible, or totally absent, they can also be intentionally or unintentionally cruel. In *Mean Girls*, Cady's parents send her off to high school as if she is going to kindergarten. While this is hardly cruel behavior, it is a complete ignorance of the totally different environment that Cady will encounter on her first day of school. The fact that they look down on her (an effect achieved by the camera angle) and talk to her in "baby-talk," only reinforces their level of ignorance. A more acerbic representation of this is portrayed in *Welcome to the Dollhouse*. Dawn's parents know exactly how to treat her—like less than a child—and her mother uses things like Dawn's siblings and chocolate cake to manipulate her. But sometimes this control and interference comes from caring, involved parents like both sets of parents in *The Incredibly True Adventures of 2 Girls in Love*. Randy's aunt and her partner are concerned about her failing math grade and Evie's mother is oblivious to her daughter's closeted sexuality and conflicted feelings. She reminds her over and over again that she's perfect while she imposes her high expectations. Both girls are struggling to find themselves in the midst of loving, yet unconventional families, which is still a painful process.

Parents are sometimes completely absent in girls' films, but even when parents are around, they are not always available or accessible. In *Saved!* Mary's mother (Mary Louise Parker, left) is focused on her own problems and interests, and doesn't notice that her daughter is pregnant. Mary (Jena Malone) deliberately hides it from almost everyone, including her mother. Here the two share a mother-daughter moment as they paint their toenails together. This act represents some of the superficial familial relationships that can't deal with reality, on and off the screen.

While parents play this designated role, they are rarely seen simply as people, as humans with their own flaws. In some cases parents are so bogged down with their own problems that they fail to be there when they are needed. This is the case in *Saved!* where Mary's mother is so unconcerned about her daughter doing "bad" things, and so consumed with finally finding a love interest for herself, that she only superficially inquires into her daughter's life when she asks, "Should I be worried about you?" And answers her own question before Mary can even avoid it. Once in a while we glimpse a child's understanding of and acceptance of her parents' failure, like in *Whatever* when Anna has a cigarette with her mother. Or when Vivian, in *Slums of Beverly Hills*, reunites her quirky family with their Sizzler tradition. And in *Confessions of a Teenage Drama Queen*, Lola's understanding of her mother, and her urge to protect her from "suburbia" causes her to lie about her father's death in order to legitimize her mother's status as a single parent. Other times parents' egos, or their version of love for their child, gets in the way of parents' ability to see their teens as adults. For instance, in *Dirty Dancing*, Baby must come to terms with her father's middle-class hypocrisy, a realization that changes Baby's view of her father forever, and a realization that greatly impacts the person she is becoming.

Coming to terms with parents' flaws is one rite of passage, but such a realization is not easy when parents are unavailable or they misunderstand. However, physical and ideological separation from parents is a necessary step for American adolescence. As Evie tells her mother in *The Incredibly True Adventures of 2 Girls in Love*, "Every time I try to separate from you, which is a totally normal adolescent impulse and in fact crucial to my adult development.... I'm an adult now and I have to traverse my own landscape." This is, after all, what coming of age is about. Even Lola in *Confessions of a Teenage Drama Queen* realizes the necessity to do her own thing, despite the fact that she finds a way to do so with her and Ella's parents' permission and assistance. She may claim that her father's presence would be social suicide, but he ends up being a connection to her rock star idol, reinforcing the need that teens have for their parents.

The conventions that define the role of parents and the trope of authority in teen films are important not only because of the ways in which they reflect myriad roles that parents may play in real life, but also because this larger theme helps to define the parameters a teen faces when she makes choices that go against authority. While this dynamic of girls' film will be discussed in more detail in the next chapter, it is important to note here that the space of girls' film acts separately from the sphere of authority. Girls are free to be whatever the narrative, within the confines of the political economy, allows them to be. These possibilities are often more limited in mainstream films and in films where teens without parents search for a new form of authority. While many more of these films end with the contrived narrative of girl gets boy and lives happily ever after, in other films, like *Thirteen*, the protagonist, Traci, is left spinning in a blur for the last few shots, symbolizing the adolescent feeling of being out of control, but also symbolizing the difficulty of getting close enough to her to stop the spin. However, many films also offer girls more space and possibility such as films that leave the future open, like *Girls' Town* where the train out of town becomes the main focus as the final scene fades into the hum of the train and the film's credits. In the mainstream, these kinds of spaces are more likely conventional, often based upon stories with staying power—like the story of Cinderella.

Fantastic Spaces: Remaking Cinderella?

In essence, all films provide fantastic spaces to a certain extent; this is part of the magic and power of film, and particularly for this genre where creative spaces must be found. These are the spaces where girls can use their power or become empowered. Some of these spaces of fantasy include Cinderella stories, makeover stories, and stories about "making it" in the music or film industries. These fantasies are limited in what they allow the girls to achieve, even if their rhetoric—their lines, songs, and scripts—proclaim the opposite. Thus, many empowering films for girls are empowering only for a certain kind of empowerment—that which is traditional or familiar—and is available only to very certain girls, especially conventionally pretty, sweetly smiling, white girls. These limits, and the ways in which some female protagonists push these limits, become much clearer when the fantastic spaces of girls' film are more closely considered.

Sometimes this magic is more obvious, particularly in films marketed toward children or family audiences like *The Princess Diaries, Raise Your Voice, A Cinderella Story*, or *Confessions of a Teenage Drama Queen*, two of which are Disney films. And all of these films follow what the cover of *Confessions of a Teenage Drama Queen* reads: "a wonderful, entertaining teen fantasy" and a "hip and hilarious coming of age comedy for the whole family!" But these spaces of fantasy are very specific to a certain kind of fantasy, one accepted and embraced by the mainstream. And as pseudo coming-of-age stories, these films all include a love interest and a happy ending. Most of these family films focus on a protagonist finding herself, and this becomes the primary element of the coming-of-age story, and often happens without many stock rites of passage, particularly sex or drugs, or rebellion against mainstream conventions and paradigms. For instance, as family films none of these films include sex, but they all include boyfriends as part of their happy endings. And in *A Cinderella Story*, Sam lets her stepmother walk all over her and strives for perfection in her grades as her only way out of her (mildly) horrible life. Only the magic of the Cinderella story, and her father's estate, pull her out of this life of exploitation.

While all of these stories are romantic, this proliferation of Cinderella tales—from the Disney version to Drew Barrymore's *Ever After* to Hilary Duff's *A Cinderella Story*—is, perhaps, explained by the necessity of fantastic space in films. Likewise, this space is necessarily connected to the traditional and familiar in mainstream girls' family coming-of-age films. While some of these films like *Ever After* work to skew the conventions of the traditional tale, others like *A Cinderella Story* help to cement the same myth in a modern setting. Still others, like *What Girl Wants*, complicate this tale and infuse it with attitude. Another film, *Ella Enchanted*, takes the fairy tale format and weaves several fairy tale themes together in a film about a princess who has been given the "gift" of obedience by her fairy godmother. While this plot sounds like it could be an interesting "adult" film, in the "family" version, Ella is, like her fantastic counterparts, a strong female protagonist who finds her way. All of these films challenge and cement the Cinderella story.

Regardless of its adaptations of the Cinderella story, there is a handsome prince who awaits Cinderella at the end of the tale, even if she, like Sam in *A Cinderella Story*, says that they lived happily ever after, "for now." After all, she assures us, she's only a college freshman. This final line is surprising in that it splinters the traditional tale of romance where there is only fate and never only a "for now." Similarly, *The Princess Diaries* offers the boyfriend a summer visit (with her sister, Mia's best friend) in the final narration, but no long-term promises. And in *What a Girl Wants*, the boyfriend is her father's "gift" toward reconciliation. And while there is no long-term pledge here either, she goes to Oxford (like her father). Considering that these are family films, it's not totally surprising that the girls' futures would not be locked into these relationships. After all, none of them have had sex and sex is barely implied. However, despite some of the elements that make this story more complicated than other Cinderella stories, *A Cinderella Story* is the same recycled plot, with the same basis of a makeover tale—only when the girl is transformed into a princess, or in Sam's case, Cinderella, is she worthy of being noticed. Through this transition she finds the power to stand up to her stepmother and to the boy who broke her heart (temporarily, of course), "both in the same day," as her best friend remarks. There are, however, more complicated events in Sam's life—her dreams of college, her attic room, her stepmother's torture, and her stepsisters' plots to humiliate her. Sam is not planning on going to prom, she's not focused on graduation, and she's not looking for a boyfriend, until her Princeton chatroom buddy appears. Instead, she's focused on finishing high school a year early so that she can go to college a year early and get out from under her stepmother. But while *A Cinderella Story* might challenge what it means to live happily ever after, it finds its mainstream convention, and its highly conventional plot, in its "fashionably hip" revision of the traditional Cinderella story. Sam does all the right things, rewarding all the right people and punishing all the bad ones, with a smile on her face—perhaps one of the blandest protagonists in an "empowering" teen film.

This message is similar to that found in *The Princess Diaries*, a film with a bit more depth in places and less in others, as Mia is made over into Princess Amelia. While this film is not a Cinderella story, it does follow many similar conventions through its themes connected to royalty. For instance, Mia's grandmother is a kind of fairy godmother as she provides her with money for her "baby"—a Mustang convertible that she's fixing up—and protects Mia from punishment by the law. But this fantastic space promises more power to Mia who is not marrying into royalty, but is taking her rightful place as heir. She isn't just a princess for show (which is part of being a princess), but for her job, as her grandmother tells her. Thus, through this fantastic space, a girl with no power gains the ultimate power and responsibility with only a "blood" qualification. This "girl-power fairy tale," while it is supposedly empowering, is disturbingly skewed to mainstream ambitions and definitions of success. Mia doesn't earn power, it is handed to her, like many dynasties. Should we accept this grant of power because Mia is set up as being liberal and humble? Because she'll listen to the voices of people who are smarter than her? This is yet another empty form of girl power.

What a Girl Wants has more awareness of the problems with the tropes of royalty and self-sacrifice, although its criticism and subversion of these are overshadowed by its reinforcement of other tropes like fate and romance. This film is also a fairy tale of sorts, but most of its fairy-tale qualities are underscored by Daphne's strategic references to Cinderella. Daphne can't fall into the same traps as the Cinderella characters because she knows the story. Invoking the power of myth, Daphne knows that her stepsister, because she is clearly an evil stepsister, will not win out over her. She stands up to her and tells her exactly who they both are ("you're designer, I'm vintage") and that she should "get over herself and stop trying to be *my* daddy's little girl." Unlike Sam who submits to the Cinderella storyline, Daphne has all the power in this relationship but never abuses this power. In the end, she gives her tiara to her stepsister-to-be because she "deserves it." Further, Daphne's prince charming is not the typical prince, riding a motorbike and working odd jobs to survive. But Daphne reinforces the Cinderella trope as she assures him that she's not going to disappear again without even a glass slipper because "this Cinderella has a daddy now." However, Ian is also not typical because he has already figured out the lesson that Daphne needs to learn. As Ian explains, his mother married beneath her and his grandparents took pity on their half-breed grandson. He went to all the right schools and had all the right connections, but "one day [he] realized the hypocrisy of it all." Daphne learns this lesson too, but it takes her own story to learn it (as she hopes in her narration at the beginning of the film). But the most romantic fairy-tale element of this film comes through in the story about her parents, a story that is told to her as a fairy tale by her mother on every birthday, much in the same way that Sam's father reads her fairy tales before he dies. But unlike Sam and Amelia's fathers, Daphne's father is alive, and she, ultimately, rescues him when he finally decides that his career is not as important as his long-lost family, making this a coming-of-age story for father and daughter (which I will return to in the final section of this chapter) that follows and reconfigures Cinderella's story.

Ever After, a film that is often cited as feminists' favorite Cinderella tale—and I have to admit it is probably the best Cinderella story circulating in film—both reinforces and subverts some of the myths surrounding this story. Like A Cinderella Story, this film gives Cinderella a real name and identity—Danielle. As the story goes, Danielle is also abandoned by her father's death and left to serve her evil stepmother and stepsisters. However, while A Cinderella Story is a "fashionably hip" revision, Ever After is a historical revision, one that allows Cinderella's story to be told not by the Brothers Grimm but by her great-great-granddaughter. In fact, this granddaughter is positioned in the beginning of the film talking with the Grimm brothers and setting the story straight, clearing up any confusion caused by the fairy tale version. While this is a powerful element of the film, and it allows for a revision of a classic tale, it also cements this story not in the realm of fairy tale, myth, or film, but in "real-life," in history. Thus, despite the improvements to the story, like Danielle's critical analysis of the conditions of the peasant working class, her ability to speak her mind, her loyalty to family, tradition, and land, and her practical sensibility, many elements of the tale are presented less critically. For instance, Danielle is strong-willed and she isn't exactly looking for a man when she pummels the prince with apples when he steals a horse. However, the narration poses the prince as "another man" entering her life 10 years after her father died. In the opening scenes of the film, Danielle's father dies and in the next scene she is 10 years older and meeting her "prince charming." Thus, like What a Girl Wants, this film sets up the father-daughter relationship as a kind of model for the daughter-lover relationship, a parallel that is disturbing and under theorized. However, despite this element, Ever After subverts many stock elements and expectations of the fairy tale.

One of the most progressive elements of this film is Danielle's class analysis and her struggles for the working peasants who suffer under the luxury and decadence of royalty. This film, unlike A Cinderella Story, is not about going from Cinderella's rags to the riches of royalty, or like for

Sam, revenge and self-reliance. In fact, riches are written into the Cinderella story. When she marries the prince, she is instantly transformed into a princess and future queen. Think about the Disney version when the placement of the glass slipper not only unites the prince with Cinderella, but restores her to her appearance at the ball. So, while Sam's recovery of her father's (more modest) fortune and legacy is a feminist revision because she recovers what is hers without having to marry the prince, it also reinforces the idea that love isn't enough—you've got to have money too. In *Ever After*, however, the prince's money is a source of contention between Danielle and the prince who wishes to be free from his "gilded cage." In fact, to Danielle, it doesn't matter if he's the prince or a commoner, and she brings him down a little closer to the people.

Throughout the film Danielle's identity stays true to her statement that she's "just a servant in a nice dress." And she uses this nice dress not to gain entry into the prince's domain, but to rescue a long-time family servant from being exported to America. Thus, Danielle is truly a champion for the poor as she faces off with the prince telling him that "a servant is not a thief" and those who are "cannot help it." In fact, her passionate speech on behalf of the poor wins the freedom of her servant and the interest of the prince who is struggling with some of the obligations that come with the privilege of his birth. Before Danielle (and after), the prince argues with his parents that an arranged marriage should not be covered under the "certain obligations" that he is required to fulfill by birth. But after Danielle, Henry frees indentured servants, invites gypsies to his ball, and proposes a library where anyone would be free to study. However, while Danielle pushes the prince to consider his privilege in ways he hasn't before, and while she urges him to see beyond the labels and assumptions that come with a person's social position, he cannot, at first, overcome his class prejudices when he discovers that she is nothing more than a servant who has been pretending to be royalty. But, of course, the happy ending comes, and myths of romance are reinforced as da Vinci urges the prince that there is only one true love for him. Thus, arranged marriage is revealed as archaic while "true love" is represented as timeless. Because this film sets the myth of Cinderella as a real story from the past, it undercuts the fact that the very class dynamics that Danielle speaks so passionately about are at crisis level in the globalized world of today. These class dynamics might not be between peasant and royalty, though they often are; instead, they are between what is considered the first and third worlds, between the industrialized countries of the North and the underdeveloped, exploited countries of the South. In the U.S., and in other industrialized countries, we are all born to privilege, if not the to the level of privilege that the fictional royalty of fairy tales enjoy, and the third world is born into an economic system that puts them in a subordinate position (like the poor in the U.S.), much like the peasants Danielle defends. Further, the gender stereotypes that this film subverts are also set in the past. Thus, when Danielle rescues the prince from the gypsies she not only proves that she is witty and physically strong, but she also opens an opportunity for the prince to shed some of his preconceived notions. And Danielle's mouth, which the prince claims has him hypnotized, doesn't lead to further conversation, but to a first kiss, at which point this conflicted relationship becomes romantic. But Danielle's wit is also buried as all of her good ideas become the inspiration for the prince who introduces radical new ideas to his father. She tells him that with his privilege he has the opportunity to do all sorts of good things for his people, but it is not these opportunities that this film ends on. Instead, the prince tells Danielle that they are supposed to live happily ever after. And when she asks, "Says who?" he tells her, "I don't know." Thus, while the prince is not given the final word, and his authority is tempered with her question, their happily ever after does not reflect the good they did for their people. Instead, in saying that what's important is, simply, that "they lived," the privilege that comes with the position of prince and his bride is clear. They lived happily ever after, but did the people?

Like *Ever After*, *Ella Enchanted* provides a strong female protagonist and subverts some of the conventions of fairy tales, in many of the same ways as Danielle. For instance, neither Danielle nor Ella follows the traditional fairy tale storyline of waiting for their handsome prince, waiting to be rescued. Both of these girls go about their own somewhat politically charged existence and are pursued by their own handsome princes largely because of their free and adventurous spirits. But *Ella Enchanted* also goes beyond the Cinderella story by bringing together elements of several fairy tales, including the egotistical and out-of-touch fairy godmother who gives Ella the gift of obedience. This film also fuses both the "fashionable hip" and "historically grounded" approaches of *A Cinderella Story* and *Ever After*. Of course, like *Ever After*, this "historical accuracy" is far from accurate. In fact, *Ella Enchanted* is a fairy tale simply because it includes magic, ogres, giants, elves, fairies, evil stepsisters, and a handsome prince. It also gets its fairy tale quality from its medieval setting, a setting which is modernized by some of the tropes of mainstream teen culture, such as fan clubs, celebrity worship, and "Medieval Teen Magazine." But this fairy tale is also infused with modern values, behaviors, styles, and even (more subtlety) politics. For instance, Ella's stepsister, Hattie, is not just the power-hungry sister of *Ever After*, she is the president of the prince's fan club and can barely speak in his presence. And the king is really Char's power-hungry uncle who killed Char's father and plots to kill Char in order to retain his power over the entire subjugated kingdom.

But more personal political issues are worked in just under the surface of this film. For instance, before the death of her mother, and for the first few scenes of the film, Ella is being raised by her mother and their "household fairy," Mandy, in a situation that appears to be like a same-sex marriage. Just before Ella's mother dies she tells Ella that no one except she and the not-so-skilled fairy know about her gift (or curse) of obedience, and that she's not to tell anyone about her gift. Despite this gift, and perhaps because Ella is raised by women, she has strong ideals and personality. Further, in most Cinderella stories the Cinderella character is close to her father before he dies and leaves her with her (evil) stepmother and stepsisters. But in *Ella Enchanted*, her father is just weak and inconsequential, and has little power to protect his daughter. He doesn't have to die for the evil stepmother to take control of the household and Ella's life. And after her mother's death, when Ella's father comes back with his new wife and her two daughters—the evil stepmother and stepsisters—Mandy is relegated to her spot as household fairy and made a servant. But, of course, this subtly unconventional family is not only disrupted by the return of Ella's father, but also the later discovery that Mandy has a boyfriend who has been stuck in a book for years, as a result of her not-so-accurate magic. In the end, she turns him back into a man, and lives her own happily ever after.

This is only one example of somewhat progressive politics in *Ella Enchanted*; the others are similar to Danielle's class politics in *Ever After*. Like Danielle, Ella develops a relationship with the prince outside of his official role and duties. Like Henry, Char is struggling with the demands of his birthright. However, unlike Henry, who questions his place partially because of the hypocrisy around him, Char has just returned from college and is out of touch with the needs of his people and the conditions of his kingdom. While Danielle adds critical commentary to Henry's emerging consciousness, Ella opens Char's eyes to the obvious problems that, as the prince, he doesn't have to see. Ella's conversations with Char sound much like Danielle's with Henry since Ella, despite her gift of obedience, has developed a strong will and compassionate politics. On her first encounter with Char, Ella tells him to do what his people do— "destroy my land and destroy my livelihood." She, like Danielle, uses Char's complaints of the unfairness of his position to point out how many other people are also unfairly constrained by their lack of choices. But unlike Danielle's passionate Marxist politics, Ella's politics are more of a feel-good, multicultural politics. In fact, at one point one of the ogres asks, "Can't we all just get along?" These words not only echo Rodney King's words, but also reflect some of the ways in which this plea has been appropriated, particularly by superficial multicultural politics. Like her character in *The Princess Diaries* (Mia), Ella's politics are framed within the current paradigm of mainstream oppositional politics. Ella is "pro Ogre" and tries to convince the ogres of this by telling them that she recently held a rally in their honor. While this moment in the film could provide a sound critique of protest and its connected politics, it is a moment, instead, rescued by Char as he shows up to do his duty and rescue the princess.

But while Danielle's class analysis provides the prince with ideas that he proposes to his good-hearted father, Ella's "dangerous ideas" threaten the evil Edgar since she is "filling our prince's head with dangerous thoughts." Thus, in *Ever After*, the promise of a better, more equal future is contagious—it infects the royal family, even if this promise seems to be forgotten by the time the story is retold by Danielle's great-great-granddaughter. This promise is not present in *Ella Enchanted*, a world that is in far worse shape than the fictional France of *Ever After*. When Char reveals his love for her and his plan to propose to her, and when Ella's stepsisters plot against her, Edgar tries to use Ella's gift of obedience against her and Char so that he can retain control of the kingdom and control of the giants, ogres, and elves—the workers and the entertainers. While this evil plan does not come to fruition, the only mention of a better world is Char's toast "to a nation of equals." This nation of equals includes his good friends (including ogres, elves, and giants) and his true love, Ella. Thus, power is once again subsumed by a fairy-tale version of love and reinforced by the rhyming narration, "you just can't go wrong if you follow your heart, and end with a song," another opportunity for a modern element, as well as the music that so many coming-of-age films (to be discussed in this sections and the next chapter) utilize.

While *Ella Enchanted*'s fusion of the modern and the fairy tale provide comedic relief, like Lucinda's FWI (flying while intoxicated) and the evil stepmother's use of "bat-tox" which leaves her face obscenely stretched, this fusion also, like *Ever After*, skews the important political messages of this film. The politics are once again subsumed by the romantic plot. Further, modern-day stereotypes still find their way into this tale as Lucinda, an African American fairy godmother who is progressive because of her skin color, also plays into the stereotypes of the black woman with attitude. In fact, Lucinda isn't simply spunky and unconventional; she is selfish, arrogant, and unhelpful. Thus, the characteristics that could make her a strong and admirable character, make her into another stereotypical black woman who parties hard and doesn't care what people think of her. While these character flaws lead to Ella's empowerment—her ability to, as Lucinda tells her, "take care of [her] own problems," and rid herself of her gift and curse—these flaws also elevate Ella above Lucinda. In fact, as her mother reminds her before she dies, what is inside of Ella is stronger than any spell. Thus, Lucinda's power cannot be overcome by Ella's inherent strength and goodness and this fairy godmother only inadvertently helps Ella discover her true potential, a potential that cannot be wasted on anything except her fairy-tale fate—the handsome prince. This is yet another way that politics is subsumed by fairy tale. While we can assume that the "a nation of equals" will emerge under the rule of Char and his true love, Ella becomes the typical Cinderella as Char makes a toast and she is whisked away to her honeymoon by carriage, obedient now by choice. This film, like so many others, ends with a wedding scene, but also a song, reinfusing this film with its modern style, but divorcing it from its modern politics. These politics, instead, become reflected in the love found between a giant and an elf; the reunion with Ella's best friend, Arita (one of the few faces of color, another mostly empty multicultural inclusion); and the unity found in a recycled song. The future, then, becomes about not breaking anyone's heart. And if this song and dance ending wasn't bad enough, the music video, "It's Not Just Make-Believe," performed by Kari Kimmel, also reinforces the romantic tropes of this film.

All of these films skew the fairy tale conventions in certain ways, but do so with little awareness about the problems of these mythical stories in the first place. And this is one of the problems with fantastic spaces; they allow a fluid space for the manipulation of stories and myths, but often reinscribe these myths. This is especially true of Cinderella films as well as films about "making it." Both of these types of mainstream girls' films provide very narrow, but still negotiable, fantastic spaces.

"Making It" Through Music and Dance

Like Cinderella and fairy tales, coming-of-age films that utilize music and dance are also a popular theme for a variety of reasons. In addition to the popularity of music and dance within youth cultures, music and dance have often acted as a means of rebellion for youth as portrayed in films like *Grease, Rock and Roll High School, Dirty Dancing,* and *Shake, Rattle, and Rock!* Further, these films harness the power of music and dance to affect the mind as well as the body, a dynamic that serves the coming of age theme well. For instance, in *Dirty Dancing*, dance acts as a means toward a sexual and social awakening for Baby but also helps develop her intellect as she is able to recognize and analyze class dynamics. And in *Save the Last Dance*, the fusion of ballet and hip hop portray a simplistic merging of cultures and, by extension, races, extending this coming of age theme to a cultural coming of age. But in the mainstream, music and dance are used not only as symbols of rebellion or of sexual or social development (as will be discussed further in chapter three), but also as means toward mainstream acceptance. For instance, in *Confessions of a Teenage Drama Queen* and in *Freaky Friday* (both starring Lindsay Lohan), music is used as a means toward inclusion in, and acceptance from, the adult world even if this music is on the girl's terms and in her own words. Many of these films also have the theme of making it, though what exactly this means varies. Despite this variation, "making it" rarely means simply struggling on one's own to break through a barrier or achieve one's dreams. Instead, it almost always means fame, if not fortune, or at least a desire for such.

Confessions of a Teenage Drama Queen, a story about making it, has many elements that make it more complex than many similar films. Lola does not need to find herself through any kind of physical transformation; as a drama queen she is always in costume. At the beginning of the film, when her family moves to New Jersey, the young drama queen, Mary, insists that she be called Lola from now on, a name that she thinks is much more fitting for a star. Not only does this name change ring true to adolescent experience, but it also rings of adolescent sexuality as Lola is a name that is often used to describe Lolita, the sexualized child of Humbert Humbert's fantasies in the book and films by the same name. This connection is, perhaps, only for the adults, if it is not simply a coincidence, since even the most sexually charged elements of adolescence—boyfriends and rock star idols, are intellectualized and pushed to the realm of friendship in this film. In fact, sex, not surprisingly, is not an issue in this film, and is only hinted at rarely, like when the queen bee, Carla, calls Ella, "Ella never had a fella," or when Lola's confession that she's a "love child" turns into a confession not of unsanctioned sex, but that her parents were married, but like, "totally in love." Thus, Lola's name may give her the (sexualized) makeover fitting of a star, even if she is not yet sexual.

This fantastic film also has some class implications. Like other teen films, Lola is portrayed as a (lower) middle class fish in the midst of peers with money. Her nemesis, Carla, is the daughter of a rich and powerful lawyer who gets tickets to the concert and party that Lola and Ella want so badly to attend. Lola recognizes this inequity when she wants something absolutely killer to wear, but her mom (a potter) has just fixed the car and paid for a new kiln. At some points Lola lies to try to put herself on the same level as Carla, saying that her mom has connections, to which Carla remarks sarcastically that she must be a really good potter. These little digs, along with Ella's parents' assumptions about her strange and unconventional mother cause Lola to stick up for her since "single motherhood is a transitory state" and her mother is "merely a victim of fate." Despite these challenges to status quo assumptions, the norms stay in place when Lola's challenges are interpreted simply as lies. All of Lola's lies not only threaten her friendship with Ella, they also come back to bite her when her truth is spun by Carla to look like lies, leaving Lola unsure of herself and only a shell of her former self, unarmed of her attitude and her confidence—two things that have helped her to succeed in this fantastic space.

In the end, with renewed confidence and a more mature attitude, Lola's experience is summed up matter-of-factly: "Here's what I learned: when you're happy the whole world's New York and that dreams are important. Someday when you're not even looking they find you." This ending lesson reaffirms the fantastic space that is the core of this movie. Here she conflates her fantasy city, New York, which was previously the "center of the universe," into the "whole world," erasing everyone in the world, except for herself. Thus, she is the center of the universe and only *her* dreams matter. Further, she equates the act of dreaming with the acts of reality when she says that "absolute reality could be so much more fun than fantasy." Again, this fantasy and this reality are alike only in the space of this film, and are not the same as the reality of the girls in the audience. And, of course, this space of fantasy is augmented by Lola's realization that Sam, the love interest in the film, has been there "the whole time." And she accepts him only on her terms: "Now that my career is launched maybe I could have a boyfriend." Focused on launching her career, Lola has been unconcerned with romance throughout the film, except for a few subtle looks at Sam. Thus, this acceptance, despite its terms, plays right into the requirements of any romantic mainstream film. Granted, this ending is more realistic, and perhaps more empowering, than if she had ended up with a rock star boyfriend, but it also undercuts Lola's free spirit and supposed originality. In the end she must conform to mainstream standards in proscribed ways, and she must have a boyfriend to make this fantastic space fittingly romantic.

In addition to Ella's star-studded adolescent fantasy-reality, this film offers a more down-to-earth coming-of-age narrative through Lola's friend, Ella. However, Ella's coming of age, her awareness, her ability to be "brave enough to be different," is subsumed by the narrative focused on the protagonist. Lola, who may inspire Ella to a courage to be different (while how she is different is unclear), succeeds by being different enough to fit into the standards set by mainstream Hollywood, standards that rule both the fiction and reality of this movie. The fact that Ella figures out, with Lola's help, that "everyone's life" is not just like hers—"doing everything you're supposed to do when you're supposed to do it, never questioning anything"—means little since what Ella does and when she does it barely changes with this otherwise compelling realization. It is unclear whether she can expect "a life like her parents" or something different. Either way, she is only an observer to the real story as she sits back and watches Lola as the center of everyone's attention—from the students who gawk at her and Stu Wolf, to the audience, who can't help where we direct our focus. And while Ella's goodness influences Lola's wildness, neither girl really changes much in the end, making this not so much a coming-of-age film, as the cover promises, but a film that is simply about learning a mainstream lesson. This is, no doubt, part of coming of age— an early stage, fitting of these family films' versions of coming of age.

The music in *Confessions of a Teenage Drama Queen* helps to reinforce and supplement the tenets of the story in important ways. The drama queen's space is not invaded since the music of Lola's favorite band, Sid Arthur, and her music idol, Stu Wolf, is not central to the film. In fact, the only time we clearly hear any of this poetry is when Lola sings one of his songs for her audition. This song becomes hers and the rest of the music is not simply background to the film, it is central. For instance, the song "That Girl," which Lindsay Lohan performs and is included as a music video on the DVD special features, urges young girls to believe in themselves while focusing on the trials of the Lola character. While this does not immediately appear contradictory, the fact that "that girl" was a teenage drama queen at one point and a "wild child" and a "dreamer," perfectly describes how the character shrinks this experience to her particular situation. Lola is, according to the song, armed with an attitude that she knows how to use, one of the strengths of many teen girl protagonists, and she has the power to change her destiny, also like many teen girl protagonists, but the message in this song is clear—to be yourself, to not be a wannabe, you have to be somebody, and this is a category reserved for the Lindsay Lohans and Britney Spearses of the world. Further, the role that Ella plays in the narrative brings irony to the lyrics of "That Girl." The song implies that she'll find herself because she is the only thing that she believes in. Not only does this imply that finding one's self and achieving success are, and must be, an individual pursuit, but they also imply that it's okay to leave your best girl friend behind in these individual pursuits, a message that conflicts with the overall, feel-good messages of the film. These are some of the contradictions that emerge from mainstream fantastic spaces. But these contradictions are also important tenets of empowering coming of age processes and narratives.

Further, these fantastic spaces are necessary and are often the only safe spaces that are available to girls. And in these spaces girls are allowed to be girls, to have fun and be fun, as the producer of *Confessions* notes about Lindsay Lohan, even as they are becoming women. In fact, this space is so safe that it is available to girls like Britney Spears who have very few safe spaces within the public eye. Britney Spears has been subjected to plenty of criticism; like all stars she is subject to rumor after rumor and a host of tabloid scandals. In light of some of this gossip, her film *Crossroads* seems like yet another piece of media aimed at rescuing her public relations and promoting her work beyond "Oops!... I Did it Again." *Crossroads* reinforces those things the public already loves about Britney: her abdominals, her sweet charm, and her singing (some of the same things we love about Hilary Duff and Jessica Simpson). But it also attempts to quell some of those detrimental rumors, showing us that Britney can have friends, sex, and fun, as she has since tried even harder to demonstrate since *Crossroads* through her commercials and MTV appearances, which has only put her under more public scrutiny. This fantastic forum is safe since she is playing a fictional character, Lucy. Despite the parallels she and this character have, these parallels include both those the audience already knows, as well as those (fictionalized elements) they long to know about.

This film, like *Confessions of a Teenage Drama Queen*, provides the story of making it with another established star. Immediately Britney (Lucy) is singled out as the protagonist, as well as star. Lucy is the nerd, destined to go on to college, and then medical school, if her father's plans work out. Kit is beautiful, popular, and a real bitch, destined to be married to her fiancé who is away at college. Mimi is rough, "trailer-trash," destined to have a baby several months down the road (she is already pregnant). Mimi talks Kit and Lucy into accompanying her on a road trip to Los Angeles for a record audition. When Mimi gets stage fright on the way, Lucy takes the stage. Her singing alone (the girls do very little in the way of a show), as well as their sexy appearance, which Kit insists upon before they go on stage, earns them enough to finance their entire trip. The girls celebrate with some "brief teen drinking" in their plush hotel room, and finally put their differences behind them. This small move, and its outcome, is representative of Lucy's character, and Lucy's role as a vehicle for Britney. Thus, from the beginning of the film it is clear that Lucy will make it. She has the most going for her. And since Lucy is not looking to make it in the business, when she succeeds in the music industry, this version of making it is even sweeter.

But while this film gives Britney room to play, it also gives her a version of her same role. We've already seen her nearly naked, so it doesn't take long for the audience to see Lucy in her underwear. (Perhaps the director chose to open with this scene so that all of the boyfriends dragged to the film would stick around hoping to see more.) The film also takes this opportunity to make a direct parallel and a direct contrast with Britney's predecessor, as she sings along to Madonna's "Open Your Heart," prancing around half-naked on her bed. In an interview on beatbox-betty.com, Britney says that she wanted to do this scene because it is so real. And similar scenes certainly do happen in real life as well as in other girls' films. The difference here is that this scene has different baggage from film to film. In *Shake, Rattle, and Rock!* for instance, Carol's dance is frenzied, an expression of her desire to escape the confines of her place in society. Lucy's dance, on the other hand, is emulation. It is a conscious attempt to portray Britney not only as Madonna's heir, but also as a normal girl.

Perhaps to remind the audience of Lucy's realness, another trope of teen films is used through graduation day, and as her father nags her about her valedictorian speech, both her intelligence and her father's dominance over her life become apparent. The former is something Britney is not known for: brains (perhaps because she has yet to prove this aspect of her anatomy?). And the latter is material for tabloid gossip. Regardless, this trope sets up both Lucy's right to pursue her womanhood, a right she means to claim on prom night, as well as her right to squirm out from under her fictional father's control. Both of these are crucial rites in this film as well as other films, including Hilary Duff's *Raise Your Voice*. In both of these films, music is a way of wiggling out from under Daddy's thumb. Further, these rites set up the societal permission for Lucy (and Terri) to pursue their dreams, her desires, and her perceived deficiencies (in this case her long-lost mother). Because these fathers are too controlling, the girls' struggles are more sympathetic, and more representative of patriarchy.

This fantastic space of *Crossroads* gives Britney the opportunity to recast her real self in a fictional light in a variety of personal and professional ways. It is no coincidence that the film is called *Crossroads* when Britney is at the crossroads of her career, as one of her many Web sites

Lucy (Britney Spears) and her friends hit the road with Ben for their own reasons, but the story's real focus is, of course, Lucy. *Crossroads* gives Britney a coming of age through Lucy who rewrites and revives her, perhaps in the hopes of also rewriting and revitalizing her career. The shift from a girl performer to a woman performer seems to mean more skin and more sex. But at the very least, *Crossroads* gives Britney an immortal moment to claim her adolescence, her coming of age, and her sexuality on her own terms, even if these terms are constructed and manufactured. Clockwise from left to right: Anson Mount as Ben, Taryn Manning as Mimi, Zoe Saldana as Kit, and Britney Spears as Lucy.

proclaims. If the film was not intended as a PR boost, it was certainly meant as a boost to her career. The songs in the film, "Not Yet a Woman," and, in the closing credits (amidst the montage of outtakes), "Overprotected," both clearly illustrate the direction her career is moving—out of the teenybopper world, the base of most of her fans, and into more serious things, at least she hopes. In this fantastic space, the songs from Britney's most recent album become the poems in Lucy's journal, as well as the song that she sings for her audition at the end of the film. This gives Britney a chance to go back to a fictional space that gives a deeper meaning to her music. But in Britney's real life she writes her prayers, not her songs, in her journal, and she doesn't write her own music or lyrics. Certainly this job is left for someone more attuned to public relations. For instance, Max Martin, who also writes for the Backstreet Boys and *NSYNC, won an award for Britney's song "Baby One More Time."

Crossroads gives the impression that these songs are more personal than professional. But when an interviewer from beatboxbettie.com asked Britney, "What about writing songs and that kind of thing?" she answers, "Yeah. Yeah, I write poetry and stuff." But she doesn't say whether this "poetry and stuff" appears in her music or not.

Crossroads also gives Britney the opportunity to be sexual in a romantic, rather than a sexualized, objectified context (though the film also delivers on this front, as noted above). Before the film, the parental warning is especially large. It warns of "sexual content and brief teen drinking." Obviously this warning is strategically placed because so many of Britney's fans are preteen girls and this film is rated PG-13. This warning not only warns of the film's content, but it also warns of two of the themes that comprise rites of passage in girls' films and lives. This film, like *Where the Boys Are*, provides stock female archetypes and a girls' story of lasting friendship, as well as a mainstream negotiation of romantic sex. Kit is a stock female archetype in that she puts her fiancé (not simply her boyfriend) before herself. Her future plans all revolve around him, even though he has been away at college for a year and keeps brushing her off. As a pregnant teen character, Mimi is already an oddity, as we shall see later. And Mimi, unlike most other pregnant teen characters, especially in the mainstream, came about her condition through rape. Britney is the only stock character worthy of romance, and while this film may include sex, it squelches real discussions of sex through its mainstream reductions of sex and sexuality.

Of course, like other mainstream Hollywood films, sex for Lucy is intimately connected to romance. She had planned to have sex with her lab partner on prom night because he was really upset about what might happen to him if he went to college a virgin, but the circumstances are just not the way Lucy planned it. But they are, as he says, just the way he imagined it. Sex doesn't happen until a real romantic figure enters the film—the shady guy who drives the girls to LA. There are rumors that he killed a guy; and the girls are nervous for days, until Lucy finally asks. It turns out to be quite the opposite. He was in jail for a technicality of the law after rescuing his sister from his abusive stepfather. He isn't a scary, shady guy. He's a knight in shining armor. And he's very good-looking, which means he fits all of the requirements. Despite the perfectness of this guy, or perhaps because of it, he innocently takes on a patriarchal role which extends from the fatherly role he's been playing as he drives the girls in his car. He writes music to go along with the poem that Lucy reads to him (from the book she is constantly scribbling in while the other two girls are arguing). And when it comes down to the act, he asks, "Are you sure?" and she nods, while romantic music plays in the background.

For the other two girls, sex is a different story. Through conversation (during the "brief teen drinking"), it is obvious that both Kit and Mimi have far more experience than the virginal Lucy. However, all three girls talk frankly about sex as well as their best days and worst days, which really aren't all that bad for anyone except for Mimi who confesses that the reason she doesn't drink is because she was raped. It turns out that the father of her baby is the rapist, and that Mimi is planning on giving her baby up for adoption. This helps to unite the girls, but Mimi is keeping the most important secret of all, a secret that Kit uncovers when she decides to surprise the fiancé who has been dodging her. Luckily Mimi has taught Kit how to throw a punch, and when she realizes her fiancé is the rapist, she punches him out. At the same time, the distraught Mimi, whom Kit has dragged up to his apartment with her, falls down the stairs. With one fell swoop the two peripheral issues (peripheral to the Lucy-Britney story) have been easily resolved. Kit realizes her dog of a fiancé really is a dog, and Mimi's pregnancy is absolved with the cliché fall down the stairs, and just after she has decided to keep her baby. All that's left is for Lucy to stand up to her father, sing her song, and kiss her boyfriend happily ever after. The film ends with Lucy singing Britney's song at the audition for the record company with her supporting cast all behind her as her back-up singers (her best friends once again) and band (including her now-boyfriend). They all cheer wildly for her and her abdomen, and a star is born while another is reborn. This romantic, fantastic space delivers for Lucy, if not for Britney.

Despite my criticism of Britney, and the derision she suffers at the pen and mouth of countless others, the fact remains that she has been an influential role model for many young girls. And if one can forget for a moment all of the other baggage that goes along with Britney, like her image and her commodification, her songs (and perhaps even her film), like Lohan's "That Girl" and *Confessions of a Teenage Drama Queen*, have empowering messages for young girls. If Britney is not the perfect role model, perhaps she is a better mouthpiece, especially if young girls acquire more self-respect, more self-understanding, or more shared cultural experience as a result of listening to her music. And while messages and images, interpretations and projections, may contradict each other, this film, and Britney's songs, offer some mainstream space for discussions about coming of age. For instance, the song she sings in *Crossroads* is about the space in between girl and woman, a space that any preteen and teen girl thinks about a lot, if not in so many words or from such a perspective. The chorus argues that she is neither a girl, nor a woman, and that all she needs is her own time and space while she is in between these two worlds. In the film, this moment could be a number of different moments, or the combination of the moments when: she loses her virginity, she stands up to her father and takes control of her life, or when she sings her poem set to music and receives a ton of adoration. The first is common; the second is slightly less common; and the third is stuff movies are made of. In the film, this moment comes too easily, as if Lucy has transformed into Britney during the course of the song. The end of the film fades into credits, outtakes, and a performance of "Overprotected." Maybe Britney is the woman Lucy becomes. Or maybe the song is a kind of plea to the media to give her some space, a moment that the public doesn't own, so that she can find herself without being prematurely made or remade by the media. Of course, all of this is interpretation, and what Britney's lyrics mean gets transposed every time another girl hears this song and makes it her own.

More recently, Hilary Duff has taken on the realm of film as an additional site for her music career in the film *Raise Your Voice*. While this film, like its other mainstream counterparts, certainly has an uplifting and empowering message for young girls, it also sets up unrealistic expectations for girls who will never be a Hilary Duff, Britney Spears, Paris Hilton, or whatever star emerges from the mainstream money-making machine. However, at the very least, this film ends with a message of overcoming difficult times and finding oneself as it does not end with Terri reaching stardom. However, this film is highly contrived and also presents Terri-Hilary as a girl who writes lyrics, but whose boyfriend (in this case platonic) writes the music. Thus, despite the empowering message, girls are once again disposed of this kind of power—a power usually assumed and reserved for men. Conversely, as we'll see in the next chapter, in *Shake, Rattle, and Rock!* Carol not only sings, but also composes and plays piano.

Only one mainstream film, *Coyote Ugly*, makes this dream a little bit more gritty and a little bit more achievable though her means are not much different as her climb requires her to use her sexy "schoolteacher" looks and the film requires romantic convention. In this film, Violet is a struggling songwriter (a working-class Jersey girl) who can't get her songs heard because she has stage fright. Her dream, unlike the girls who dream of the lights and cameras and fans, is to sit in the dark while someone great sings her songs. But in order to survive, she has to shake her stuff on a bar where she is able to overcome her stage fright, if only because she is singing along to a jukebox and not singing her own songs. Through a variety of trials, Violet finally makes her stage debut, a success in itself.

Most importantly, Violet makes her own success with the other characters in supporting roles. No one makes Violet's success for her—all they
can do is be there for her. For instance, her dad and best friend urge her
to continue on even when she turns around and her boyfriend is there for
support when she really needs it. Like Derek in *Save the Last Dance*, he
shows up despite the fight and break-up they had. But unlike Derek,
Kevin does not need to invade her space—the stage—he simply turns out
the lights and makes everyone disappear.

Because this film, like other mainstream films, relies on a happy ending, Violet achieves her dream, gets the guy, makes up with her dad, and
finds a support circle among the coyote girls. This story, instead of being
a story of one individual's success, is truly a story about finding one's voice
and place through the negotiation of, rather than subservience to, mainstream expectations, even though mainstream convention wins over in the
happy ending. And Violet's dream is achieved through the film as well
since Piper Perabo only lip synchs while star LeAnn Rimes sings the
songs that a real songwriter wrote, including her hit song, "Can't Fight
the Moonlight." But this film isn't an adolescent coming-of-age story. It,
like the films discussed in the following two sections, takes place post–high
school, post adolescence, and often post–having to make it on their own,
often with less magic and less fantasy.

Extending Adolescence Beyond High School

Many films that are marketed to teenage (and wider) audiences have
various, similar conventions of the mainstream teen films I've described,
but are moved to a college setting, or a life-after-college setting, rather
than a high school setting. This makes sense since the space between
childhood and adulthood has expanded for many teens and young adults
in the U.S. Not only are kids growing up faster, as adults like to lament,
but those who are fortunate enough to go to college can also have this
time expanded, particularly if their parents pay their way. Even if young
adults have to work their way through college, like Dora in *Loser*, some
of the other responsibilities of adulthood are still delayed. Mainstream
films in this genre rarely deal with those who can't or don't go to college
and few deal with teens or young adults who choose alternate paths,
though both of these scenarios will be further explored in the following
chapters. In the mainstream, this space between adolescence and adulthood can become the space of freedom, experimentation, and growth like
similar spaces: summer vacations, trips abroad, or girls' schools. But more

often, this space makes the demands of adulthood, and their inevitability, the central outcome like in *Girls and Boys*. Or, like in *Loser* and *Can't Hardly Wait*, this adolescent space is extended, creating more space before the inevitable adulthood.

Perhaps because of this manipulation of adolescent space in many mainstream films that take advantage of this space, some of the crucial differences between high school and college, or post college, are not reflected in the change of setting. Thus, it is not surprising that these films rely upon the same romantic and other conventions of mainstream films. While the films discussed in this section are only a small sample, they show some of the patterns of teen-themed films and post-adolescent coming-of-age stories. For instance, in some sequels, like *Bring It On Again*, the high school characters go to college, but college is a new space for the same old battles. In *Bring It On Again*, the varsity team is the enemy and the competition, and all of the stars who played the key characters have been replaced by actors who don't shine so brightly. And, in *American Pie 2* the high school characters are still pursuing the same shallow goals and using the same sexual jokes and innuendoes. And further, all of the strong female characters like Jessica, Heather, and Vicky make only small appearances. They, unlike most of the boys, have moved on. This is, in a way, a powerful statement about the girls.

After the success of the teen films of the late '90s and early 2000s, many films came out that resembled successful teen films, and also had many of the same stars. *Loser* and *Boys and Girls* are two of these, and both carry high school over to college and star the idols of the teen genre. In *Loser*, Mena Suvari and Jason Biggs play "losers." For him this is not a big stretch and for her this means darker, messier hair and rattier clothes. As losers, both Dora and Paul suffer the same kinds of punishments that they had to endure as losers in high school. For instance, Paul's roommates use and abuse him. Interestingly, but uncritically, both of these characters are losers because of their lower socioeconomic status. She is trying to put herself through school by working as a cocktail waitress, and he is from a small town and is not hip on the trends, lingo, or attitude of his roommates. Dora is so poor that she eats the free packets of honey that she gets at the school cafeteria. And when Paul gets duped by his roommates he has to live in the animal hospital. While they begin as friends, together, these two losers find their place, though this path is not exactly a coming-of-age narrative.

In *Boys and Girls*, Jason Biggs and Freddie Prinze Jr. star as roommates. Biggs' character, Hunter (aka: Steve) is not a far cry from his other roles, but Freddie Prinze Jr. is not the same popular icon he was in *She's*

All That. Instead, he's a nerdy guy. How can we tell? Glasses and braces. But this film is not as much about the boys as it is about the girl, Prinz's nemesis and love interest. And while both Hunter-Steve and Ryan go through a kind of coming of age, this film is focused on her coming of age. Despite her struggles throughout the film against submitting to the mainstream's expectations concerning love and romance, Jennifer finally must accept these conventions, if only so that she stops running away from them and from Ryan. As the title reflects, the characters are not yet adults, and the adult world these characters enter at the end of the film is just as contrived as many teen spaces. This film assumes that love means having to compromise and sacrifice, which it can and does. But it also assumes that to have love, and to have a real relationship, one must also be an adult, in the narrow mainstream conceptualization of this term.

Another teen film, *Can't Hardly Wait*, also plays up this extended high school theme in a different way as it takes place primarily at a party on the last night of high school before the protagonist, Preston, leaves for college. However, he can't leave until he finally tells Amanda that he loves her. This film plays up the angles of unrequited love and fate as several misunderstandings and coincidences happen until, finally, Preston gets a chance to express his love. And Amanda realizes that all this time she's not only been missing out on being herself, but also has been missing out on this "great" guy. Though neither of these characters can wait for college, they seize their window of opportunity briefly as Preston puts his plans on hold for a few extra hours—a gesture toward their future. Not only does this moment reflect (limited) personal sacrifices, a must for a long-distance relationship, but it also reflects the ability to push adult responsibilities and demands off until later. College provides one of the best opportunities to avoid adulthood while still pursuing some acceptable, if not mandatory, mainstream-sanctioned avenues toward adulthood.

Legally Blonde also takes this space to create one of the best examples of a girls' coming-of-age film, which, not coincidentally, relies upon stock makeover plot elements and high school themes. When Elle's boyfriend breaks up with her during their senior year because she is not serious enough, she decides that she's going to apply to Harvard Law School (the school where he is going) in order to prove to him that she is, in fact, serious, and, thus, win him back. The plot she undertakes at Harvard Law School varies only slightly from those of several teen films. In trying to prove herself to him, she ends up proving herself to herself. But of course this comes with help from her soon-to-be boyfriend. Further, the same petty games that the popular crowd plays in high school are played by Elle's peers at Harvard as they ban her from study group and make fun of her eccentric dress (by Harvard standards). Of course her genuine sweetness, and her later-discovered smarts, help her to convert her enemies into her friends and to win a more mature and enlightened beau. As Mitchell and Ford discuss the positive aspects of this makeover story, it is clear that this film does not stray far from mainstream expectations. Further, this story line, not by any means unique to *Legally Blonde*, reads much like cries of reverse discrimination. Poor Elle is stereotyped because she is from California, she's blonde and she likes to dress in frilly, impractical outfits. Somehow this experience pales in comparison to the stereotypes that, say, Brandon Teena has to deal with. Thus, this film, like too many others, displaces real discrimination—the kind of discrimination that doesn't lead only to hurt feelings, but can lead to a total lack of any opportunity (let alone Harvard Law) and especially not far worse forms of oppression and even death. These are hardly the stakes for Elle.

Unlike many of the films above, *Never Been Kissed* and *Romy and Michelle's High School Reunion* don't pretend not to be teen films. When Josie goes undercover as a high school student she finds that she is just as nerdy in the present as she was in the past. She is still "Josie Grossie." And when Romy and Michelle decide to go to their high school reunion, they imagine all of the ways they can get back at the popular girls who made their high school lives hell. For Josie, this time high school holds the potential to further her career, but also holds the key to love in her life. And for Romy and Michelle, their high school reunion provides a kind of redemption that even Romy and Michelle couldn't originally imagine. Thus, Josie finds her true love in her return trip to high school—a teacher who would have been off limits, and off her radar, the first time around. And Romy and Michelle find the success and popularity they have always craved. But, better yet, this success and popularity propel them out of their high school frame and into an adult world where success and popularity are far more valuable. This success and popularity is partially derived from their undiscovered talents, but is also reliant upon help from a man and his money.

As is clear from the various mainstream patterns and tropes I have discussed thus far, these films are romantic not only because of their romantic love stories, but also because they make use of a time and a space between adolescence and adulthood that is only available to those who have the privilege to remain in this space. Only from this privilege does this type of romance follow. Another kind of privileged space is found in *Love and Basketball*, a coming-of-age film that not only follows Monica from childhood hoop dreams to the WNBA, but also provides a coming-of-age film that is focused on an African American protagonist and a cast of African American characters. Like some of the films I will discuss in the following chapter, this film provides characters who represent a variety of stereotypical and nonstereotypical characters. And it provides a strong female protagonist who succeeds in her dreams, at least as much as societal structures will allow. But while this film is focused outside of the mainstream in these ways, it is also a film that fits squarely within mainstream American and African American films. Monica loves basketball, but she also loves Quincy, or "Q." Perhaps because of her fairly comfortable middle-class existence, most of Monica's struggles result from her place as a woman, while few of these struggles are connected to race, at least overtly. She is not allowed the same access to basketball as Q is; he has his gender and his father's legacy to follow and Q's struggles are also not overtly connected to race. Further, Monica's emotional responses often get her into trouble on the court while, as she points out, Q's similar responses don't. All of these elements, and others, allow this film to confront many of the challenges that women like Monica face in a variety of social locations and relationships. She has to work harder. She has to face her personal struggles, particularly the many different expectations that people have of her. She has to fight for what she deserves. Thus, Q is not the one who is ultimately successful (and he provides parallel critiques of masculinity and professional sports, for instance). And in the end, Monica wins. She has it all—a supportive husband and baby, who cheer her on from the sidelines, a family that loves and supports her, and a career playing basketball. And while Monica's dreams were always focused on being the first woman in the NBA, this is a dream that is only available through the female version, the basketball league that holds little prestige compared to the institutionalized NBA.

This film is a good example of a film that walks the line between mainstream and independent, particularly because some of its most important critiques are buried or barely touched upon. For instance, Monica's mom and sister make her "pretty" by doing her hair and make-up for the Spring Fling dance. And later, when Monica gets a job at her father's bank, she dresses in dresses and high heels. In both cases, she is seen as being beautiful, but also as out of her usual element, at least by Quincy. However, when she joins the WNBA at the end of the film, an organization that is often criticized for its insistence upon the players' sex appeal, Monica's hair is straightened and she fits right into the glamour of the WNBA. And despite Monica's recognition of gendered stereotypes and expectations, these are, ultimately, expectations that she fulfills without too much question. She can have both love and basketball, but only through romance and only in predetermined contexts.

In the following section I discuss some of the films that take advantage of this in-between space for meaningful coming-of-age stories that reveal the not-so-romantic characteristics of the space between adolescence and adulthood. These films rely upon mainstream conventions less, and reveal some of the challenges that young women face when this space is not romantic. Thus, these films, like *Love and Basketball*, also challenge the conceptions of coming of age as merely an adolescent process.

Coming of Age Beyond Adolescence

Several films, like *American Beauty, Party Girl, Go,* and *Ghost World,* make much better use of this in-between adult and teen space, making them more powerful coming-of-age narratives than many of the films described in the previous section. In these post adolescent coming-of-age narratives, the lack of patterns recognized by adolescent psychologists becomes more apparent in the lives of its post adolescent protagonists because these characters are often mired in responsibility and sacrifice. Many of these films also include the theme of suburban angst as the protagonists struggle to find meaning in their boring, pointless, go-nowhere, mean-nothing lives. Sometimes this struggle is a reaction against the comforts of privilege, like in *American Beauty* or *Splendor,* but often protagonists are trapped by their circumstances like in *Go.* Other times, these films directly confront the promises of the previous generations or the limits of the American Dream, like in *Reality Bites,* one of the Generation X films of the '90s that embodies the angst of this (or, one wave of this) generation. Struggling, post college, this film offers a critique of white, middle-class, suburban angst, but still stays within sanctioned and acceptable limits of critique. Thus, in *Reality Bites,* and other films in this section, these issues are still romanticized and reduced, if to lesser degrees than the films discussed in the proceeding section.

Mary, in *Party Girl,* lives as the title suggests—focused on clothes, sex, and partying. She's great at organizing social events, but terrible at organizing her own life. When she gets arrested, she turns to her only family member for help. But since she has tapped her aunt too many times, her only recourse is to get a job working in the library where her aunt is a librarian. She takes this job out of desperation, but also as a way to prove herself. Through the narrative Mary not only discovers her aptitude (and soon, her passion) for library work, but also finds love outside of her usual crowd. While she has to struggle and sacrifice and prove herself, she has more help in doing so than, for instance, Ronna, in *Go.* Mary gives up the party life for a more serious adult pursuit, one that helps her to find herself and to find love. Thus, this post-teen coming-of-age story relies upon many of the same conventions as mainstream girls' films, but because the character is already an adult, legally, she has more at stake than many other similar protagonists like Cher in *Clueless* and Lola in *Confessions of a Teenage Drama Queen*. Her rites of passage cause her to find a way to be herself while also being responsible for herself.

Go, unlike the other films listed above, focuses on the lives of teens, but these teens are living in a space in between the youth and adult worlds. While this film has three divergent, but interconnected plots, my focus here is on the only strand that focuses on a female protagonist, Ronna, who is struggling to make ends meet, living on her own and working at the age of 15. When her story begins she is already responsible for herself, a subject she is almost silent about as she tells her friend, Claire, that she knows she can't go home. Ronna has few choices and when she is threatened with eviction, and an opportunity arises, she sees no other recourse than to sell drugs, an endeavor that she has neither the experience, nor the capital to undertake. She is a customer, but not a supplier. And as Claire cautions her, she shouldn't ask for trouble by trying to disrupt the drug hierarchy. To do so, she must play the part of the dealer, and, at times, adapts Todd's attitude and words to fit her own style. This role creates many obstacles that Ronna must navigate from Todd's hard personality, to the cop's undercover strategies, to her innovative ways of working out sticky, even life-threatening, situations.

Very few teen films deal with drugs as a means toward survival, if they deal with drugs at all. But in this narrative, drugs are not portrayed in the typical fashion—as something that's okay to experiment with as long as it's not a hard drug, like in *Clueless*; as something that helps one cope with pressure or boredom, like in *Whatever*; or as something that causes an inevitable downward spiral, like in *Thirteen*. Instead, Ronna enters a game she's not exactly ready to play and finds herself only slightly worse off in the end. And while she learns to innovate, to take risks, and to keep her cool, there is no magical happy ending that restores Ronna or rescues her overdue rent. Instead, ironic coincidence saves her life, bringing the three narratives together. And her life continues with the beep of the grocery scanner.

A similar kind of go-nowhere existence exists for the protagonists in *Ghost World*, though these characters are more sheltered than the teens in *Go*. They, more than other films in this section, illustrate the space between adolescence and adulthood for two girls who have little to look forward to and little to motivate them. However, both of these young women have the time and space to wait for something to happen, and the style and narrative progress of *Ghost World* mirrors its themes as the characters seem to go nowhere and do nothing, finding pleasure in making fun of people. Like in *Go*, the events that have meaning in these characters' lives are not augmented as important coming-of-age rituals. In fact, at the end of both of these films the characters seem to have changed little and are still stuck in their same go-nowhere lives. If any of these girls did have dreams, they faded a long time ago. But, in these films, that's okay. That's life.

While these films are coming-of-age stories that take place at the edges of adolescence, some films, like *Freaky Friday*, include both adolescent coming-of-age stories and adult coming-of-age stories in the same film. Two such films, *American Beauty* and *What a Girl Wants*, vary in several significant ways. The similarities and differences between these two films, particularly in the ways in which the coming-of-age narratives are constructed, reveal some of the key differences between mainstream films and independent films, adult and teen coming-of-age films, and male and female coming-of-age narratives. First of all, *What a Girl Wants* is focused around the adolescent while *American Beauty* is centered around the adult. Both of these films have attributes as coming-of-age films, but since *What a Girl Wants* is a family film, and is rated PG, one can expect it to be quite different from *American Beauty*, an independent film, rated R. While the focus of this film is on Lester, and is not, thus, a teen coming-of-age film about a girl, I choose to include it here for this very reason. This film not only reveals important aspects of coming-of-age films, but it also reveals the typical focal point of (white) men for films more generally and the tendency for such films to catch the attention of critics more often than films that focus on teens or girls. Further, this film reveals some of the more sinister mainstream conventions of some teen films. And, finally, this film shows the promise of breaking free from mainstream conventions that the next generation holds—a theme that is much more pronounced at the edges of the mainstream. These comparisons set the stage for the second half of this book.

During the midlife crises of Lester and Carolyn Burnham, they fall apart at the same time their daughter is establishing her own sense of self and trying to be autonomous from them and from the life they have provided her with. Both Lester Burnham and his wife, Carolyn, face the pitiful state of their seemingly perfect, but desperately lacking, suburban lives, a theme that comes up in a number of films including many of those in this study like *The Virgin Suicides* and *Splendor*. Similarly, in *What a Girl Wants*, Henry, while well-off and successful, has had to bury himself in the codes of behavior required by his royal position. He has been sleep-walking just as long as Lester. Conversely, Daphne's mom, Libby, knows who she is, but because of her self-knowledge and her need for independence, she is forced out of the royal family by one of Henry's advisors. She raises her daughter on fairy-tale stories of her father, expecting her to be independent and secure in herself. Thus, the only thing Libby is missing is Henry and the only thing Henry is missing is, it turns out, Daphne (and Libby). Daphne's appearance has a direct effect on Henry (not totally unlike Angela's effect on Lester), reminding him of what his life was like with Libby. This family scenario is easily fixed with a romantic, sentimental plot. And because this film is a fairy tale of sorts, not only do Daphne's dreams come true, but Henry's do as well. But the condition of the Burnhams' lives is not so easily mended.

Despite the fact that Lester will be dead less than a year after the narrative begins, he is in control as he narrates from beyond death, a power that girls can only joke around with in e.g. *Nikita Blues* and *The Opposite of Sex*. He tells us that his death does not matter because, in a way, he's dead already. And no long-lost daughter is on her way to save him, even if she could. Lester and Carolyn both deal with their crises in their own ways. Lester lifts weights, pursues his fantasies (which include telling off his boss, which he does, and having sex with Jane's friend, Angela, which he doesn't), and escapes from reality by smoking the government-engineered pot that Ricky sells him. This is a subversive element of the film since the key to Lester's enlightenment is both engineered and outlawed by the government (and Carolyn despises it). Thus, Lester subverts the government while Henry simply escapes it. And, Carolyn can only partially escape the trajectory that her life has followed. She pursues her self-discovery through an affair with the successful real estate king she worships. Rather than free herself from the demands and expectations she structures her life upon, she finds only a temporary reprieve. Her crisis, unlike Lester's, continues to be ruled by American myths—an appearance of success at all costs. Henry is also driven by appearances, and after her behavior is interpreted as scandalous, Daphne temporarily conforms to his, and his country's, expectations long enough to turn his election around. But her muted appearance and expected behavior also causes her to bury herself, and she's no longer willing to sacrifice her essence. She leaves and tells Henry she's tired of waiting for him to do the same.

Compared to Daphne, Jane seems to have no effect on her father. She is going through the demands of adolescence at the same time her parents are going through their respective midlife crises and neither parent pays much attention to her unless they are fighting about her in terms

of her place in their lives. When Carolyn drags Lester to see Jane perform in a high school basketball game's half-time show, Lester is bored
until he sees Angela, and immediately his gaze is compromised. Suddenly
the camera sees nothing but Angela as she gazes back at it seductively.
The half-time show is narrowed to Lester's focus and Angela dances as
if she is dancing only for his gaze. She begins to unzip her shirt and
instead of being greeted by her body, a stream of rose petals bursts from
her chest. Lester snaps out of the gaze, and it has permanently altered his
view. When Lester and Carolyn meet Jane after her performance, Lester
continues to stare at Angela and stumbles over his words, which, of course,
embarrasses Jane. And Lester continues to act like a dork when Angela
is around. She has aroused in him more than sexual interest, she has
aroused part of him that neither Jane nor Carolyn could—himself.

This Lolita figure acts as motivation much like Henry's daughter
acts as his motivation for allowing himself to truly be himself. And while
this film is a romantic, family film, perhaps for this very reason, this story
about a relationship between father and daughter takes on some disturbing Lolita tones, tones that are overt, exposed, and rejected by *American
Beauty*, even as Angela fulfills and exposes the Lolita myth. At the beginning of *What a Girl Wants*, Daphne is longing for her father; she tells her
mom that she's known for a long time that what she is missing is her father.
She can't know who she is, she argues, until she knows about her other
half. Despite the fact that her mom assures her that "getting to know
someone because they share the same DNA with you isn't the answer,"
Daphne is sure that she can't get to know herself until she knows her
father, reinforcing American's narrow conceptualization of family. Almost
simultaneously Henry is renouncing his spot in the House of Lords so
that he can run for parliament as a commoner. He asks the media "why
should an accident of birth allow me to make decisions," but questions
about what one is entitled to from birth become twisted when Daphne
arrives. At first their relationship is awkward, but as Henry gets to know
her, he's reminded of what he's sacrificed. This arousal culminates in
Henry and Daphne making a motorbike escape from a political function
after she shoves a persistent suitor into the water. As long as the two are
free, they spend their time together and Daphne takes her father to some
of the same spots where her boyfriend took her in previous scenes. Thus,
as the father-daughter-spending-time-together montage plays, Daphne
models several outfits for her father while she only modeled a skirt for
her boyfriend. While this scene is showing how playful and carefree
Daphne is, and includes a stock element—the fashion show—in many
similar films, it is also slightly disturbing, particularly when viewed in

In *What a Girl Wants*, Daphne (Amanda Bynes) and her father, Henry (Colin Firth), bond after their "date." Henry is invested in his job, his responsibility, and his legacy, but Daphne shows him a glimpse of what his life was, and could have been, without royalty. In these ways this film is not only a coming-of-age story for Daphne, but also second chance for Henry. His service to his country, and to his political conventions, become secondary to his chance at real love, romantic and fatherly, and a real family, American style. This mainstream version of a father-daughter coming-of-age story calls attention to *American Beauty's* darker elements, as *American Beauty* exposes some of the underlying problems with *What a Girl Wants*.

the context of *American Beauty* where Angela is made into an idealized sexual object in Lester's gaze. Lester stammers to find words that will impress Angela (and fails miserably—"Do you like muscles?"), but through his fantasy gaze, he continues to seek out the fantasy Angela and she lives up to his expectations. Under the influence of the gaze he seduces her, kisses her, and pulls a single petal from her mouth. He also finds her in the bathtub surrounded by rose petals. But the fantasy Angela cannot live up to the "real" Angela, and even this Angela is a construction of a myth. Lester's gaze makes the fantasy Angela seem like "Lolita," but the "real" Angela is actually closer to Nabakov's Lolita. (The characters even share the same last name.) They are both "vile and disgusting" (Wurtzel), but seductive nonetheless. She is the Lolita that is often left out of mainstream conceptualizations. She is the Lolita that Daphne isn't. But she is also the Lolita just below the mainstream's obsession with girls' bodies and sexuality. Discussions of Britney's and Christina's abdomens and J Lo's bootie, and rumors of Spears and Lohan having breast augmentations reveal some examples of this obsession, which sometimes plays itself out through other obsessions—like fairy tales.

While *What a Girl Wants* presents itself as a modern fairy tale, and has many similar elements as *A Cinderella Story* and especially *The Princess Diaries*, it also complicates this story in many important ways. For instance, Daphne has far more attitude and personality than Sam or Mia, and she doesn't want to be a princess or a Cinderella. She wants to be free. But she can only be as free as a mainstream narrative can allow; so, she gets her "own happily ever after." She gets her father-daughter dance, which "got interrupted when my boyfriend showed up and my parents started making out, but sometimes things aren't exactly as you imagined— they're even better!" Her father, in the end, may surrender his self-sacrifice and his loyalty for his country, but he plays right into mainstream convention when he shows up at the perfect moment—a wedding—with the perfect prize—"prince charming." To further romantic mainstream conventions, the "happily ever after" is temporarily interrupted by Daphne's narration, assuring us that all of the "bad" people got their due, much like Sam's final narration. Thus, this film relies upon the same conventions as the other Cinderella films, and mainstream films more generally—everyone gets what they deserve. And perhaps because the good-evil binary is so entrenched in mainstream convention, few of these films question who gets to decide who is good and who is evil and whether what they get is really what they deserved. Not only is this questioning imperative for contemporary politics, but, as *American Beauty* shows, this lesson is not so simple.

The lessons learned in *What a Girl Wants* are far simpler than those in *American Beauty*. In his opening narration, Lester says that he would like to tell Jane that her insecurity, anger, and confusion will end, but he can't. By the end, he has changed his opinion and, like Ricky, he sees true beauty not in any of the manufactured beauties of American culture, but through the camera that can find beauty in the most ordinary object, or something that is not an object at all. Lester has lost the gaze and can see true beauty—beauty in life, beauty in an inanimate object, beauty in his daughter and wife—because Ricky's view has become his own. What Lester had with the gaze was an idealized, sexualized version of girls. His gaze, as both a personal fantasy and as symbolic of the masculine gaze of culture, turned Angela from a girl into an object, from a virgin into a Lolita. But when he stops gazing, she is exposed for what she really is and seems nothing more than an ordinary girl. Just as Lester's gaze is an illusion, the "real" Angela is also an illusion. Both of these illusions are shattered when Angela tells Lester she's a virgin. He can no longer go through with his fantasy of having sex with her and the viewer can no longer go on believing in the fantasy of the "real" Angela either. After her confession, she becomes, not a Lolita, but an average teenage girl and Lester makes her a sandwich.

This moment is like many other moments in teen films when the attitude or stress is set aside and the girl is exposed. For instance, in *Saved!* when Mary wants to talk to her mother but they end up painting their toenails together. Or, in *Nikita Blues* when Nikita comes into the kitchen to ask for cake and confesses to her mother that she misses her father. Or, in *The Princess Diaries* when Mia and her mother paint with paint-filled balloons and darts. These moments are revealing of some parents' relationships to their teens—they are there, but they can't be there all the time, and they probably won't be there when the hard decisions get made. In the mainstream films discussed thus far, teen protagonists aren't usually faced with the real hard decisions, especially those decisions that require a girl or young woman to stand up on her own, and especially not those hard choices that require her to stand up against structural forces. There are, of course, exceptions, like in *Ella Enchanted* when Ella not only breaks the curse that has confined her to obedience all of her life, but also challenges the king's policies of segregation and discrimination.

Thus, some moments provide space not only for vulnerability, but also for a challenge to the conventions that rule mainstream culture and film. For instance, *American Beauty* begins with what seems to be a typical teen, shown through Ricky's camera, in what appears to be a foreshadowing of what is to come. But this opening scene is yet another subversion of the dominant culture's myths. The camera is focused on Jane, in her underwear, telling Ricky (and his camera) what a jackass her father is, and asking Ricky to kill him. But this footage is a trick. The same footage is shown in the context of the narrative and it is clear that Jane does not want Ricky to kill her father. The difference between the beginning camera footage and the same footage in the course of the narrative juxtaposes the two different contexts that the same piece of film can have depending upon its placement and its interpretation, but it is also the difference between the expectations of dominant, mainstream culture and the free will of its narratives. This film could have easily been about a teenage daughter who, with the help of her crazy boyfriend, kills her father. It certainly seems like this is the direction the movie is headed. But this would be a plot that surrenders to conventions and stereotypes and compromises Jane's character. It would also be a plot that would allow dominant culture's myths to triumph. It also could have been a film about a frustrated wife who kills her husband, but it is not this narrative either. This film is an adult's coming-of-age story, a story that ends in that adult's death because he cannot control the actions of the other people in his life. But this film is also a coming-of-age story for Jane, a story that underlines and augments her father's story.

While this film seems to be determined by the thoughts and actions of the men, it is Jane who is the central figure and it is Jane who will continue to oppose culture on the same grounds as her father. Jane's coming of age is interrupted by Lester's awakening, but if not for this interruption, Jane may have followed the fate of so many other girls (and boys) who do not question the people they are becoming. When the film begins, Jane is annoyed by both of her parents. In his narration Lester describes Jane as a typical teen, and he only really begins to become interested in her life when he wakes up to the pitiful state of his own. But Lester has not established a pattern of caring and he cannot just walk into her life because he wants to. Jane continues to try to avoid her parents' strangeness until she is confronted with a strangeness that is more intriguing—Ricky. He seems to be a pervert, always taping her, but when she asks him to stop, he does. Jane cannot figure Ricky out, but soon she stops trying to decipher him, and decides to get to know him. (And Ricky is violently misunderstood by his father, a misunderstanding that eventually leads to Lester's death.) The two complement and comfort each other and fall in love. At the end of the film, when Lester is talking to Angela, he asks her if Jane is happy. Angela tells him, with a bit of jealous eye rolling, that Jane thinks she is in love. This news makes Lester happy, not simply because Jane is happy, but because Lester knows that the person she is in love with will not let himself (or Jane) be sedated. Because Ricky helped him to see true beauty, Lester knows that Ricky can also see true beauty in Jane and neither Ricky, nor Jane, is ordinary. Thus, while Lester's opposition to dominant culture is the impetus of the movie it is Jane and Ricky who will continue this opposition.

Obviously, considerations of what coming of age means cannot be restricted only to films that portray adolescence, as these examples show. Understanding some of the ways that coming-of-age narratives happen in extended spaces helps us to better understand the ways in which coming-of-age narratives can be applied to various processes in life. As *American Beauty* shows, it's never too late to question convention and seek freedom. However, with Lester's death this point seems to be moot. But because Jane, when she becomes the focus of the story, demonstrates promise and possibility, this film illustrates one more important point. Girls who are often overlooked, underutilized, or over sexualized also hold the key to understanding coming of age processes more deeply, completely, and unconventionally. The films in this study, rooted in girls' struggles with mainstream expectations and conventions, provide a map with a variety of paths toward coming of age, in and out of the mainstream, and in and out of film. The next chapter looks at some of the ways in which girls' film, in and out of the mainstream, challenges the conventions of mainstream films that have been outlined in chapters one and two. Many of the same themes are revisited as girls flip convention on its head and negotiate new spaces, strategies, and resistances. In some cases these alternative spaces offer little power and in others these spaces offer more powerful rites of passage, and even empowerment. And some resistances offer small, personal victories, while some subvert powerful mainstream forces. Likewise, some strategies work in and out of the mainstream, but are more complicated and conflicted at the edges of, or outside of, the mainstream. As we will continue to see, it is impossible for girls to negotiate anything, including their own rites of passage or coming of age outside the confines of the mainstream. But, together, these films show that there are many ways and means toward individual and collective empowerment, and individual and collective coming of age.

PART II

NEGOTIATING AMERICAN CULTURE: TRAVERSING OUR OWN PATHS

THREE

OPPOSITIONAL POWER
AND EMPOWERMENT
Girls' Experiences from the Margins

Formal, institutional powers like school, family, religion, and law make rules that girls are expected to know and follow, but the informal rules of adolescence that come from these structures also restrict girls' behavior and social and sexual development. And while institutional powers confuse and contradict each other, the rules of teen culture are, appropriately and ironically, adapted from the structures of adult culture. Thus, both informal and formal rules are subject to mainstream conventions and definitions, like those detailed in the first half of this book. Together these structures might make girls feel as if they are "crawling out from under a complex web of affection and alienation, woven largely by their own insecurities, fantasies, and confusions" (208), according to Sara Shandler, author of *Ophelia Speaks: Adolescent Girls Write About Their Search for Self* (a book she wrote and compiled in response to Pipher's book *Reviving Ophelia*). They fight battles in their heads that can leave them powerless to oppose, or even identify, the larger scale. But within these webs, largely woven by mainstream culture, girls do negotiate the larger structures of society as well as the "insecurities, fantasies, and confusions." According to Lyn Mikel Brown, "Early adolescence ... disposes girls to see the cultural framework, and girls' and women's subordinate place in it for the first time." She argues further "that their reaction to this awakening would be shock, sadness, anger, and a sense of betrayal is not surprising" (16). This shock, sadness, and anger come up against the very culture that begot them, and girls feel confused about, and powerless against, its expectations. However, this shock, sadness, and anger are some of the most potent tools that girls have, in life and in film. These tools are one of the subjects of this book, particularly as they are used to negotiate both the informal and formal rules of adult and teen culture in their most benign and malignant forms—from rules that structure teen culture to those that deny girls an autonomous coming of age, and from those rules that define a girl by her appearance and status to those that structure her life possibilities.

These rules are not as easily negotiated as Lola implies through her song "That Girl" in *Confessions of a Teenage Drama Queen* when she sings that a girl can make her life anything that she wants to make it and that she doesn't have to play by anyone's rules. However, all girls have to play by someone else's rules at some time in her life, especially Lola. The success she achieves is not on her own terms, not by her own rules, but on the layers of rules that structure families, schools, and Hollywood itself. For instance, she lies about her father, but appreciates him in the end. At school, and in the school play, she wants to stand out, but she also wants to fit in. And she wants to be a big star because that's what she's destined to be. However, what's important is *how* a girl not simply plays *by* the rules, but *how* she *plays* the rules. Since Lola plays by all the rules, her song loses some of its edge. But this edge is central in many girls' films, especially when dreams, fate, and happy endings are not stock elements.

Tools of the Trade: Attitude, Voice and Awareness

The tools of negotiation for girls' coming of age are similar in film and in life. Attitude, voice, and awareness are three things that every girls needs if she wants a fighting chance of survival, let alone success, but these are also three tools that are feared, and thus often belittled or reduced by mainstream adult culture. Thus, while these three tools are important, they can also be emptied of the true potential of their power. For instance, sometimes the importance of voice in girls' film is given more weight than it deserves, like in Hilary Duff's *Raise Your Voice* or in *Confessions of a Teenage Drama Queen*. In these films, voice is a way of participating in the forums where girls are allowed to be heard—on the stage, as commodities. And sometimes attitude gets constructed as an aspect or ethnic identity like Ella's fairy godmother and Denise in *Raise Your Voice*. In *Welcome to the Dollhouse* Dawn's "attitude" gets her in trouble at school and at home. And in *What a Girl Wants* Daphne's attitude is portrayed as what makes her unique even though this attitude is, at least sometimes, an extension of her teen energy or American ignorance (both of which are also endearing). Finally, awareness, while it comes in many forms, is often only seen in small doses in girls' film. The kind of awareness that gives girls a structural insight into their circumstances, or the kind that gives a film irony, is not utilized often in girls' film, and is not always as effective as it can be when utilized in other genres. Regardless of the failures or limited successes of attitude, voice, and awareness, these tools, as they are used in girls' film, reveal the kinds of battles that girls undertake in film, and the ways in which these battles influence their coming of age.

Voice is one front among a short list of both defensive and offensive strategies that girls have in life and in film. It can be used to negotiate conflicts with peers and parents, individuals and structures. Sometimes this front acts as a way of dealing with harsh conditions, like in *Girls Town* when Patti struggles not just to graduate from high school, but also to provide her daughter with the necessities, or in *Nikita Blues* when Nikita tries to bury her sadness about her father's death. And as previously mentioned, this front is a means of survival in the face of both state and underground authority for Ronna. But at other times this front can be a way of appearing to be cooler. For instance, because Angela, in *American Beauty*, does not want to be ordinary, she puts up a front. She tells Jane all of the graphic details of her sexual escapades, but neither Jane, nor any other girls at school are really that impressed. When Angela brags about sleeping with a fashion photographer, one girl at school sees right through Angela and tells her off in an attempt to shatter Angela's preoccupation with her looks and her dreams of a successful future in modeling. And when Angela hounds Jane for her own dirty details, Jane refuses to cooperate and tells Angela that "it's not like that" and that she wishes Angela wouldn't tell her everything she does. What Jane thinks it is like is left ambiguous. She has no front. The friends in *Coming Soon* also front as they talk about sex as if they are far more experienced than they actually are. Stream feels like she is lagging behind Jenny and Nell when, in reality, she is learning more about herself—sexually and socially—than any of her friends are. Thus, sometimes voice and attitude only attempt to hide vulnerabilities.

Other times, voice (often infused with attitude) is used to give girls a means of expressing opinions that are not always welcome by parents, teachers, social conventions, or other power structures. For instance, Chantel challenges her teachers and her Eurocentric education and when she wants to graduate early, the principal tells her she's not ready. First she has to "behave more like a lady" and "tone down that mouth." The principal's advice is unsatisfactory for Chantel because he is, at least in her mind, speaking for the status quo. He cannot convince Chantel that she is too immature for college because his only reasons are her behavior and her mouth. These aren't good enough reasons for Chantel because, to her, her mouth and her behavior are her essential self. To tell her that these things will keep her from achieving her dreams is not a legitimate claim because her mouth and her behavior are the only things she can use to survive. If she has to behave differently, she'll be a different person, and she's not willing to sacrifice herself. Emma, in *Girls Town*, finds another way to express her voice when she writes on the bathroom stall, "these guys will fuck with you." Similarly, Carol, in *Shake, Rattle, and Rock!* expresses her voice in the only form where she will be heard, in the appropriated words that epitomize the "devil speak" of rock and roll that her mother is so worried about—"awop boopa loo bob awop bam boom." Even if she is not heard, the permanence of the paint on her parents' walls speaks volumes. And while girls in film often use their voices in individual struggles, they also use their voices in collective struggles. For instance, in *All I Wanna Do*, Odetta uses her voice to rally the girls of Miss Goddard's together, not to try to speak for the girls, but to give each girl a democratic stake in her own future. This stake, however, is small and relatively inconsequential in the larger picture of politics and democracy. But this film doesn't let such realities stand in the way of its characters' futures. All of the girls are, as a result of finding their voice, successful in the career dreams that they had as teens, even when unforeseen circumstances, like Tinka's coming out, change the nature of these dreams. But in girls' film, voice is taken to more powerful and empowering levels through narration as voice negotiates with the conventions of the film and the genre.

Virtually every girls' film includes narration, particularly the most transformative narratives. Narration provides details about the narrative as well as details about the protagonist's internal struggles and negotiations. Without this internal dialog many films would lack their irony, their edge, or their deeper meanings. And without narration, many girls would lack a voice. In fact, in films like *The Virgin Suicides*, one of the boys narrates, reinforcing the fact that in the book, and by extension in society, the girls have no voice except through the male narrator and through dominant, masculine culture. Thus, in many girls' films narration is also a means of control—not only control over the narrative, but also control over the girl's coming of age. For instance, in films like *What a Girl Wants*, the narration is used to give Daphne complete control over the narrative, using her narration to mold both her and her parents' stories. However, control is not always what it seems to be. For instance, in *Ripe*, Rosie's narration is all she has left as the movie opens and she looks back on the impending narrative, talking about her sister in the past tense. She tells us, "I'd do anything for Violet," but her anything is, like so many other similar promises, a conditional anything—she'll do anything as long as she is in control. And Rosie cannot control nature. By the end of the movie, Rosie's voice is gone again. In fact, both girls are silent. And, finally, control is not always achieved through narration. For instance, in *Slums of Beverly Hills*, Vivian controls the narrative in many ways, but she doesn't narrate until the end. Her character and her attitude are enough to give her control over her coming of age even if she can't control all of the elements of the film. In fact, like in *What a Girl Wants*, power over the film's narrative gives her less freedom and power since this film is strictly contained within mainstream romantic convention, while *Slums of Beverly Hills* is not.

In most girls' films, narration details the narrative, and it is the narrative that is empowering. Sometimes narration looks back on a situation and offers the wisdom of experience as the narrator adds to the narrative. Other times the narration is simultaneous as if the girl is talking as we are watching. But narration always gives a girls' film a female perspective and an orientation specific to that character. For instance, when Chantel in *Just Another Girl on the IRT* narrates, she talks directly to the camera. She exposes herself for what she is; she is on the verge of womanhood, and childbirth is a wake-up slap in the face. She uses the camera as her confidante, telling us all of the things that she can't tell anyone in the movie, and her narrative carries her out of adolescence and into motherhood. In *Manny and Lo*, Laurel (the pregnant teen) isn't the narrator. She is too close to the narrative to have enough distance to narrate her story. Instead, her younger sister Amanda (Manny) allows us to see Lo for what she is and we like her despite her adolescent flaws. Manny is on the verge of adolescence, and her position gives her a clarity that her sister doesn't have while her narration acts as a model from which she can construct her own adolescence. Dedee's narration in *The Opposite of Sex* comes, as we find at the end, from the depths of adolescence, but she is narrating from a new beginning, a new point from which she can come of age on her own terms instead of on the terms that her story began with. Thus, Dedee's narration, while it constructs her story according to her discretion and acts as a front or a buffer between her and her audience, also opens space for her to come of age beyond the restrictions of her self-constructed narrative.

Like Chantel and Dedee, some girls use attitude in conjunction with narration, a combination that is powerful, and sometimes empowering. However, in the mainstream, this combination is often effective only within set parameters and expectations. For instance, as Lola in *Confessions of a Teenage Drama Queen* sings and argues, she's armed with an attitude and she knows how to use it. In this film, Lola's attitude allows her to combat the powers of the popular girls like Carla, and this attitude rubs off on her friend, Ella. But her attitude also softens when she realizes that her lies, a part of this attitude and persona she wants to portray, hurt the people close to her. And in *What a Girl Wants*, Daphne is all about attitude. Her attitude briefly awakens the staunch aristocracy of England, makes a disenfranchised English rebel fall in love with her, and helps her father to realize who he is and where he needs to be. And, in the end, this attitude so defines Daphne that she chooses to turn her back on her royal blood and return to a life where she can be herself. Her attitude is not portrayed as being simply an American phenomenon, as some characters initially think, nor is it explained away as typical teenage behavior, it is what makes Daphne "unique" in the course of the film. But she is unique only in comparison to girls who lack a voice or an attitude, girls like Dawn in *Welcome to the Dollhouse*, who suffer miserably because of their lack. Dawn can't defend herself without being whiny. She can't talk back to her parents without being shut down. She can't talk to her only friend, Ralphie, without being mean. She can't talk to her sister without contempt. And, most of all, she can't talk to Steve without coming across as a naive child. However, other characters without attitude are far less dynamic than Dawn. For instance, Marci in *Jawbreaker* is, as her father puts it, a follower. She doesn't do anything for herself, let alone think for herself. All of her attitude comes from her friends, whose attitude is derived from status and self-absorption. This character is a trope in the genre, appearing also as Karen in *Mean Girls*. She is the Plastic, the Heather, the queen bee who follows along empty, except as she is (ful)filled by her master.

Conversely, in some films girls are not confined to the "proper" language of PG ratings and aristocratic bloodlines; it is their narrative, and they can say whatever they want to say, even if they don't say it as well as they could have. Thus, attitude is needed to back up the narration. But attitude is especially needed for girls whose voices are not the dominant voices or the narrating voices in the films. For instance, for some girls who do not possess the wealth or status to float by, like Karen in *The Smokers*, attitude is, presumably, all that they have going for them. She's not like the other girls—not just well-off, but filthy rich—though she aspires to reach their financial status. She uses attitude to deal with the principal when he threatens to expel her and she uses attitude to deal with her lack of sexual power. Such attitude is also needed by characters like Chantel in *Just Another Girl on the I.R.T.* as she confronts her Eurocentric education, or by Elin in *Show Me Love* when she introduces her new girlfriend, or by Treasure in *Stranger Inside* when she has to negotiate the prison structures to try to get closer to her mother. And this attitude, this ability to fight for herself, is what Monica's mother most admires, and is most envious of, in *Love and Basketball*.

Another kind of attitude that is successful in some contexts and some doses is that of the "bad girl." This characterization also fits Karen since she is lower class, which is only one reason why the "bad girl" label may be attached, as it is to Suzie in *Wild Things*, for similar reasons. Or, the "bad girls" are not powerful at all like in *Girls Town* where Patti has to deal with the physical, mental, and verbal abuse of her baby's daddy, until the girls, together, get revenge. The label of "bad girl" may also be attached because of "deviant" sexualities like in *Cruel Intentions* or *Jawbreaker*, or perceived sexualities like in *Mean Girls* or *Saved!*. Other times the "bad girls" are the leaders, the means toward power and empowerment, like in *Foxfire*. But much of the time "bad girls" are bad because they are too powerful, and, thus, they are "mean girls." For instance, the too-powerful characters like Regina George in *Mean Girls*, or Lana in *The Princess Diaries*, or Hilary Faye in *Saved!*, are one type of "bad girl." Their attitudes, however, only cover up their insecurities, like any other front. The ways in which these "bad girls" negotiate this identity beyond attitude, voice and awareness will be taken up again in chapter four.

Beyond voice and attitude, many girls' films share an awareness of their genre like *Heathers*, *Scream*, *The Opposite of Sex*, *Jawbreaker*, *10 Things I Hate About You*, *Saved!*, *Mean Girls*, *But I'm a Cheerleader*, and *Girls Town*. The awareness shown in these films often comes only in particular varieties and small doses, and only sometimes challenges mainstream conventions. One bit of awareness that peeks through every once in a while comes through "feminism." At times this awareness is light, like when Kat is proclaimed a "feminist bitch" because she wears black, listens to indy rock, and sees the futility of an empty, consumerist lifestyle. And *Mean Girls* offers a pop feminism when one of the Plastics, Gretchen, tells Cady that friends can't date ex-boyfriends because "that's just like the rules of feminism." But one unexpected portrayal of a feminist happens in the unlikely narrative of *American Pie*. Oz goes on a date with a "college girl" and he brags beforehand about how he is sure to score. But this college girl is nothing like Oz expects. He tries to spout off lines that seem romantic and then follows up with the line, "Suck me, Beautiful." This line ends the date, but only after this Postmodern Feminist Thought major gives him a lecture about women.

Other films embody feminist ideals whether or not these ideals are painted as being feminist in nature. For instance, *Foxfire*, a film based upon a short story by Joyce Carol Oates, has feminism at its core. Legs is almost too stereotypically feminist as she brings the girls together to empower and defend themselves. In the end, however, her brand of feminism is not strong enough to forge bonds stronger than friendship. Likewise, in *The Craft*, the girls bond around their power and their witchcraft. However, jealousy and abuse of this power not only splinters this coven, but also requires Sarah's natural powers to reign in Nancy, the baddest of the bad girls. Other films, like *All I Wanna Do*, display their equal rights brand of feminism loudly and proudly as the girls demand a right to vote on whether or not their school goes co-ed. This liberal feminism is the kind most often portrayed in girls' films, after the pop feminism found in the family films previously discussed. Films like *Virtual Sexuality, Coming Soon,* or *Slums of Beverly Hills* push more current strands of feminism as the girls take control of their sexuality instead of waiting around for a boy to initiate sex. But few films that consciously utilize feminist ideals push the boundaries of mainstream feminism.

While these films show various inklings of feminist consciousness, a kind of awareness, other types of consciousness are sometimes used as conventions in girls' film. This awareness, in the form of allusion, is shown in *Girls Town* when the two popular girls are referred to as "Heather and her other friend Heather," which not only shows an awareness of its genre, but, in this case, also gives the girls who aren't "Heathers" the chance to confront this celluloid and real-life manifestation. This position reveals another kind of awareness inherent in films like *Girls Town* and *All Over Me*—an awareness of what a girl's position is on the margins of her culture and society, and what kind of treatment and life chances they have available. Thus, it is this awareness that gives girls some space for negotiation of these limitations, which will be discussed throughout this and the following chapter.

Another type of awareness utilized in popular culture, particularly movies and television shows that challenge mainstream expectations, is parody. *Not Another Teen Movie* challenges many of the conventions of the teen film genre; however, this parody is done in a masculine space and often makes fun more than it makes waves. Few girls' films, with the exception of *Heathers*, whose parody has been unparalleled by many girls' films (approached only by *Scream, Saved!,* and, perhaps, *Mean Girls*), use parody as a convention. And the awareness that parodies like *Heathers* and *Scream* rely upon for their plots is used in other teen films to briefly parody a specific convention like in *10 Things I Hate About You, She's All That,* or *Mean Girls* when the mandatory introduction of the cliques is done. Thus, many films that do involve satire or sarcasm can be considered as what Frederic Jameson and Chela Sandoval describe as pastiche. Parody "mimics, ridicules, and transforms" (26) dominant structures, while pastiche lacks an awareness of the dominant order it mocks. Thus, films like *Clueless*, a parody of mall culture and the Beverly Hills lifestyle, lacks an awareness of the larger structures that need a makeover. For instance, Cher makes herself over by organizing a clothing drive and becoming interested in vague "global issues." This is the way in which rich people get involved; and while it is admirable, it is also the easiest and least costly way to get involved (at least personally). Cher doesn't confront what it means for her to have so much, and she doesn't have to sacrifice anything to become a "better person." This lack of awareness is also shown in *Mean Girls*, which parodies the conventions of high school and teen films. However, while reviewers note that this film parodies many "politically correct" conventions through its portrayal of teen girls as wild animals, not unlike those in the jungles of Africa, this use of "Africa" invokes cultural stereotypes without complexity, and with assumptions of racial and cultural superiority, as discussed in chapter one.

Despite some of the awkward attempts at parody in girls' films, the recent film *Saved!*, a film that is not exactly a girls' film though it shares many of the same conventions and themes, not only takes up the rare convention of parody, but also takes up other mainstream taboo subjects as well, such as religion, homosexuality, disability, and teen pregnancy. In this film, many stereotypes are subverted including the token wheelchair character, the bad girl and the good girl, and the conditions surrounding teenage pregnancy. Through its parody of a born-again Christian high school (American Eagle Christian High School, a name that reflects the mainstream American nature of this Christian school as well as its version of Christianity) this film is able to tackle one of the more extreme versions of mainstream culture's values, expectations, and limitations—that of the religious right. While this film's choice to parody the religious right was offensive to many people because of the stereotypes of religion that the film confronts, parody must utilize stereotypes to some extent. And exposing the limitations of stereotypes, as well as the truth about stereotypes, is part of what good parodies do well. For instance, the narrowly conceived dogma of the "in-crowd" (teens and adults) at American Eagle Christian High is challenged as a specific example of Christian dogma gone awry. Thus, *Saved!* does not simply parody Christianity, but a certain form of Christianity that breeds insecurity, haphazard application, and strict adherence to ideals without considering context, or more specifically, "free will." And though it reinforces the institution of Christianity, *Saved!* also questions the ignorantly zealous, a challenge that is especially important in its time.

The primary character for this film's parody of Christian righteousness is Hilary Faye. In her role as Hilary Faye, Mandy Moore does not differ much from the role she plays as Lana in *The Princess Diaries*. She is popular, mean, controlling, part of a musical group; the only difference is, in *Saved!*, she plays this role in a parodic Christian context. Because of this context, this stock popular "bad girl" character, a character who does not fit with Christian dogma, is already ironic. And while Hilary Faye's cruelty is a means for her to try to control everyone and everything, and while she really seems to be trying to live according to her faith, her ignorance of this faith, and of anything outside of it, makes her easy to mock. For instance, Hilary Faye likes to remind her brother, Roland, and everyone else, about how she was "the miracle that saved his life," even while she asks him why he has to "make everyone feel so awkward about [his] differently-abledness." Hilary Faye may talk the language of "political correctness," but this language does not reflect her ideas, only those ideas she has been taught to accept uncritically. Thus, *Saved!* pushes a parody of political correctness much further than *Mean Girls*, especially since Hilary Faye's political correctness does not overflow into her opinions about and treatment of "gays." For instance, when she finds out that Mary's boyfriend, Dean, is gay she remarks that "we've never had a gay" at American Eagle Christian High School. And she extends this ignorance when she says that it's a good thing that they can't reproduce because "the gayness would be passed on." Later she holds a prayer meeting for Dean and "all the perverts" who just haven't found the "right girl." Again, Hilary Faye recycles phrases that she's heard used so often that she repeats them without question. This political correctness also appears and disappears in an international context. For instance, when Patrick returns to high school after doing missionary work in Africa, Hilary Faye assumes that he has been working to bring religion to "the heathens," since this is her conceptualization of what missionary work is. When she asks Patrick "what part of the world has the worst heathens?" he just looks at her as if she were crazy. Thus, this invocation of Africa, unlike that in *Mean Girls*, is used to confront the stereotypes of Africans as "heathens" and to challenge the place of "Christians" in bringing them religion, even if this challenge is underscored by the Christian cultural capital that Patrick's work affords him. He is the type of Christian that Hilary Faye tries to be, even if she tries too hard. And in the end, her brother asks, "You have everything Hilary Faye; what are you so afraid of?"

Saved!'s solution to the subjects it parodies is a lighter, feel-good, kind of Christianity, one that innovates upon narrow or hypocritical mainstream versions, but also reinforces them. For instance, at the end of *Saved!*

another form of feel-good equality (and "multiculturalism") is espoused by Mary as she narrates, "No one fits in 100 percent of the time." Besides, "why make us so different if [God] wanted us to be the same?" But Mary's question really only begins to get to the deeper issues that this film touches on throughout the narrative. And this exploration is even more bleached when she remarks that she was "not the first person to get the message mixed up," erasing a historical legacy of violent repression and brutal enforcement of Western Christianity at the expense of many different groups of people. And if Mary's "mix-up" is a means toward growth and understanding for herself and her faith, as it is in this narrative, where does Hilary Faye's mix-up lead her? In the end, the "good" Christians (Mary and Patrick) are the winners, and they, of course, forgive the "bad" Christians (Hilary Faye and Pastor Skip) for their sins. And they, in many ways, recreate their ideas of a Christian family and, to a lesser extent, Christianity itself, as Mary remarks, "What would Jesus do? I don't know, but we'll be trying to find out together." Thus, *Saved!* may question, but does not ultimately challenge the role that religion plays in mainstream society's expectations and history, including its disavowal, marginalization, or banishment of any and all people, ideas, or cultural texts, particularly those that don't fit with their vision and truly challenge the mainstream's social and cultural, individual and structural, authority.

Attitude, voice, and awareness are all means toward empowerment as well as a way in which some girls can establish control over their narratives and, thus, power, or an illusion of power, over their celluloid lives. However, these games of power and empowerment pale when we consider how power can be achieved in teen narratives with or without empowerment. For instance, in *The Princess Diaries*, Mia accepts the job of princess because if she were princess of Genovia, "my thoughts, and the thoughts of people smarter than me, would be much better heard, and just maybe those thoughts could be turned into actions." This statement is supposed to hold more weight because we've been shown clues to the princess's humanity throughout the film. She and her friend, Lily, are much less shallow than their schoolgirl counterparts, taking up primarily environmental (and some human rights) causes like those of Greenpeace. It is Lily who reminds Mia that the price of the new bag she has "could feed a third-world country," and who first reminds Mia about the power that a princess has "to effect change." However, one can't help but wonder what kind of real power a princess can actually have. Has Mia undergone a proper coming of age, and a deeper understanding of herself, not just a heel-popping kiss? Does her revelation about the power of ideas, which, within the context of the film sounds empty and unconvincing without specific examples, simply sound like liberal, humanist jargon?

Enforcing the Rules of Fashion

One example of the way the formal, institutional powers make laws and rulings that punish and confine girls is the way schools use their power to control girls' sexuality. For instance, schools often restrict "distracting" clothing, which suggests that controlling the sexuality of boys and men is the girls' responsibility, like the stubborn assumption that it is a girl's fault when she gets raped. She was dressed provocatively; she invited it upon herself. Again and again girls are reminded of this responsibility through such formal and informal rules. And they are faced with this reality whether they are sexually assaulted or abused themselves or whether they simply hear the horror stories. But the rules of teen culture are not always so severe, particularly in mainstream teen films where the informal and formal rules are often mocked or satirized. Despite this playful character, fashion and appearance are tropes in teen films that are ruled by the formal and informal rules of teen culture, reflecting and refracting what these things mean in real life. Fashion is also one space of negotiation where girls in film develop a sense of self, a power over themselves and others, and even a means of expression and subversion; however, this space is often corrupted by corporate and other interests attached to the fashions in a film, making this space as conflicted as any other adolescent or cultural space. And like these spaces, representations and negotiations of fashion and appearance converge and diverge in and out of the mainstream.

In the mainstream, issues of fashion and appearance are always a part of the film in some way, often through a fashion show montage or shopping spree. Most often fashion and appearance are connected to struggles for popularity or acceptance, and are sometimes used consciously or ironically. However, regardless of whether the protagonist is a queen bee, where fashion is key to popularity, or an outsider, where fashion can be a means toward or away from popularity, fashion plays a role in her narrative. For instance, in *A Cinderella Story*, a film with a lower socioeconomic character, she models an array of Halloween costumes—many awkward and unappealing—before finding the perfect dress for a Cinderella. This fashion show scene is similar to those in other films like *What a Girl Wants* when Daphne playfully models outfits for her father, and *Confessions of a Teenage Drama Queen* when Lola searches through her entire closet to find the perfect outfit for the concert. But this also reflects Dunn's sentiments that girls can reinvent themselves through new clothes and make-up. At the edges of the mainstream, fashion can also play this role, but fashion and appearance are often used in more unconventional ways that more deeply connect to adolescent issues beyond popularity. For instance, in the 1980s setting of *Whatever*, Anna and Brenda dress in ways that they think are more adult, but watching this film from a modern conception of teen fashion, their clothing gives an added element of, perhaps, nostalgia, to the other awkward visual indications. And Anna also goes through a fashion show; however, this show is for herself as she searches for something that she's comfortable in—quite a different function than the fashion-show montages previously mentioned. But regardless of whether a film is mainstream or independent, fashion and appearance are important not only because of their connections to the film industry and to teen culture, but also because of how girls negotiate these elements in girls' film.

The role most familiar for clothing and fashion is as a marker of status. High fashions mean money and since many teen films are set in upper-class locations, fashion becomes a must in the game of popularity. In some cases, fashion as a marker of status is taken to an extreme when it takes on some characteristics of costume. For instance, in *The Smokers*, the girls are not simply upper class—they are filthy rich. This distinction is shown not only in some plot elements, but also in the elaborate fashions that the girls wear. Part of this elaborate fashion signals a desire to fit into the adult world, offset by the oversized hats and jackets and the high heels, whose awkwardness visually signals adolescents dressing up as adults. And ordinary fashion as clothing is not enough for these girls who paint their faces to match their clothing, or wear wigs when it suits them. This costume trope is taken to a more literal level in *Confessions of a Teenage Drama Queen* when "costumes are sacred" to their drama teacher, but are also the only option for a really cool outfit for the hottest party of Lola's young life. The fact that Lola has to wear a costume to a party to which her nemesis, Carla, can just wear a regular dress subtly underlines the difference in these characters' status.

But fashion also acts as a marker of status between the stars and other characters as it does between Lola and Carla. For instance, when Bianca and her friend pass by the boys in an opening shot, Bianca is describing the difference between love and like (key since the boy who has a crush on her is listening). "I like my Skechers," she says, "but I love my Prada backpack." Her friend answers, "But I love my Skechers." To which Bianca insists that "that's because you don't have a Prada backpack." While this is clearly a joke, it also reveals a lot about Bianca's shallow character. She may choose the "right" guy, the guy who is nice and sincere, but she doesn't develop any respect for those things, or people, whom she considers herself above, whether its the reasonably priced, common teen fashion—Skechers shoes—or those "crack whores" who, she argues, should have made their "skeezy boyfriend" wear a condom. To reinforce this, Bianca, despite her ignorance and classism, is still triumphant, while her friend gets what she "deserves"—Joey.

Partially because of the importance of status, makeovers often hold the key to other kinds of transitions. These kinds of films are described as teen makeover films by Elizabeth A. Ford and Deborah C. Mitchell in their book, *The Makeover in Movies* (which includes a chapter specifically on the role of the Cinderella story as makeover). In this book, they focus on four other teen films that are also included in this study: *Clueless, She's All That, Josie and the Pussycats*, and *Legally Blonde*. While their study is, for the most part, parallel to mine, it also diverges in various ways. First of all, to look at makeovers in teen films, there are more films that have makeovers as central or minor themes. For instance, in *Jawbreaker* Fern is made over into Violet, a "nerd" who takes advantage of an opening to become one of the popular girls. Violet is eventually exposed, but only after she threatens Courtney's power. As Violet, Fern embraces the very behavior that she once idolized, the same behavior that kept her at the bottom. Further, while Cher's makeover talent in *Clueless* may give her a sense of control, it does not give her any real power, except the power to temporarily change something's surface. When she tries to change what's on the inside to match the outside, as she does with Tai, the results are not as dramatic. Thus, while makeovers can give both power and empowerment, neither of these are guaranteed. As Cher finds out, her makeover power only really matters when she finds she needs to makeover her inner self, a task she really doesn't have the tools for.

The second divergence in our studies is the limited treatment of race, class, and sexuality in the authors' analysis. Their analysis is focused on the way in which these films fit into the makeover genre and what kinds of messages they send to their audiences; thus, much of their analysis centers on whether the film's message is positive or negative. And one of their primary questions is why progressive women continue to return to such conventional plots. Further, their analysis also seems to take place from some post multicultural space that does not yet exist. They mention, for instance, that Valerie in *Josie and the Pussycats* is the "tough but sensitive African American girl." Her race is half of the description about her in their summary. In fact, all three girls are described by their appearance, but only Valerie is described by her race. Josie and Melody are described as the "red-headed wanna-be star" and the "ditsy blonde fluff kitten." While the bulk of the film centers around Josie, and Melody's character relies upon her ditsy and fluffy qualities, Valerie's character seems to have little to do with her race. But since Valerie has a smaller and less crucial part in the film one can't help but wonder if her character's place has as much to do with her race and appearance as Melody's character does. Both of these girls may be made over during the course of this film, but in no case is the makeover powerful enough to erase the traps that identity creates for them. These traps are some of the same ones that girls deal with through film and life.

One important point about the makeover is that it is a popular plot element in teen films, perhaps because the makeover can symbolize the transition from teen to adult—a transition that is difficult to make without internal or external help. The makeover trope is usually connected with changes in fashion and appearance, making the makeover intimately connected to females, despite the popularity of makeover shows like *Queer Eye for the Straight Guy*. The dynamics of the makeover as a trope that empowers and changes girls for the better are not usually the focus of discussions about makeovers. Thus, a simple analysis of whether a film has a positive or negative message, like that offered by Mitchell and Ford, does not deal with the complexities of the makeover film as a trope in coming-of-age films. As we see throughout my analysis, here and in the rest of this book, the makeover trope reveals some of the problems with superficial transformations.

A change in clothing often signifies a change in attitude, and sometimes in personality and actions as well. In *What a Girl Wants* Daphne's spunk and sparkle are captured through her quirky (but still mainstream fashionable) clothing and accessories. They are something that set her apart from the drab clothes of the upper echelons of English society, including her (evil) stepmother and stepsister-to-be. But when Daphne must look past this part of herself, she also sacrifices part of herself—and the rest of it too. In order to fit in better and help her newfound father's political career, she must look the part, making her boyfriend remark that she should call him "when Daphne reinhabits your body." But her grandmother, in giving Daphne her first tiara, reminds her that "it's not the crown that makes a queen" but what's inside. While similar advice, given to Mia in *The Princess Diaries*, causes her to look inside and realize her responsibility to the people of a country she has never known, the same advice helps Daphne to remember who she is. But Mia is supposed to become a princess and Daphne is supposed to reject her ties to royalty, not just because of the belief of fate that the girls' mothers instill in them, but because these are the set plots for the film. In discovering herself as princess, Mia is connecting with a father she never knew. But she also gains a ready-made future and a new image. While her makeover is somewhat a result of finding herself, and is reinforced by her grandmother's urgings that she'll make a fine princess, the physical transformation is necessary for Mia to fit the part. And while the importance of Mia's appearance is underscored by several elements of the narrative, in the end she's cleaned up and repackaged in the way that a princess is *supposed* to look, despite the fact that Amelia's grandmother attempts to shatter the princess stereotype when she tells her that "people think princesses are supposed to wear tiaras, marry the prince, always look pretty, and live happily ever after." But it's so much more than this, she assures Mia, "it's a real job." However, the grandmother's "princess lessons" ensure that one cannot do this job unless one looks, and acts, the part, which Mia is able to do "naturally" in the final scenes of the film. Unlike Mia's discovery, which brings her closer to her father via her grandmother, her job, and her position as princess of Genovia, in discovering that she doesn't want to be a princess, Daphne is reminding her father of what's most important in life. Mia undergoes a makeover in appearance which helps her come out of her (glasses and frizzy hair) spell and realize who she is always meant to be, but Daphne's fashion reflects who she is from the beginning of the film. For her, it's the makeover into something that she's not, represented by clothing and accessories (or lack of accessories) that mute her appearance as well as her spirit. In finding herself in someone else's clothes, she finds that she's known herself all along.

This importance on appearance and fashion is underscored in one of the DVD extras for *A Cinderella Story*—"Cinderella Couture: The Making of a Fashionably Modern Fairy Tale." The costume and makeup artists go on and on about how difficult it is to make Hilary Duff look ordinary. They talk about how they chose blues for the mood they express and as she gains more confidence throughout the film, so do her colors. This is an obvious example of unrealistic expectations as the "before" images are always attempts to make stars shine less bright, often adding glasses and frizzy hair and frumpy, shapeless clothes to get the right effect. Thus, fashion in teen films is used to make over not only appearance, but also social awkwardness. A red dress (and some help from Zack's sister) transforms Janie in *She's All That* from a nerdy art student in overalls and glasses to a hot potential prom queen. In *Clueless*, new clothes take Tai from rags to designer style but those clothes don't change her personality, nor her character, since she rediscovers herself when she hooks up with Travis. And for Violet, in *Jawbreaker*, new clothes take her from outcast to in girl, but in adopting a new attitude to go along with her new identity, Violet as is exposed as Fern, and she resigns to an improved version of her old self. But despite the power of clothing in a makeover plot, clothing can be just as important for a certain look, like the dress for Cinderella (Sam) in a *A Cinderella Story*. The film's stylists describe how Hilary Duff's mom knew right away that she had found the perfect dress when she saw a picture of it. And in *Confessions of a Teenage Drama Queen*, Lola must have a "drop dead gorgeous dress" that makes her look at least 25. When her mother tells her it's not in the budget, she searches her closet for anything that will work. Despite the mound of clothes she sifts through, as many girls and women know, nothing is acceptable. So, she conspires with her (future-ish) love interest to borrow her "Eliza Rocks!" costume, a short, tight, shiny red dress.

While clothing can be connected to identity, status, or appearance, it can also be a way to portray a character's identity, positively or negatively. For instance, in *10 Things I Hate About You*, Kat is assumed to be a feminist because she wears all black, but when her sister finds her black underwear, she has a different interpretation. And in *Mean Girls*, Janis is assumed to be a lesbian because of Regina George's accusations, thus she dresses "weird" as a means of coping with her marginalized identity. As both of these examples show, clothing can also be a marker of perceived sexuality, and this perceived sexuality is usually that of a "slut," as is consistent with dominant ideology about what girls and women can and cannot wear. This is a means of social control that is often treated lightly in films like *Mean Girls* when the Plastics have real rules for the social control of their group—no ponytails more than once a week, jeans or sweats only on Fridays, and pink on Wednesdays. Or, often, more serious situations are deflated like in *Clueless* when she is "sexually harassed" and robbed at gunpoint, but is more worried about her designer dress. Thus, in this example fashion becomes a joke in what could have much more dire consequences, but this is expected in films like *Clueless* because girls (characters) like Cher are beyond such harm.

On the other hand, when girls of lower socioeconomic status dress less fashionably in the same kinds of clothes as many of the popular girls, they are more often perceived as "sluts," in film and in life. Short skirts, tight clothes, and cleavage can all be sexy or slutty depending upon the dominant's ideology-laden expectations. Brenda, the classic "slut" in *Whatever*, dresses sexily with confidence while Anna's discomfort with her body is subtly obvious as she searches for the perfect outfit for a party where Martin is supposed to be. But this discomfort is negotiated differently by Vivian in *Slums of Beverly Hills*. In this film Vivian's discomfort is in the forefront of the film, as represented by the full-frame opening shot of her in her bra while her father and the saleswoman argue about her in the background. Vivian's family can't afford the latest fashions, so she has to borrow from friends. But fashion is not the foremost issue for Vivian, who is dealing with many complex issues on top of her physical coming of age, something that makes her father uncomfortable so that he lashes out at her "revealing" shirt and makes her put a bra on underneath it, which ruins the "classy" fashion. But clothing also represents Vivian's discomfort as she suddenly worries that Eliot (the "building guy") might stretch out her friend's sweater. Not only does this suggest a discomfort with letting Eliot feel her up in the laundry room, after the dryer buzzer wakes her to reality, but it also expresses her discomfort with her class situation.

While in *Slums of Beverly Hills* and *Whatever* clothing reveals the markers of puberty, in other films clothing is used to hide signs of puberty as well as other markers of sex and sexuality, like pregnancy. For instance, in *Just Another Girl on the I.R.T.* Chantel strategizes about ways to conceal her pregnancy from her mother. She buys clothing in both her old size and her new size, and puts the old size in the laundry and lying around her room so her mom won't get suspicious. But pregnancy is a far less severe marker to conceal than "gender dysfunction." In *Boys Don't Cry*, clothing is used in order to hide Brandon's physical biology of a girl, so that he could live as his gender—male. When clothing can no longer conceal, Brandon suffers the most severe punishments—not chastisement or banishment, but rape, abuse, and death. But issues of fashion and appearance that arise in *Boys Don't Cry* are as rare as those that appear in *Party Girl* and, to a lesser degree, in *Nikita Blues*. In *Nikita Blues*, Nikita sells clothes that she steals from her job in a popular store in order to make some extra money on the side. For much of this film, this side job acts as a source of power and empowerment for Nikita. But when a couple of her friends voice their disapproval, Nikita starts to have second thoughts. However, just when she decides to give it up, a coworker, who reaped the benefits of Nikita's business but none of the risks, turns her in. While this might be an opportunity for redemption in many teen films, in this film, it is cause for Nikita's world to implode. On the other hand, clothes are also an economic means for Mary in *Party Girl*. As she grows and changes throughout the narrative, the clothes that were so important to her at the beginning of the film, the clothes that gave her status and identity in her party-girl life, become the only means she has to pay her rent as well as one of the few connections she has to her dead mother, as we find out when the saleswoman refuses to buy a few of her "vintage" items. Thus, this becomes one step in her coming of age as she transitions into the "adult" world.

By looking at the role of fashion and appearance in girls' film, the dynamics between mainstream and independent becomes more clearly defined, but the connections between and among these films also make this line more blurry. All films rely upon the same conventions, but it is how these conventions are negotiated that make the biggest difference as we shall see in the next section which looks more closely at films that pose their narratives as stories of rebellion and resistance.

Negotiating Adolescence Through Music and Dance

Rebellion is one of the most fundamental elements of adolescence in academic studies, common knowledge, and in film. The films discussed thus far have various elements of rebellion, but the films in this section (and throughout this chapter and the next chapter) have more overt elements of rebellion. These films present a variety of tactics for negotiating the structural forces in girls' lives since the girls in these films are not simply fighting against those forces that are most immediately stifling. They are also fighting the interlocking structural forces that pattern our lives, what bell hooks calls White Supremacist Capitalist Patriarchy—the effects of which are detailed throughout this book. However, many mainstream and independent films that are specifically about girls' rebellion, like *All I Wanna Do* and *Shake, Rattle, and Rock!* are strictly limited to straight, white, upper-class girls—the only girls who are allowed to oppose structures overtly. Further, these films are often nostalgically set in the past, removing them from the immediacy of the issues the films raise. But in films that do not focus on rebellion, per se, like *Girls Town* and *Foxfire*, girls are more creative in their tactics because they have to be. Their enemies are less forgiving. However narrow the characterization of girls in these films, the girls make important statements against the structures that confine girls, sometimes considering larger issues than their individual circumstances, like in *Shake, Rattle and Rock!* While the 2004 film *Mean Girls* isn't specifically about rebellion, it helps to illustrate the dynamics of the mainstream films in this chapter.

In *Mean Girls*, Cady is not simply rebelling against her overprotective, unconventional, out-of-touch parents. Nor is she fighting against other symbols of authority in her life, at least not intentionally. Though Cady is able to deal with the power structures of adult authority as she exposes her math teacher and principal as the human beings that they really are, she is not fighting against adult culture or adult authority. Instead, she is subversively fighting against the authority in the teen world—in this specific manifestation, the Plastics. Cady calls this world "girl world" and opposes it to the "regular world." In "girl world," there are tons of rules, even more rules than in the world of school and the adults. When Cady gets to school she remarks that she "had never lived in a world where adults didn't trust me." She can't go to the bathroom when she needs to, let alone use the wrong kind of pen or read ahead, or anything else she has not specifically been told to do. The rules in "girl world" are just as frivolous and strictly enforced. You can't wear your hair in a ponytail more than once a week. We wear pink on Wednesdays. And we only wear jeans or track pants on Fridays. These are parallel worlds, both highly structured and highly policed.

Cady, with the urging of her new friend, Janis, infiltrates the "girl world" to find out its secrets (a strategy that, not coincidentally, parallels the role of the scientific researcher in Africa). Cady is supposed to report back all of the stupid things that Regina says and does. Despite Janis's constant warnings about Regina's evilness, Cady continues to think that Regina and the other Plastics are nice, until Regina takes back her ex-boyfriend, Aaron Samuels, the boy that Cady has a crush on. This is when Cady, Janis, and Damien begin to plot ways to bring down Regina George by targeting the things that make her powerful—her boyfriend, her "hot body," and her "army of skanks." Janis makes an interesting case to persuade Cady, telling her that there are two kinds of evil people—people who do evil stuff and people who see evil things being done and don't do anything about it. The latter, it is assumed, have the power to change the former. And Cady learns quickly that "in girl world all the fighting had to be sneaky." But Cady also quickly learns that she doesn't have as much power as she thought she did as her sabotage of Regina makes her into the evil she has sought to destroy. Aaron tells her that she is "just like a clone of Regina," and Janice tells her that she's not pretending anymore, she is a mean girl, a bitch. And when Regina gets hit by a bus, the power is out of Cady's hands. She realizes that, just like when you're bit by a snake, she now has to suck the poison out of her life. She has to make good on the bad things she's done, specifically to Regina and to her teacher, Ms. Norberry.

Cady's subsequent coming of age is both a renewal of herself and the emergence of the woman she was raised to be, as Cady says at the end of the film. She went from being "home school jungle freak to shiny Plastic to most hated person in the world to actual human being." These stages all happen over her junior year. She is introduced into a foreign culture— the U.S. public high school—and she succeeds in navigating these waters as well as changing the nature of them. Thus, her coming of age is also a dismantling of the forces within adolescent culture that cruelly ruled the lives of girls throughout the junior class at Cady's school. By dismantling the Plastics, via their most Plastic leader, Cady creates freedom from stereotypes for herself and some of the other narrowly defined cliques. At the end of the movie she proclaims that "all of the drama from last year just wasn't important anymore"; her school "used to be a shark tank," but now she can "just float." She proclaims that "finally girl world was at peace." And when junior Plastics are spotted, Cady remarks that "if any freshmen tried to disturb the peace. We know how to take care of them." One more of Cady's violent fantasies surface as three junior Plastics are hit by a bus, but of course Cady is only kidding. Has a new order really been established? Or has Cady only temporarily disrupted the system? She can float, but can everyone? And is floating really the ideal state? What about those who are treading water?

Cady's new vision of, and for, her school is, perhaps, a more enlightened view of power. But it is not really much different than any other power over people or power to influence people. Cady is portrayed as, finally, being above the competition and cruelty that takes place amongst the girls in this film. This competition and cruelty is portrayed as if it were the natural product of a corrupt social order, a social order that seems to be autonomous from the adult world, the very culture that helps to define and confine teen cultures. Further, this corrupt social order is not contested by Cady, whose privilege plays no small part in her ability to dismantle the Plastics and to bring a feel-good quality to their Spring Fling dance. But Cady's privilege is also not challenged even as she has the power to change the power structures at her school without claiming power and without appointing a new leader. However, as much like a utopia as this final scene might be, Cady has clearly not relinquished power as she recognizes the next generation of Plastics and squashes them with a bus in her final mental fantasy.

A similar dynamic is at work in *Josie and the Pussycats* as the girls battle the corporate MTV machine, expose its inner workings and bring down the evil, insecure woman who has used corporate power to enact her personal revenge on popular teens everywhere. The corporate freedom fighters in this film are rebels only to the extent that they refuse to sacrifice their art, themselves, or their friendship to become corporate whores. The tone of the film is sarcastic as it pokes fun at boy bands and it takes issue with product placement, and while it spoofs record executives and the mindless drones who buy anything, and everything, they're sold. But rather than bringing down corporate structures, they bring down two evil individuals. This not only reinforces the mainstream convention of individualism, but romance is also utilized as these two former nerds find love and solace in their similar situations. Further, popularity and success are reserved and preserved for the beautiful and the cool as the two evil executives are actually just nerds enacting their personally motivated revenge on the youth. Thus, the youth in this film are not exploited and contained by some kind of nebulous, hegemonic, manipulative cultural force (like their real-life counterparts). Instead the youth endure the wrath of two wannabes. Thus, *Josie and the Pussycats* also reinforces the very corporate structures and rules of popularity that its plot is set against.

But *Josie and the Pussycats* does not only reinforce corporate structures through its plot line. More obviously, this film also reinforces corporate structures through its use of advertising and corporate control, both ironically and not. Further, the very group the movie makes fun of is also its main audience. Thus, this film must show that the youth portrayed in the film were not simply mindless drones, but that they were being manipulated by misfit individuals, not the compassionate corporate MTV. To further drive this element into the film, MTV personalities like Carson Daly and Tabitha Soren appear as their MTV personalities, as well as outside of these personalities. This is one type of person-product placement in this film that is ironic and not. But even if ironic, the product placement, like Target's logo plastered all over everything, is an effective advertising strategy regardless of the film's message. Further, this mainstream film may offer a kind of rebellion that suggests subversion of the dominant, but the film's rebellious impetus is, perhaps, not as effective as it is within the fictional space of this film. This speaks to the fact that rebellion in an age of globalized capital and rampant consumerism is not as easy as it may have been in the less complicated cultural and political terrain of the past. This helps to explain why rebellion in girls' film, and especially mainstream girls' film, is often set in the past.

Most mainstream films about rebellion are, for the most part, set in the past, like *All I Wanna Do*. And many of these films include dancing or music, particularly *Shake, Rattle, and Rock!* which is set in the '50s and recycles many of the themes from the 1956 film of the same name, and other such films—the "evil" of rock and roll, the ways in which parents and society view rock and roll compared to how their kids embrace it, and the racism inherent in parents' and society's disapproval. In both of these films, the specific negotiations of the structures that girls undertake in the past have relevance for today. The rebellion in these films is usually directed toward parents or society, but in some cases this rebellion has a larger goal to dismantle the structures, as we'll see in the following chapter in films like *Girls Town* where the girls set out to "subvert the patriarchy." Films like *Girls Town* that tackle current (and timeless) issues must do so in a modern and relevant setting while films like *Shake, Rattle, and Rock!* and *All I Wanna Do* address their issues in a time when these issues can be isolated into a specific context. The former deals with issues of racism and segregation in ways that films set in current times can't and don't, and the latter deals with feminism and women's rights in ways that films of the '90s and 2000s cannot. While *All I Wanna Do* is not a film that uses music or dance, it has many of the same nostalgic elements of films like *Shake, Rattle, and Rock!* or *Dirty Dancing*. In all of these cases, rebellion is strictly located in the past.

In *All I Wanna Do*, the girls at an all-girls' school, Miss Goddard's, rebel when (and before) the board of trustees decides to go coed and merge with a boys' school that does not meet the same academic or social standards as the girls' academy. The girls at Miss Goddard's have opportunities that they wouldn't have at other schools. And as Verena points out, the girls at Miss Goddard's have everything going for them; they have everything they need in order to be successful—education, looks, money, etc. And despite all this, most of them will end up submitting to the expectations that have been set for them. They will settle down, have two kids, and a collie and live in a colonial-style house. But despite all of these opportunities, Miss Goddard's cannot survive financially. And since alumni are more generous in their support of boys' schools, because, as the headmistress argues, they can assure the continued domination by men in politics and other powerful fields, the only choice the board of trustees sees is to merge with St. Andrews. As the headmistress says, "It won't be the first time women have had to marry for money."

Some of the girls are in favor of this merger, but others know that coeducation means that the girls become second to the boys. They know that the real world is not "boy, girl, boy, girl," as one of the girls states, but it is "boy on top of girl," as Verena rants. While Verena and Maureen (Momo) plot to keep the merger from happening, some of the other girls discover just what it will mean when the girls are forced to move into the boys' school. Not only does it mean that the girls will want to change to please the boys, not only will it mean fewer educational opportunities for the girls, but it may also mean that the girls will be humiliated and used by the boys, as Tweety is when the boys take a picture of her exposed breasts as part of a bet. After this happens, not all of the girls want to "sell out the school ... just because they're horny," as Verena accuses them.

Consistent with mainstream definitions of rebellion, Verena's plots to save the school could be considered to be at the level of adolescent pranks. She and Maureen plot wildly, considering what kind of boys their

parents would never allow them to consort with—like drunks and perverts—so they spike the punch at the dance and seduce the boy, Frosty,
who has connections to the board of trustees. But such plots do not work
when the forces they are fighting against are economic and structural.
Instead of changing the minds of the trustees, Verena's plan gets her tossed
from her "home," and the plans to merge move forward. However, Verena's plan also exposes some of the problems with the merger and inspires
other girls to take more organized and collective action. Odie, who has
an interest in politics, but has been pursuing her interest in sex instead,
takes up Verena's battle, but not with underhanded plots. Instead, as Miss
Goddard's girls are known for, Odie organizes the girls and they demand
a vote. Since the girls have been taught to govern themselves, this seems
to be the logical course of action and the girls, in their collective struggle, succeed in securing a vote and a student representative on the board
of trustees. Thus, while Verena's passionate politics are ineffectual, Odie's
democratic ideals are a much safer rebellion.

Despite their setting in the past, these nostalgic rebellions are fighting forces that are still issues today. However, the mainstream appeal of
these films keep them from a radical restructuring of the forces that girls
struggle against. For instance, we could consider Verena's battles to be
juvenile, or we could consider them to be radical and to be the only means
through which the girls have a chance to fight. For instance, when the
girls want to expose what a pervert their teacher Mr. Dewey is, they concoct a plan that does not work because the headmistress is able to identify Verena's handiwork. Not only are they caught, but they are not given
a chance to explain why they put this plan into action in the first place.
They have a teacher who attempts to seduce and coerce the girls to have
sex with him and often uses their "genuine interest in political theory" as
a means to his ends. Instead of looking into this teacher's behavior, Verena is lectured about how difficult it is to get male teachers to teach at
Miss Goddard's since they consider girls' schools to be second rate and a
waste of time. Once again, the girls' are put in their place since they are
fighting against a more rigid structure—male privilege. And despite the
headmistress's similar feelings, she is also powerless to fight these structures, at least by herself. With the girls behind her, even after she tries to
get them to back down, the headmistress is finally able to do what she
has been trying to do all along—preserve Miss Goddard's and all it stands
for. Thus, Odie's solution, one that works within mainstream structures
and expectations, one that forces these structures to change, is the tactic
that succeeds. And she goes on to be a congresswoman to "wage war on
the tobacco industry," as the ending credits tell us.

Other interesting elements play out in this narrative like the relationship between Tinka and the townie, Snake. Tinka, who has a fortune and a future to match it, runs off with Snake, only to come out years later in a Hollywood interview. This is the only reference to homosexuality besides Odie's narration at the beginning of the film when she states that her parents are sending her to Miss Goddard's because they think she'll be safer "surrounded by walls and lesbians." Despite the setting of the girls' school, sex is talked about only in heterosexual terms, and it is expected that all of the girls are heterosexual, especially Verena, who is the only one who "still has her hymen," as the girls inform Odette. Since Odette's plan (before and after she arrives at Miss Goddard's) is to have sex with her boyfriend, Dennis, the girls decide to help her carry out this plan. But Odette realizes the futility of her sexual rebellion, and develops her political consciousness as a result. And unlike many female protagonists in girls' film, Odette ends the film without a boyfriend. However, Verena, who has been antimen throughout the film, finds the one man who is right for her—Frosty, the grandson of an influential member of the board of trustees, who, like Verena, is on thin ice. And like Daphne in *What a Girl Wants*, who finds her perfect match in a boy who disavows the same things she does (before she does), Verena finds a boy whose parents are divorced and also has no "home." Together they find a better space at a coed school. Thus Verena, the rebel, the radical, the natural leader, conforms and "sells out" her past beliefs for a more "mature" understanding of the way things work. The fact that she achieves her dream of starting "Moi" fashion magazine only reinforces her success in an "acceptable" domain, with a magazine that helps her, and other women, focus on themselves, primarily their outer selves.

Finally, Verena's (and later Frosty's) critique of the American Dream, and their observations that everyone is "marching off the same cliff," spills over into the critique that Odie offers to the rest of the girls at Miss Goddard's as inspiration—"no more little white gloves," the slogan of the DAR, a group that the girls invite Odie to join after her attitude matches theirs. However, through the final frames, and the girls' future careers, as well as the school's future legacy, it is clear that all of these girls are working for equality for women within the structures and expectations of the mainstream. For instance, Maureen, a famous scientist, is working on the first male oral contraceptive. And Tweety, who struggles with bulimia throughout the film, becomes a famous psychologist who writes a book called *The Fatal Purge*. This fight for equality and struggle for healing is obviously not a bad thing. They are important. However, these solutions do little to dismantle the male supremacy that the girls struggle against and challenge. And further, these do little to challenge the interconnected systems that keep women without white privilege and economic privilege from achieving similar gains. Odette does not become a congresswoman who wages a war on poverty; she becomes a congresswoman who wages a war on the tobacco industry. Clearly the latter is important as it is connected to the corporatization of America, but fights against the tobacco industry do not deal with some of the more pressing concerns, the issues that continue to affect people's lives despite how many women are in Congress, or are doctors, lawyers, or business women.

Like *All I Wanna Do*, *Shake, Rattle, and Rock!* is also a film centered on women's experiences, with the majority of the characters being women and girls. Also like *All I Wanna Do*, *Shake, Rattle, and Rock!* is a battle between an older generation which doesn't want to change and a younger generation which wants more freedom, though this generational split is much more pronounced than in *All I Wanna Do*. In *All I Wanna Do*, generations are bridged by parents wanting the best for their daughters and believing that an all-girls school is the best environment. But in *Shake, Rattle, and Rock!* this bridge never meets. Instead, the tensions between youth and adults, and the "straights" versus the "juvenile delinquents," join the tensions between black and white, and in all cases, the status quo is strictly enforced by those who have the power to pose and impose the rules. While the strategies of democracy work as the board is forced to surrender to the demands of the girls, the youths' attempt to prove rock and roll's innocence through a mock trial fails when the "not guilty" verdict is overturned by the conservative judge, at the demand of the mothers who fight against rock and roll throughout the film.

As discussed throughout this book, few films deal with racism and related issues, partially because these are difficult issues to deal with, and particularly because the privilege of those with power in the industry allow them not to engage beyond "multiculturalism." However, *Shake, Rattle, and Rock!* is one film that does deal with racism. Because of its setting and its rock and roll theme, this film has to tackle these issues to some extent, though it still falls into many of the traps previously discussed. For instance, despite the film's inclusion of African American characters and singers, the focus is still upon the white female protagonist. Further, only one of the black characters actually has a name, Sireena, and the rest of her friends and band members are credited as "the sirens" as they are part of the singing group Sireena and the Sirens. Also, this film provides plenty of opportunities for the white characters to stick up for, and fight for, the black characters, who are mostly portrayed in an all-black space, in Sireena's mom's diner in the black neighborhood of this segregated town. For instance, Carol stands up to a butcher who tells Sireena and the Sirens that they've "got their own place." She tells him to go back to "Nazi Germany" because that's the worst thing she can think of. And, Danny Clay, the town's celebrity troublemaker and equal-opportunity music promoter, argues to his boss that "they're part of our community" and, thus, also deserve a space to enjoy and perform rock and roll. These defenses come in the face of the overt racism of the white adults in the town who not only want to keep the town segregated, but also want to keep their children from being exposed to that dangerous negro music. In fact, on more than one occasion, the women of the town argue that this music is dangerous because it is African music and the drumbeats work on the libido and cause grinding. "Grinding! Think about it!" they cry. And at one point, Carol's mom even argues, to Carol's disgust at her mother's "perversion," that this music is a form of foreplay.

But in the case of the protagonist, and her black foil, Sireena, this argument goes far beyond Carol's mother and her clique's opinions about rock and roll's sexual influence. For Carol, rock and roll is not connected with sex, per se; it's connected with her body, from "head to toe," as the music touches her in places she never knew existed. And for Sireena, rock and roll is her chance at a real career, a way to pursue her dreams to be a famous singer and make her own way without staying in the house, having 12 kids, and peeling potatoes all of her life, as she argues to her supportive, but realistic, mother, who tells her to stick to her books and stop dreaming because "sometimes it's better that way." Thus, for Carol rock and roll is rebellion, while for Sireena it is a means toward inclusion and success. However, this dynamic is not one of the foci of this film, though more than one character points out how lucky Carol is; she has such a nice home and such nice clothes, her mother argues, "can't she just be content?" Instead, Carol's rebellion (made necessary partially through how "lucky" she is) is the focus. Sireena's family accepts who she is and supports her and her dreams, even if her mother wants to protect her from disappointment. Carol's mother, on the other hand, wants to control not only Carol, but all the kids in the town. And, ironically, it is Carol's mother who is brainwashed, not by the music she fears, but by her best friends, one of whom is shown burning books that she deems are "inappropriate." These women have all the power in town, showing that when women do have power this power is often backed by claims of morality and propriety—these women in charge are conservative, not progressive, a fact that contests simplistic gender politics.

Carol's struggles with her mother's misunderstanding culminate in several confrontations and Carol's father is too spineless to stand up to his wife, even if he doesn't agree with her. Thus, Carol's rebellion is a means of separating from her mother, who just wants a daughter she can dress up and show off, but it is also a means of self-discovery and coming of age. These processes aren't connected to sex or sexuality until her mother interferes and destroys Carol's healthy outlet of music, forcing her to run away with a "juvenile delinquent" because he, unlike her parents, "understands." When Lucky, one of the Desperados, pursues Carol throughout the narrative, she tells him off several times, even though she confesses to her friend that she thinks he's cute. At one point she tells him that he's desperate, and he tells her to get used to it. At another point she tells him that she has plans and that he doesn't fit into her plans. But Carol doesn't seriously entertain his offer to run away until she realizes that she too is desperate. She can't go home, as she sings about longingly earlier in the film. And she has nowhere else to go. But rather than just being a lonely teenager, she becomes part of a pair of like-minded rebels. As she tells her friend Cookie when she asks where they'll go, "We're desperate. Get used to it."

And clearly Carol is desperate. After all, her mother threatens to tear up all of Carol's college applications, her only way to get out of town and out of her mother's house, forcing her to go to city junior college and continue living at home. But Carol's desperation comes not only in the face of a controlling, unbendable mother, but also a society of the same kind. The only way out is on the back of a boy's bike, not riding her own bike, as her own driver. This is another desperation. And while "not the end" is superimposed as Carol and Lucky drive off, the future is still uncertain. Carol finally has her wish to "get out of here" and "be somebody," though she does so without graduating and without having anything to run to. With this focus on Carol's story of rebellion, however, the larger structures she is struggling against fade into the background. Sireena, on the other hand, has a potential offer from a (black) record executive who sees her on TV in her mother's diner. But Carol has nothing. In some ways she has a privilege that allows her to run away, to escape her immediate circumstances. But how much will this privilege help her with no money, no high school diploma, no autonomy, and only a love for rock and roll?

Unsanctioned Rites of Passage

As explained earlier in the section about unrealistic expectations, high school graduation is considered a standard rite of passage in life as well as film. And with this rite comes those other rites like prom, SATs, admissions decisions, and other rites that can also comprise plots and subplots in teens' and girls' films. For instance, the SATs cause much anxiety and in films like *The Perfect Score*, "multicultural" teens work together, for a variety of reasons, to steal the results rather than study. This is an unsanctioned rite of passage, and while it's a collective process, it's still for individual gain. Further, this film doesn't address the more structural problems with the SATs like its racial, gender, and class bias, for example. Or the fact that such a meaningless test holds so much weight not only in some college admissions, but also socially and mythically. This mythical status is also connected to things like prom and graduation. While prom is often an important coming of age device, partially because of its connection to sex, prom is not always a key rite of passage for the protagonist, like for Kat in *10 Things I Hate About You* where prom is just another dance, another event that she attends so that Bianca can also go. But for some girls, like Anna in *Whatever* and the girls in *Girls Town*, prom is inconsequential and even undesirable. It's something that other girls do while Emma, Patti, and Angela are focused on bigger problems and issues. Like prom signifies an end to high school, symbolically and realistically, graduation is an event that propels a teen forward into the rest of her or his life. However, there are several factors that qualify graduation as a rite of passage. If there is nothing to look forward to after graduation, then it loses its power as a rite and becomes a frightening shove or an inconsequential event. Also, because coming of age is a process, graduation does not necessarily equal adulthood. A teen can graduate and still have many trials ahead of her as she passes out of high school and into college or the "real world." But regardless, graduation is a rite that is often a must for a girl who wants or needs to move on. It's a hoop to jump through, often one of many such hoops a girl jumps through on her way toward adulthood.

Despite the necessary presence of school in the lives of teenagers, many films completely leave it out like *The Opposite of Sex*, *Manny and Lo*, and *Ripe*. These movies, along with *Slums of Beverly Hills*, take place during the summer so school is not a factor, but what this also shows is that girls do plenty of growing during the summer when they are free from the rigid confines that school puts on them. Other movies totally romanticize high school, like *Clueless* and *American Pie*. In *Clueless*, Cher can argue her way to better grades and make over and fix up her teachers. But in *Whatever*, Anna, like the girls in *Girls Town* and Dawn in *Welcome to the Dollhouse*, despises school. Anna hates school because it seems to drag her down. Her guidance counselor is easily appeased and she is rude and disrespectful to her English teacher because he is rude and disrespectful to her. She does, however, find a mentor in art class where she excels. In *Girls Town* Emma and Angela do well in school and Patti just barely gets by, but after Nikki's death, school means less and less to them, mainly because school does nothing but contribute to their problems. Dawn hates school because the way she is treated there, and she is only in junior high. In *Just Another Girl on the I.R.T.*, Chantel doesn't despise school. She sees it as her only means to an end, so she does well in school despite the frustrations she has with her "Eurocentric education." And for the girls (and boys) in *American Pie*, high school graduation and prom are definitive markers because the boys (and some of the girls) make them so. Graduating is simply a marker that signals more freedom to grow in college. But what happens when there is no college to look forward to, when there is only an uncertain fate ahead? What happens when graduation holds no particular promise? The film *Whatever* does not make the assumptions of college not only because it deals with a different social class than films like *Clueless*, *American Pie*, *10 Things I Hate About You* and other high school coming-of-age films like *Can't Hardly Wait* and *She's All That*, but also because the protagonist, Anna, cannot be defined by her class and because her high school experience is not romantic. Further, in *Whatever*, prom is never mentioned and, because of Anna's struggles in English class, graduation is not an automatic fact.

At the start of the film, Cooper Union, a prestigious art school in New York, has had Anna's portfolio for two months. She's getting restless as she waits for a reply because she has pinned all of her hopes on Cooper Union (and its scholarship) and her romantic notions of being an artist in New York. Like Chantel in *Just Another Girl on the I.R.T.*, Anna has big dreams, but a reality that makes those dreams difficult to realize. Like Randy Dean in *2 Girls in Love*, Anna does not do well in school. But Anna's problem is not with math, it is with English class. And it is not because she *can't* do the work, it is because she *won't*. Anna understands that her future does not depend upon the work she does for her patronizing English teacher, but the work she does for her mentor, her art teacher. Anna's mentor tells her that she is the most difficult, and possibly the most talented student that he has ever had. He feeds her dreams of art school at New York's Cooper Union and he is the only positive encouragement Anna has at school or at home. Because of these, and other circumstances, Anna's rites of passage don't come through the sanctioned means like graduation, prom, or the SATs, but through the unsanctioned rites she experiences mostly with or through Brenda. Thus, Anna's biggest encouragement and discouragement in matters of coming of age

and sex is her best friend, Brenda, the "classic slut" character that I have
mentioned several times. Brenda is everything that Anna is not. She is
confident, sexy, directionless, and, most of all, easy. Throughout the first
part of the narrative, Brenda supplements parts of Anna. Brenda helps
her put on eye makeup and encourages her in the matters of men and sex.
Brenda coaches her on how to act in front of Anna's crush, Martin, and
how to dress when they go to New York. One scene shows the difference
between these two girls as they get ready for a party; Brenda controls her
image and Anna is annoyed by hers. Anna tries on outfit after outfit in
front of her mirror, trying to look good for the "boy" she likes (Martin).
She is displeased with outfit after outfit and her snotty little brother comes
in to tease away her confidence, calling her fat and ugly. In direct contrast, Brenda stands in front of her mirror as she dresses and applies makeup like a pro. She gives herself sexy looks and kisses in the mirror. She
dresses sexy (bordering on "slutty") and knows she looks good. Anna puts
on a skirt and she looks different enough that her mom and a friend (and
later Brenda) comment on how nice she looks, though she takes this com-
pliment with some embarrassment.

While Brenda gives Anna advice and guidance that she cannot get
anywhere else, Brenda also drags Anna into potential trouble on more than
one occasion, trouble that also acts as rites of passage. Brenda's ability to
find trouble stems directly from those elements that make the two girls
different. Brenda takes Anna (literally and figuratively) on a wild ride that
reveals to Anna what kind of future she will have if she follows Brenda.
It is a future that is completely undesirable, but also a last resort. When
Brenda mentions going to New York with Anna, Anna makes it clear that
she's not interested in the idea of moving to New York with Brenda.
Brenda's desire to move to New York expresses her desire to get away from
her life as well; however, Brenda's fate follows her wherever she goes.
Anna can be friends with someone like Brenda because she knows (or at
least unconsciously hopes) that she will soon leave Brenda (and everything else in her life) behind for New York. But throughout the film, this
future is as uncertain as Brenda's, and it takes many unsanctioned rites—
from sex and drugs to dealing with her mother and her future to come of
age.

While Brenda urges Anna to have sex, Anna pursues the object of
her desires in her own nonchalant way. But Anna thinks that Martin is
something he is not. He is alluring because he is older and he is an artist
who has just recently returned from a (bogus) journey to find himself. Martin knows Anna is a virgin, and he stalks her in a way that is not unsim-
ilar to A. Friend in *Smooth Talk*. He waits around by the keg at a party

and then says lame things to Anna until he pushes her up against a wall, tells her that he thinks she wants it, and kisses her. She doesn't protest and the two go inside where Martin becomes more aggressive. He is pompous and his smooth talk hits Anna right where she is most vulnerable. When he plunges his hand between her legs and she tenses up, he asks her what she is afraid of. She tells him that she's afraid of being ordinary and he tells her that it is easy to be ordinary. In *American Beauty*, Angela says the same thing to Lester. But her version of not being ordinary is quite different from Anna's. Anna wants to be a talented artist and she is afraid that she is only an average artist. This worries her mostly because being ordinary means not being able to pursue her dreams of being an artist in New York. But for Angela, it is not a question of talent—it is a question of beauty. For Angela, being ordinary is also a barrier to pursuing her dreams, but to be ordinary is to be ugly, which is, in this case, only an outer reflection. For Anna, being ordinary reflects not her outside, but her inside. Martin thinks that he is extraordinary, but the irony of his smooth talk is that he is the one who is ordinary. He offers Anna nothing except a means to an end (though she still has a crush on him). When Anna tells Martin that she's afraid of being ordinary she means it in the sense of being an artist as well as a woman. Martin is unwilling to help Anna be anything she wants to be, even if it means getting into her pants. Martin tells her that art school can't teach her how to paint. He tells her that painting is about passion, hitting another vulnerability since Anna is afraid she has no passion. Martin is more than willing to provide a taste of passion, even if it is not real passion and is less than sincere, though Anna doesn't realize this lack right away. She, unlike Brenda, is not savvy to the games that men play. These are the same games that Anna sees her mother playing with Howard.

Anna cannot find respect for her mother and it is easy to see why. In the first scene with Anna's mother, she arrives home looking hung over and used just when Anna and her little brother are getting ready to go to school. Her mother attempts to do her job as a mother, yelling through Anna's door for her to wake up. However, Anna's contempt is clear as she lies in bed wide awake, telling her mother to shut up. For the most part, Anna avoids her mothering, partially because she isn't a desirable role model. She tells Anna not to drink when she has a drink in her hand, and everything else she tries to tell Anna seems to be contradicted by her own self-defeating behavior. Anna has few weapons against a mother who has almost no clue about what is going on in her daughter's life, just as Anna has no clue what her mother's going through. For instance, in one scene, Anna and her brother are dragged to dinner with Howard, the fat, bald man that her mother is dating (under the illusion of a future for her and her children). The scene begins with Anna watching her mother dance with Howard to a lounge band version of CCR's "Proud Mary." Anna has paint on her face and when Howard tries to talk to them, neither Anna, nor her brother, are very cooperative. After Anna tells Howard she is planning on becoming a nun, he chuckles a little bit and asks why a pretty girl like her would want to do such a thing. Anna gives him the deadpan answer, "Because I want to marry Jesus Christ." Howard isn't sure how to react and he just chuckles again. Anna's response here is subversive because Howard is equating what he appreciates about Anna's mother—her looks, her lack of autonomy, her sex—with Anna. Anna undermines his thinking by offering an answer completely devoid of sex because she knows that Howard won't know what to say. But this use of wit is only a temporary reprieve since Anna's problems with her mother continue and escalate into a fight. When Anna insults her mother's plans to marry Howard, she slaps Anna, sending her running to Martin.

When Anna shows up at Martin's place after this fight with her mother, he is more than willing to have sex with her since that has been his goal the whole time. (Anna is grounded so sneaking out to see Martin is an extra act of defiance.) Martin's foreplay is as lacking as his seduction technique. Once he knows Anna is willing, he takes little time with the preliminaries. He only partially undresses her and his version of foreplay includes a prodding question, a placement of her hand, and an in-depth conversation about a penis she saw during a trip to an amusement park, which is followed immediately by penetration. Being the pseudo sensitive man that he is, Martin asks Anna if she is okay, and she lies, telling him that it feels good despite her apparent look of pain. Martin forges ahead. When Anna leaves Martin's house, she seems not to have gained anything, but, rather, symbolically, to have lost something. Anna arrives at Martin's house on the symbol of her autonomy—her bike. But when she leaves, the pain is too great to ride her bike and instead, she silently walks it home. The next day she waits, and waits, for a phone call that never comes like her mother waits for the husband who never materializes. Thus, Anna's mom's dreams offer another roadblock for Anna. When Anna arrives home late after her visit to New York, her mother is watching TV and waiting for her. Anna's mother tells her that she was going to go to Paris; she had an internship at one of the fashion houses. But when Anna asks why she didn't go, the answer is chilling in terms of her own life and her mother's life—because she got pregnant. Suddenly Anna is staring not at the woman she despises on a daily basis, but at the woman she could easily become. She is faced with this version of her future just as her mother gives Anna her rejection letter from Cooper Union. Like Sireena's mother, Anna's mother tells her not to expect so much; it's easier that way.

After Anna gets a rejection letter from Cooper Union, her situation seems even more hopeless. The art teacher gives her a bag that he had in New York and she cannot bring herself to tell him that she didn't get in. As she takes off he senses the disappointment in her face. After she leaves the art teacher, she has no one else to talk to and shows up at Martin's place. Surprised to see her, he puts on his smooth talk and asks her what he can do. She begins to tell him that "things aren't really happening the way [she] planned" and he pontificates: "Life's what happens while you're busy making other plans," just as his date walks in. Martin has failed her once again—philosophically as well as personally. This time when she leaves, not only can she ride her bike, but her mobility is a defiance as well as he offers her the only thing he can—a ride on his way out with a woman much older (and probably more "sophisticated") than Anna. Anna's refusal and her icy stare are her only revenge. Once Anna realizes what a snake Martin is he becomes a far more important unsanctioned rite of passage than he was through sex, even if it takes Anna a few more rites to realize this.

Brenda is the only option that Anna has left. As undesirable as that path is, Anna isn't sure what else she is going to do. She shows up at a party looking for Brenda. In contrast with earlier party scenes, at this party, Anna is clearly out of place. She sits and waits for Brenda and Zak sits down next to her and lights her cigarette. When he asks her what she's doing there, she answers honestly—she doesn't know. Brenda decides to go to Florida with her boyfriend and Zak, and Anna follows Brenda because she thinks she has no choice. Before they go, they stop by Brenda's and while she is trying to steal her stepfather's money, he comes down and catches her and begins to hit her. A scuffle starts and Brenda's boyfriend hits him and takes him down to the ground. Brenda beats him with a fireplace poker as her mother, Anna, and the guys look on. As she beats him, she repeats what he said to her in the darkness of her room. "Make Daddy feel good. Daddy loves you." When Brenda finally stops, she looks at her mother and tells her she hates her. In this brutal and violent rite of passage, Brenda gets revenge, but she also forces herself into a certain fate. She has come of age in her own way, and she is hardly able to control her enthusiasm.

On this revenge high Brenda becomes more and more annoying as the four of them share a hotel room, and Anna turns to the substances that have helped her cope with the pressures in her life throughout the whole movie—pot and alcohol. She rummages through the guys' drugs until she finds a joint and smokes it adamantly. Her vision becomes altered and the scene fades to black as she and Zak kiss. In the next scene Anna awakens lying naked on a beach. She jolts upright and hugs her legs to her body. In an echo of the first scene, Anna collects not Brenda's clothes, but her own clothes. When Zak approaches, she yells at him and cries, but finds out that she has gotten lucky once again. Zak didn't do anything except search for her and try to keep her from hurting herself. She accidentally smoked a joint laced with angel dust and in doing so, she put her world into a spin for which she wasn't prepared. As Anna and Zak stand on the beach, Zak makes things easy for her. He tells her that there is a bus station nearby, and these minimal words are all she needs to hear. The two barely speak as she boards a bus for home. Zak ends up being not the scary, tough-guy, ex-con kind of character he could have been. Nor is he the lover Anna could have had. Instead, he is one of the few people Anna comes into contact with who has her best interests in mind. Thus, Zak is another "bad guy" character whose appearance doesn't match his character. Like Patrick in *10 Things I Hate About You*, Zak is watching out for Anna. And Zak is one of the few people who recognizes that Anna has potential and a future beyond her immediate circumstances.

But even this awakening, Anna's rebirth, does not complete her process. When she returns home she still has her mother, her art teacher, and school in general to face. Her mother is again waiting, burning holes into the plastic that surrounds a fruit basket—Howard's "going away" gift to her. (He got a new secretary.) Anna sits down and stares at her mom's cigarette, and when her mom offers Anna one, the two share a moment unlike any they have shared before, a moment of understanding, and Anna even hugs her mother to console her.

Fighting another battle, in one night Anna writes the term paper that is her ticket to graduation. When she turns it in, she shrugs off her teacher's threats that it's an hour late. She discusses alternative plans for art school and asks her mentor if he'll still let her have his art bag. Finally, at the end of the narrative, after Anna has weathered all of the turmoil of her adolescent life, she is ready to move on, not to the future that she so carefully planned, but to whatever the future may bring her, because now she is ready to take on anything. She rides her bike away from school, past the band marching in unison, rejuvenated after surviving her many rites. Instead of being frozen in time, Anna is moving toward her future.

In *Whatever*, sex is only one rite among many others like police chases, broken wine bottles, road trips, essays, graduation, cigarettes, and sex. Anna's relationship with her mother, her mentor, and with Brenda all require her to come to terms with them as people. She must see that her mother is doing the best she can with her situation, that her art teacher did not fail when he left New York, but simply chose an alternate path, and that Brenda's fate is not necessarily Anna's fate as well. Most of all, Anna, like Chantel in *Just Another Girl on the I.R.T.*, must realize that just because reality conflicts with her dreams, that doesn't mean she can no longer dream. There are plenty of things that are worse than being ordinary. But by surviving and overcoming all of the barriers in front of her, Anna is not ordinary at all. But Anna is also not ordinary because she faces many of the barriers that girls face, but she is lucky enough to have the help she needs to make it through various (often dangerous) rites of passage and succeed enough to have a future to face. Not all girls, like Brenda juxtaposes, are so lucky.

While Anna has to grudgingly deal with her mother, this is easy compared to the family situation that Brenda is forced to deal with. Anna's mother is searching for a husband, but Brenda's mother has already found one. When Brenda asks to borrow her mother's car, her mom says that she has to ask her stepfather. It may be Brenda's mom's car, but it's also the family car and he, according to Brenda's mom, is the head of the family. Brenda is frustrated by the power her stepfather holds over her mother, the family, and, most of all, herself. This scene is only a precursor to what Brenda's family puts her through. When her stepfather comes into her room one night after she gets home late, she tells him to get out. But instead of leaving, he shuts the door behind him and turns out the lights. The scene ends here, but when Brenda beats her stepfather with a fireplace poker what happened in Brenda's room is clear. It is one unsanctioned rite of passage that Anna does not have to deal with. And it is these types of rites—often violent—that cause other forms of violence to be a necessary defense—and offense.

Violent Realities, Inarticulate Strategies

For the most part, the violent realities that many young girls like Brenda face are hardly mentioned in teen films, let alone are they very often prominent themes or plot lines. More often, these realities become jokes like when Cher experiences "sexual harassment" and armed robbery while only putting her fashionable clothing in danger. Or violent realities become an opportunity for a concerned parent like in *Confessions of a Teenage Drama Queen* when Lola and Ella are followed around the streets of New York by a mysterious man in black and his dog (who turns out to be Lola's real, live father). Both Cher and Lola have the means to confront violence since the means are written into the characters and plot. Cher needs Josh to "rescue" her after she is out of immediate danger and Lola's dad is key to gaining Stu's attention. Both of these examples, however, pale in comparison to what Miss Norberry terms the "girl on girl crime" that teens deal with, as well as the structures that girls need to negotiate. This negotiation is relatively easy for the innocent Cady and the rest of her junior class. After "the girls have gone wild!" as one teacher exclaims, they can solve all of their problems in a daylong assembly in the gym where Miss Norberry tries to convince the girls that they've got to stop calling each other "sluts and whores." The ease with which these structures are negotiated are juxtaposed with the violent images that Cady imagines, images that are usually verbally connected to her past in Africa, particularly to the wild animals. These are some of the articulate ways to deal with adolescents' problems, thus it is no surprise that adults are often involved in these resolutions. But, as discussed throughout this chapter and the next, when girls come up against the structural paradigms, and the manifestations of these paradigms in their lives, sometimes unconventional plots and power over narration are not enough and a more forceful method is required. Thus, the rebellion in the films in this section have both specific and personal and general and structural forces that girls are fighting not simply to challenge or rebel, but to survive. Their strategies are inarticulate, just like the unsanctioned rites discussed in the previous section, because they are not legitimized by the dominant, mainstream culture. Girls are only articulate when they can deal with specific issues like Odie and the girls in *All I Wanna Do*. They are inarticulate when they use more radical means like violence or the more watered-down example of the graffiti on Carol's wall. It's indecipherable to the adults it was meant for; however, from the adult point of view it is Carol, and not the adults, who are inarticulate. Films like *Boys Don't Cry, Girls Town, Foxfire,* and *The Smokers* take their rebellion further than Cady in *Mean Girls* or the girls in *All I Wanna Do*. The girls in these films not only push against society and culture, but they also push against the limits of what conventionally defines coming of age.

While *Boys Don't Cry* does not exactly fit the criteria for a teen film about girls, it is important to note here for several reasons. *Boys Don't Cry* is, according to its jacket, "a true story about hope, fear and the courage it takes to be yourself," but more than this, it is about trying to be yourself in a world, and in a system, that can't account for certain deviations from the norm. Clearly this version of "being yourself" has more at stake than it does for Daphne or Lola. Thus, *Boys Don't Cry* is a film that deals

Left to right: Chloe Sevigny and Hilary Swank star in *Boys Don't Cry*, directed by Kimberly Pierce. Lana and Brandon share a relationship that challenges norms as well as personal perceptions and understandings of such norms. In these ways, love transcends gender lines in ways that many cannot understand. This lack of understanding is most violently exemplified through Brandon's killers, products of an environment that is hostile to difference. But this film also brings important issues to the mainstream.

with a subject matter that is furthest from the mainstream's sight and understanding. In a world where sex is male or female, and where gender must follow sex, Brandon Teena has no choice but to live in the margins. The violent realities that Brandon faces are brought upon him not only by the ignorance and brutality of individuals, but also by the ignorance and brutality of the criminal justice system. When Brandon finds himself in Falls City, he is there because he has nowhere else to go. He's running from the law as well as from the wrath of men who are upset because, as Brandon states, he "fucked all their sisters." When he finds people whose lives are as stagnant as his, he also finds a place where he is accepted.

Throughout this film, details about what it means to have a "sexual identity crisis" are subtly and not so subtly revealed. For instance, Brandon's cousin asks him when he's going to get gender reassignment surgery and Brandon mentions not only how expensive it is, but some of the requirements such as hormone shots. Medically, the transition from female to male or male to female is not a simple or inexpensive procedure and it can be covered by Medicare only if the person is diagnosed with a sexual identity crisis. While such rules and realities are being actively challenged and negotiated today, such a "crisis" is treated by the field of psychology as a mental defect. And this professional categorization seeps into the popular consciousness. When John and Marvin strip Brandon and don't find a penis, they remark that it "doesn't look like no sexual identity crisis." In fact, Brandon attempts to explain his "problem" in a variety of different ways because it is really "too intense" to explain. At one point he tells Lana that it's a "weirdness, kind of like a birth defect," and another time he says that he's a hermaphrodite. But when John and Marvin find a pamphlet Brandon has, they also get a glimpse into what Brandon's "problem" is, according to the medical establishment. Lana's mom and John and Marvin can only ask "are you a girl or not," and "what the fuck are you, motherfucker." Thus, this film also shows the confusion and anger that arise when people are faced with something they don't understand, and with something that goes against the norms they seamlessly embrace.

An example of mainstream schizophrenia can be seen when Lana's mom is key in instigating violence against Brandon, despite the fact that she has come to love Brandon for who he is—a nice, kind, caring, loyal person. She tells John where Brandon is not only because she feels confused and betrayed, but also because she feels threatened by John even more than she feels threatened by Brandon. But even as Lana's mom and John and Marvin cannot accept Brandon, Lana and Candace accept Brandon as a human being, despite his lies and problems. But this film shows that individual acts of acceptance are not enough in a world where sex and gender lines are drawn based upon narrow criteria and where the system cannot deal with difference. More than anything, this film shows the consequences of sex and sexuality that are not mandated or approved by the mainstream, but that the mainstream helps perpetuate nonetheless.

After stripping Brandon and humiliating him in front of Lana and her mother, John and Marvin drag him away in their car to find out for themselves whether Brandon is a boy or a girl, and, ultimately to punish him for being a biological girl when he acts and lives like a boy. The scenes of John and Marvin's repeated, brutal rape and assault are interspersed with Brandon's relating these events to the local police. It is difficult to decide which scenes are more brutal—the violent rape and beating, or the barrage of probing and cruel questions that the cops ask Brandon and the tone and demeanor in which they question him. The cops ask for details for their own amusement and badger Brandon, asking him, where'd he try to put it first, until he finally answers, in tears, "my vagina." The cops also ask why he chooses to dress and act like a boy when he's really a girl and refuse to believe that he's 21 years old and has never "had sex." So after being brutally raped and beaten, the cops do the same verbally. And despite going to the police, the cops don't even try to stop the inevitable murder of Brandon, which also results in Candace's death by murder. These portrayals of this "real-life" story are not exaggerated; they speak to all the kinds of violence that are visited upon those who deviate from presumably "natural" norms.

However, this film, recognized by the mainstream through Academy Awards for Hilary Swank for best actress and a nomination for Chloe Sevigny, brings an important subject into a realm where such things are not talked about. However, there are many things that keep this film and its subject matter marginal. For instance, because all of the people portrayed in the film are of a low socioeconomic status, the events can be written off as particular to that class. And because the film does not explicitly deal with the details of Brandon's "sickness," people could watch the film without fully understanding why she is "not a dyke" and why he is not a "girl," except in genitalia. Brandon's sexuality remains cloaked and while viewers can certainly understand the physical violence brought upon Brandon by John and Marvin, they might not so readily understand the violence that the system can, and does, visit upon those who do not fit its narrow criteria.

Girls Town also deals with consequences of sex and sexuality that cannot be remedied through happy endings because the consequences are both personal and structural, and the film is realistic rather than romantic. *Girls Town* is unlike many other girls' films as the style of the film, as well as several other elements, distinguish it. At one point the three protagonists get in a fight with the "Heathers" of the school for many apparent reasons, including the fact that these "Heathers" are totally out of touch with these girls' reality. When the girls in this film, like girls in life (and in other films), try to deal with the consequences of personal and systematic violence on their own, they get nowhere. But when the girls try to understand the structural consequences by remedying their personal situations, they begin to subvert the structures that aim to keep girls and women in their place. While these acts, these rites, are "inarticulate," they also allow the girls an empowered, open-ended coming of age achieved through action.

When the movie begins, all four girls are in situations of powerlessness and the movie quickly makes this an issue when Nikki, for reasons revealed later in the film, commits suicide. While she may have seemed like a girl who had it all together—smart, attractive, on her way to Princeton—she could not keep her self together in an atmosphere that tore her apart. Among the stresses of "normal" teens, Nikki had also been raped while working as an intern at a magazine; this is a secret that dies with Nikki until Emma steals her diary from under the nose of the cold and rigid mother of Nikki (yet another clue to her suicide). Nikki tried to keep control of her self by writing "Fuck you Richard Helms" in her diary, the only place where she had total control. She could not confront her rape in life, and her journal is the only place where she can express powerful feelings with powerful language. (In *Heathers*, Veronica also uses her journal to express feelings she can't express in life.) The other girls also deal with their powerless positions in silence, without the solace of even a journal. Still, they cannot believe that Nikki would rather die than talk to them. They take it upon themselves to figure things out—about Nikki, about their world(s), and, ultimately, about themselves. First they talk about all sorts of issues from date rape to women's place in society and they argue about the very issues and arguments that society debates again and again. When the girls realize that their arguing gets them nowhere, they feel even more despondent because they realize both their powerlessness, and their inability to remedy this lack of power, at least in a forum of discussion.

While the girls don't know how to remedy their structural situation, Emma cannot let her personal situation go. Emma gets revenge on the boy (Josh) who date raped her by going after his car. After ditching a school assembly, she and Nikki and Angela deface his car with the word "rapist" and then they break windows. This vandalism is not something that they planned to do, but an opportunity that presented itself, and this opportunity opens more empowering possibilities. They realize that one of the few weapons they have is visibility since they are dealing with issues that culture pushes into the dark, like abuse and rape. But they also realize that any kind of reaction is powerful, since no action is often the response to such crimes. These two scenes parallel those in other teen films. In *Smooth Talk*, A. Friend seduces Connie and forces her to go with him in his car and have sex with him. The word rape is never mentioned (and the sex does not happen on screen), but after this incident, Connie quietly accepts her place as a woman. His car, like Josh's, was the vehicle of his violence. And in *Fast Times at Ridgemont High*, when Damone flakes out on Stacy, Linda writes "prick" on his car and "little prick" on his locker. Again, this is the only kind of effective revenge readily available to adolescent girls as they seek justice for themselves as well as their sisters.

In *Girls Town*, Patti and Emma confront Richard Helms, exposing him in the only way that they can. They call him out on the street and take his manhood like he took Nikki's dignity and sexuality, as well as (if only indirectly) her life. This "inarticulate violence" is one recourse for a system that makes reality violent, harsh, and trying for many girls, especially girls of color. (An October Films release. Photograph by: Phyllis Belkin)

The girls in *Girls Town* take their "inarticulate" acts up a notch when Emma, Patti, and Angela confront Nikki's rapist and beat him down on the street. The first act, while violent, is violence taken out on an object, not a person. It is an act meant to have an effect, but not be immediately threatening. But it is seen as a senseless act of violence by those who cannot (or don't want to) understand the purpose behind it. For instance, some of the other girls at school give Emma a hard time about trashing Josh's car. They tell her they know she did it, but they cannot understand why she did it, just like they don't understand how the death of their friend has affected Emma, Patti, and Angela. The second incident is violence taken out on a person, but in this case the girls see Richard Helms as an object from Nikki's diary. She could only curse him on paper, but the girls punish him for his objectification of Nikki and for affecting her in such a fatal way. By attacking him on the street and in front of a friend as he leaves work, Richard cannot hide. Even if people don't know why three teenage girls attacked him, he is forced to confront some level of exposure and embarrassment.

But violence is not the only form of revenge the girls use. Patti gets revenge on Eddie, the slimy, controlling, and abusive father of her child by pawning his beloved stereo equipment. He is more careful with the objects in his life than he is with the people, and Patti and the girls make him pay (literally and figuratively) for such transgressions. They make Eddie recognize them by making important *things* disappear, and they replace Eddie's prized objects with the practical things he should have been supplying his daughter, like clothes. While this act of revenge is not violent, it is still illegal and unsanctioned. But it is also the only way Patti can fight against the abusive force Eddie exerts over her and her life. And she can only empower herself this way with the help and support of her friends.

These acts are inarticulate expressions, like all violence, but they have meaning for these three girls (even if the meaning is only fully discovered when they talk about it afterward). Though what these girls do is criminal, they are also getting revenge on the criminals for the crimes that cannot be prosecuted. In many ways, this delinquent behavior is the only option that these girls have in an environment where, as Patti describes, "you [usually] don't complain. You just keep on taking it like everybody else does." The only way they see to "subvert the patriarchy" (what Emma writes on the bathroom stall, among other things) is to do so inarticulately. Thus, because their resistance is not community-sanctioned, neither is their written resistance. They write on the bathroom stall that "these guys will fuck with you," an act that a couple of snotty girls in the bathroom challenge them about, but only after they say "just because your friend is dead...." And this is all they need to say to spark the emotions of three girls who have not been allowed to grieve for their friend. Nikki and Patti end up getting suspended for fighting (but not Emma), but the bathroom walls preserve and enhance their subversion. While the girls lash out in acts that seem inarticulate, they are, to a great extent, successful in what they set out to do. They get revenge on the people who individually wronged them and Nikki, and they begin a kind of community where some other girls appreciate that they were "representin'" for all of us" and add to the written rebellion on the bathroom walls and in their lives.

By the end of the movie, the girls have worked through many of the issues surrounding their powerlessness. Rather than fighting and rather than submitting to the circumstances that attempt to define them (and in lieu of prom), the girls sit on the dugout at an empty baseball field and talk about all sorts of things, including the future, the very thing that has been such a source of stress for them throughout the narrative. As the camera slowly pans away from the girls' talk, their voices can still be heard. As the credits intersperse with the final few frames, the girls' voices fade as the train passes by them and moves out of town. Like the ending of *The Incredibly True Adventures of Two Girls in Love*, these girls are frozen in a powerful pose. They most certainly will face all kinds of turmoil in the future as they inevitably go their separate ways, but they have been empowered, and regardless of what they will face, they will be better prepared to deal with life than they were when the film began.

Like *Girls Town*, *Foxfire* deals with the structural forces in girls' lives and girls' inability to recognize, let alone alleviate, the impact of these forces. However, unlike in *Girls Town*, where the girls react and only later try to figure out what their reactions mean, the girls in *Foxfire* are led by a girl (Legs) who is aware of the structural forces and has her own ideas about how to combat them. Legs' appearance throws a wrench into the spokes of Maddy's expectations for herself and her future. She narrates the film, and when it begins, she says: "By senior year I had it covered, or so I thought. I had a great guy, sights on college—art school—and the dream of a life beyond.... Most of all I avoided the snares, skating past the obstacles, the way everybody who can manage it does." As she narrates, the viewers see her rollerblading through the halls of her school—a small act of rebellion against the structures of rule. This small act of rebellion shows that while she relies on the ease of going with the flow, she is not like any other person who just "manages." She plays by the rules enough to get along, but not enough to sacrifice her self. She is strong, intelligent, and independent within a system that allows this to a degree. She continues her narration, "But then something happened unexpected. I felt it before I knew it." This something is Legs, but more than Legs, this something is Maddy's coming of age and her realization that "managing" isn't necessarily living.

When the wandering stranger, Legs, walks into Maddy and Rita's biology class and sees the way that the teacher, Mr. Buttinger, is harassing Rita, Legs steps in because no one else will. She asks Maddy what his problem is, and she replies, "He's such an asshole." Legs replies with words that no other classmate would utter: "So make him stop." Maddy's blank stare asks the question: How? When Legs sets Rita's frog free, she sets the girls' freedom in motion and Mr. Buttinger's attempt at authority doesn't work on Legs like it works on the other girls. When he tells her she has detention, she says, "I don't even go here," as she climbs out the window.

Shortly after, Maddy comes across Legs in the bathroom talking to Rita. Rita is telling her the details of what Mr. Buttinger does to her. Other girls in the bathroom overhear and call Rita a liar. Only Legs believes her (as Maddy watches and listens silently), until Violet comes out of a stall and says that he does it to her too. One girl in the bathroom, a "typical" girl, invoking the slut stereotype, says, "You don't count, Violet. You do it with everyone." Maddy speaks up to tell her to shut up, and Legs tells them that they're all assholes "because when that son of a bitch puts his hands on her, he's also putting them on you, and you, and you," she says as she points around the room. She tells them the way to change things is to stick together. Most of the girls want nothing to do with such talk. Like so many of us, they have no personal stake in sticking together. To do so would only cause them trouble, and they aren't looking for trouble. They would rather blend in with the managing masses. They leave, but Maddy, Violet, and Rita remain with Legs.

When Mr. Buttinger gets Rita alone in detention—the consequence of Legs' frog liberation—he starts aggressively harassing and touching Rita. What would have happened is plainly obvious, but the other girls come in to break up his party. He responds violently, verbally and physically, and the girls react to his violence with their own. They leave him with a physical pain that cannot match the mental anguish he puts his victims through, but they also leave him with the pain of the failure of his power and control. Goldie walks in as the girls are leaving, remarks "cool," and joins them in their escape. The girls can hardly believe what has happened and are unsure of what to do next. Legs has disappeared, making her own escape, and Maddy tells the girls to just go home, unaware of how this one event will dramatically change their lives.

The girls' action brings a reaction from those in the film who are threatened, individually and institutionally, by the girls' show of independence. The first to react to the girls' feats is Maddy's boyfriend, who is hurt and confused. But he's not a bad guy. In fact, in the opening scene he sticks up for Rita when some of the jocks begin following the teacher's lead and harassing her. He doesn't understand, but he ultimately accepts Maddy's explanation when she puts it in terms he can understand: what would he have done in the same situation? He would have kicked his ass. But he is less understanding when Maddy, under Legs's influence, begins to grow away from him.

The next to react is the principal; he reads about the girls' feat in a confiscated note and calls them in to ask them if there is any truth in this note. The girls confess, and without hearing their side of the story—he was sexually harassing Rita and was moving on to touching her, and when the other girls interrupted, he hit, kicked, and pushed them—the principal suspends them each for two weeks. "What are you," he asks, "some kind of gang? Girls who run with foxes, that sort of thing?" This ignorant comment receives the giggles it deserves and the principal goes on to further wield his power, upping the time suspended every time one of the girls argues. The girls are suspended for three weeks and the principal refuses to let Maddy go by the art room to pick up her artwork for her portfolio, which is supposed to go out the next day. His show of power does little to deal with the issues of the situation; it is a reaction against an event he cannot, and does not, try to understand. Because he perpetuates the system, and the systematic violence, that helped to cause the problem in the first place, he does not put a stop to the girls' reactions. Instead, he pours fuel on the fire. The girls don't have a gang; they aren't even friends, but when they all get suspended together, the principal initiates a group of girls that is more powerful as a unit than the girls are individually. They need this power to come of age, but they also need this power to survive their immediate and distant futures. For instance, as individuals the girls are types. Rita is the shy, dorky one. Goldie is the rebellious drug addict (and is Asian American, though the plot does not touch on her ethnicity). Violet is the slut. Matty is the overachiever. But together they aren't types, and they forget that in school they wouldn't even talk to each other. They have nowhere else to go when they get suspended, so Maddy takes them all to an abandoned house where she hopes Legs will be.

When Legs continues to lead the girls, she finds out about Matty's portfolio, and she suggests they go get it. The girls know this is illegal. Rita says she would be in "so much trouble" if she got caught, and Violet says it would be "way risky." Goldie says she's "up for a felony." The girls break into the school, chatting and giggling like the novice thieves they are. When Goldie inadvertently starts a fire that sets off the fire alarm, the girls have to make a run for it. All but Maddy and Legs make it back into the hatch through which they entered; and they duck into a room where they are almost caught. The girls return to their house in a burst of adrenaline and chatter. But their chatter ceases when Legs says she's going to commemorate tonight and pulls out her tattoo kit. The other girls stare in wonder and awe when Legs takes off her shirt and tattoos a flame above her right breast. She says that it's so she'll "always remember you Maddy," and continues to name each girl. Legs chooses fire "because it nourishes; it also destroys," she says, "that's how we were tonight." The scene is all seriousness and silence until Rita's turn. She squirms and whines, and then she mocks the principal when she says, "we're like those girls who run with foxes," and the girls laugh together.

Through their bonding, which begins with the tattoos and continues with their friendship, each girl grows in her own way. For instance, Rita comes out of her shell and begins to develop her sexuality and her independence from her parents' many rules and Violet comes to terms with the experience that makes her a "slut" in many people's eyes. Their growth is fed by positive things, like the letter that Violet gets from an anonymous freshman thanking her for putting a stop to Mr. Buttinger's harassment, and by personalizing their house with mementos from their rooms at home as well as Maddy's pictures of them (during their montage of skating and miming tai chi, and generally hanging out). The girls gain knowledge from each others' experiences, especially Rita, who learns vital sexual knowledge from Violet's "condoms 101" and the girls' "talk about penises," as Rita phrases it. But their bonding is also enhanced by the negative things like when several members of the football team show up at their house (and interrupt their dancing) to threaten them if they don't stop what they started. The boys further extend the systematic violence when they make good on their threat. They use one of their girlfriends to lure Maddy away from the sanctuary of their house and into the car of one of the boys. (The girlfriend doesn't realize exactly what she is participating in and begins to have second thoughts.) Legs rescues her from them and they take off in the boys' car. While this escape is carjacking, it is also their only means of escape from a potentially dangerous situation. They pick up the other girls along the way and diffuse the danger of the situation they have just escaped by going joyriding. When the authority of the police steps in, Legs is clearly shaken and unsure of how to proceed. They go careening off the road and this scene cuts to a courtroom scene where Legs is sentenced to a juvenile detention center and the rest of the girls get probation. In a typical assessment of any challenge to social or legal norms, the judge says that it's clear that the girls had fallen in with a bad element. The girlfriend who lured Maddy away lied, but the judge won't listen to the girls' protest as the guards escort Legs away. And the fact that she was the one who had fallen in with the bad element is not even an issue. The difference in the parents is clear from this scene (and in others). Rita's parents are listing the extent of her punishment: no dates, no phone, etc. But Maddy's mom, understanding only part of the situation, tells her not to worry. "She'll be okay." Maddy, of course, is not concerned with herself; she is concerned with whether Legs will be okay. While this example of the criminal justice system's violence is negligible compared to Brandon Teena's experience, it does show how this system wields its power according to its own rules, and how girls can be punished by a system that fails to account for the systematic violence they often deal with on a daily basis.

In the eyes of the law and authority in general, Legs is a bad element, not only because she has helped them to break the law, but also because she has opened their eyes to the unfairness of the law and the system it represents. When the girls break into the school, they have a reason why they are breaking the law—the principal has unfairly wielded his power over the girls. They are simply righting a situation that was wronged by Mr. Buttinger's actions. When the girls carjack the boys, they are escaping a situation that would certainly have been harmful and could have been fatal. But when the law takes Legs away, it does not remove the "bad" element, it removes the glue to the girls' unity and the crutch they were using to hold themselves up.

Goldie, whose drug problem has been alluded to, goes homeless and begins to take heroine. If Legs had been around, she would have found Goldie and set her straight, but instead, Maddy steps in and goes to find Goldie. When she finds her in a drug den, Maddy tells the girl who is with her that if she ever sees her near Goldie again, she'll kill her. (Meanwhile the girlfriend who lied goes to the judge to tell her what happened, and Legs is freed from prison.) The girls don't know what to do with Goldie, who is ill and going through withdrawal. It is almost as if they are clueless about such things without Legs to enlighten them. When Legs arrives, the girls look to her to solve the problem. She concocts (or fails to concoct) a plan—the pivotal point in the plot as well as in the lives of all the girls, but especially Maddy, who has been the most influenced by Legs' unexpected arrival. Thus, this film is most about Maddy's coming of age.

From the moment Maddy encounters Legs, she is enthralled, but she is also confused about her feelings toward Legs. Legs has opened Maddy's eyes, but she isn't sure exactly what she's looking at. Legs inspires feelings of social and personal responsibility in Maddy, but she also inspires more convoluted feelings. When they're alone together, Maddy blurts out, "If I told you that I loved you, would you take it the wrong way?" Legs tells her that she'll take it however she means it. Maddy tries to explain, but she is tongue-tied by the jargon that makes talking about love entirely impossible. "It's just that I'm not ... and you're...." Maddy's lack of a language to speak about her love reflects her lack of understanding what, exactly, that love is. She feels the need to explain it, even though it doesn't need to be explained. Initially Maddy's explanation of the feelings, thoughts, and actions Legs inspires in her can only be explained through Legs' words. When Maddy tells Legs about their suspension, she uses Legs' words to explain: they were suspended for thinking for themselves. When Legs is being taken away by the guards after being sentenced, Maddy uses another of her lines: "Don't take any shit." It isn't until Maddy internalizes what she admires in Legs that she is able to use her own words, rather than spit Legs' words back at her. She uses her own words when Legs' words no longer make sense to her.

Because the other girls leave the plan up to Legs, she decides that the way to help Goldie is to get $10,000 from her father for her to go to a drug treatment center. When he refuses and tells the girls to leave his house, Legs (and coincidentally Rita and Maddy) kidnap Goldie's father with his own (loaded) gun (but only after he threatens to call the police). Legs begins making up things as she goes along, barking orders at Maddy and Rita. Maddy doesn't just take these orders; she wants to know what they are doing and why. Several times she almost disobeys, but she can see that Legs is serious about what she is doing. Instead of arguing, she keeps the situation under control by saying, "We're just going to calm down, okay?"

The girls take him to their house and Legs has Rita hold the gun on him while she thinks. Maddy says, "Talk to me. Tell me what you're doing." But Legs doesn't know what she's doing; she tries desperately to think of a way to carry out the plan. She decides that they'll call his wife and make her pay. "That's kidnapping," Maddy says. And Legs tells her, "That's just a word, Maddy. Don't let it scare you." But Maddy has found her voice, and she tells Legs, "You're what's scaring me." The innocence of the girls' previous crimes is absent and Maddy knows that "[they're] doing it wrong," despite the fact that Legs is only trying to do what's best for Goldie. She says, "I'm just trying to make him do the right thing."

But what Legs doesn't understand is that you can't force people to do the right thing; they have to do it on their own. Maddy knows that "this way" is not the way; it is not the best plan for the goals they are trying to achieve. But none of the girls know what the best way might be. Finally, Maddy says, "I want him to see Goldie…. Maybe he'll come through for her this time." But Legs disagrees. It becomes clear that Legs' judgment is clouded by her feelings for her own father, and are not driven by Goldie's feelings for her father, when she says "fathers mean nothing. They don't care. They mean nothing." Maddy's experience is different, and she knows that regardless of how much of an asshole Goldie's father is, he is her father. With compassion in her voice she tells Legs, "This isn't about you." When Goldie comes up the stairs and asks what's going on, Rita accidentally shoots Goldie's dad in the shoulder and the plan has to change. There is no time to argue and Legs tells Rita, "It's my fault." Legs is no longer doing the planning and she is no longer controlling the action. The girls just figure out what they need to do as Violet and Goldie get her dad into the car and Rita insists on driving, taking responsibility for her mistake, even as Legs tries to take the blame. As these girls find their own way, the story turns back to Maddy. She still has to confront her self— her feelings and her fears.

As they are pulling away, Maddy realizes that Legs is gone. She finds her on the bridge and asks her where she's going. She says, "You don't have to go. Stay with us; we're your family." But Legs doesn't reply to any of this; she only asks, "Do you want to go with me?" Maddy can't answer that question with words. She looks around and gives a very slight nod, her eyes brimming with tears. Legs tells her that she'll just put out her thumb. "When a car stops you won't even have to think about it. You'll just know, and you'll decide, and you just do what feels right in your heart, okay?" Maddy follows Legs for a few steps before a truck pulls over. The two look at each other long and hard and Maddy begins shaking her head before she can get the words out. She can't say no because a part of her wants to go. Instead, with a painful, tearful gasp Maddy says, "I'll never forget you." The look on Legs' face is even more painful than the sound of Maddy's words. She gasps and sighs and turns to go. She pounds her chest with her fist and says, "You're always in my heart, Maddy."

Maddy stands alone on the bridge and looks up at the structure that she refused to climb with Legs at the beginning of the film. She begins to climb and her narration reveals the happy, but not easy, ending for Goldie and her father. He claimed that he shot himself and it was "just stupid enough that the cops believed it." He put Goldie in rehab and worked things out with her. As Maddy reaches the top of the bridge and stands on top of it, she says, "I've traveled since, half the world—art museums, train stations, airports. I've never seen Legs again. The rest of us, we've drifted. But we embrace when we meet again, veterans of a sort, bound together for life." Maddy stretches her arms out, still cautious, and walks the bridge. Like the ending of other films, this is a powerful pose for Maddy. She has conquered her fear. But her stance is also even more powerful because she is no longer dependent upon Legs for strength or words. She walks the bridge alone, autonomous, and free, but her narration makes it seem as though she has spent much of her life since looking for Legs, or looking for something that can only be embodied in a search for Legs. She has an unbreakable bond with the other girls, but Legs, the catalyst of this bond, has been estranged from everyone.

At the beginning of the film, Legs is a mysterious stranger with a wisdom that the other girls don't have and probably wouldn't discover without her. She empowers them by sharing her experience with them and sharing in the new experiences they create together. However, Legs breaks down when the girls need her most, which allows the girls to find their own power, but also makes Legs no stronger than her issues will allow. Many films rely upon this character flaw to make them work. The girl who is just plain evil like Courtney in *Jawbreaker*, Lana in *The Princess Diaries*, or Regina in *Mean Girls*, or just really messed up psychologically like Karen in *The Smokers*, is often a scapegoat. In this case, however, Legs' past keeps her from fully functioning as the person she seems to be. When it comes down to it, she is not an independent champion of feminism; she is the application of feminism as a catalyst in the growth of others. She inspires the girls, but especially Maddy, to see the bigger picture, to grow a feminist consciousness. She shows the girls how to stand up to authority, but she seems to be afraid of authority every time it pops into her life. Perhaps Legs' problems speak to the weakness in all of us, or perhaps she is just another scapegoat. After her mistake she flees, and when Maddy tells her that they are her family, she doesn't even acknowledge this sentiment. She is only concerned with whether Maddy will leave everything in her life behind, including her self, to join Legs. This is truly why Maddy cannot go with Legs. As she comes of age, she becomes her own person, not a carbon copy of Legs. Instead of taking her own advice and sticking together, Legs flees. If Legs represents a feminist awakening, she also represents some feminists' inability to distinguish between rhetoric and the ways in which feminist dogma translates into real life. Legs shows the girls how to disrupt the system, but her way ends up not being the best way, at least in Goldie's case. Rather than simply mimic Legs, each girl adapts Legs' teachings to fit her own life, her own issues, and her own circumstances. But it is also a unifying factor across difference. This adaptability is one of the strengths of feminist ideology, but it can also be one of the problems with feminism, especially if this dogma is adapted and adopted unconsciously or uncritically as it is by Karen and Jefferson in *The Smokers*.

While *The Smokers* has many of the same elements of feminism, rebellion, and sisterhood as *Foxfire* and *Girls Town*, its characters are coming from a very different place. The girls in this film live in a world of money and prestige. They have been sheltered and spoiled, except for Karen who tries constantly to conceal and correct her lower-class origins. Thus the rebellion in this film is inarticulate not only because their rebellion has no real, specific purpose, but because it is misdirected, distracted rebellion. Jefferson narrates, "When I tell people I went to private school they picture ... right in the middle of the dairy state. Right in your own back yard." The girls in this film are unlike their urban sisters in *Girls Town* and their suburban sisters in *Foxfire*. Everything from the way they dress and fix their hair and makeup to their attitudes show this difference. The girls in *The Smokers* are all privileged white girls, with the exception of Karen, who tries to walk the walk and talk the talk in order to fit in. She is a scholarship girl, and she does everything she can to be part of the upper classes. And while she impacts her friends' lives, ultimately she has no place in their world.

Karen's lust for the good life is evident early on when the girls go on spring break. Karen's very impressed with Jefferson's mom's popularity and she's fixated on Dan, a sex-obsessed boy from school because, "he's the only guy at our school who's got taste." Lisa and Jefferson disagree as Jefferson names half a dozen girls she doesn't consider to be "taste," but Karen cites Georgio Armani as proof of his taste. She is easily impressed by anything that costs an absurd amount of money, evidenced later by her obsession with the Tamagachi that Lisa gave her. When Jeremy picks at the sticker, Karen explodes. That sticker is the difference between a cheap knockoff and proof of the real thing. And Karen needs all the proof she can get. But Karen's obsession with money is dangerously heightened by her insecurities and her desire for attention. At a bar, Karen overhears a man at the next table talking on his phone about two tickets to Tahiti. She gets his attention by getting him to light her cigarette, and then she holds his attention by saying things she knows will turn him on. She asks why guys like oils so much—like strawberry, cherry; then she asks Jefferson to play the smoking game, a game which consists of one girl blowing smoke into the other girl's mouth. When Jeremy asks if he can play, Jefferson tells him to "put his tongue back in his mouth," but when the stranger asks, Karen is more than happy to oblige. He offers her a ride in his limo, an offer Karen surely couldn't refuse, even though Jefferson says they'll just get a cab. Karen, in her short black wig, and costume-like clothing, rides with him in the limo, and when he drops her off, her face is stained with tears. She looks almost child-like when she demands his phone number. When he refuses ("my wife wouldn't take too kindly to strangers calling the house"), she desperately writes her number on his hand before he drives away.

When Karen arrives back at Jefferson's after her "date," she looks distraught and sinks onto the couch. Taking a break from her bong, Jefferson asks her, "Was it at least good sex?" Karen mutters that she doesn't know. "What do you mean, I don't know?" Jefferson pushes her, "Either it was or it wasn't!" Karen exclaims, "Have you ever had good sex?" With how much Karen talks about sex, this is a surprising state-ment, but also a revealing one. Her front is that she "just wants to have fun," just like Dan. She wants to get laid on her own terms. But what Karen is discovering is that for girls there is no sex on her terms. Since Karen has no context for this discovery, and she's a little bit too smart and too ignorant to process her feelings, she turns to finding her own solu-tions. And she offers her own theory of girl power.

Later, when the girls are sitting around smoking, and talking about boys and kissing, Karen wonders, "What's wrong with us? We're in a fuck-ing palace and we can't even find a prince!" But while Karen may think she wants a prince (he's got to have money, after all), she also knows that fairy tales are overrated. She and Lisa argue about the story. Lisa insists on the story's elements while Karen doesn't buy them. Karen doesn't see why Cinderella sat around waiting for the prince; she should have bor-rowed some of her sisters' clothes "and gone knocking on the palace door." She's sure that if Cinderella had just been nicer to her sisters she would have been better off. But Karen doesn't take the "nice" route. Karen groups men in the same way that she assumes men are grouping her, referring to them as "mental midgets." When Lisa (not very seriously) says, "Maybe I should get fake tits," Karen replies, "What, for some cold, uncaring guy? Please!" But Lisa wishes she could "be as uncaring as he is." And Karen has the perfect solution: "We could show them how it feels. Give the boys a taste of their own medicine. Fuck them like they fuck us." Lisa doesn't get this, so, showing Jefferson and Lisa the gun she took from Jefferson's sister, Karen explains further: "Take this big, steel shlong, and stick it in David's face the next time you have sex with him." Jefferson responds like Maddy responds to Legs' kidnapping plan: "You're talking about rape?" But Karen has an answer for everything: "I'm talking about going after what it is you want. These boys get to hunt us, to catch us, to leave our remains. It's time to change the game, girls.... These boys are hurting us, Jefferson. We have to fight back. Come on, we'll do it together. We'll do it for Lisa. We have to do this, for all women." But Karen fails to make the distinction between the "silly little schoolboy" that has turned Lisa into a wreck and the predatory man who used her and left her remains. She makes Lisa's personal problem into a problem that represents not only all women, but also Karen's own particular issues. Thus, she abuses the power that comes through collective action.

The girls prepare for their revenge as if they are preparing for prom or Halloween—they shop for just the right outfits and strut down the street licking big, round lollipops. The juxtaposition between their sexy disguises and their oversized lollipops show that these girls are playing a game, and making up the rules as they go along. Further, the line between child and adult, playful and sexy, is blurred by the girls' childish props and seductive moves. They forge a note to David from Bambi (yes, that's really her name), the girl he supposedly had sex with behind Lisa's back, and give it to him during church. While he is skeptical, his friends, including Dan, urge him to go. When he arrives the girls ambush him, tie him up, put a chicken hat on his head, and argue about who's going to fuck him. But David can't get it up, and they laugh at him before they untie him and let him go.

Later, Lisa is clearly upset about what they did to David while Karen uses it as an example of feminism in action. Lisa vocalizes these feelings by saying, "I don't think he liked the chicken hat," as she stares at it and flops it around in her lap. Even later, out at a bar, Lisa can tell something's bothering David and says she's considering telling him it was them. Jefferson tells her he'll forget about it, but Lisa's not so sure and Karen is there to reinforce her doubt. "Did you forget the first time some guy shoved a cock in your face, Jefferson?" Karen's psuedofeminism finally rubs Jefferson the wrong way and she asks, "Who was the guy who fucked you over so badly?" Karen only mumbles, "Yeah, which one?" And Lisa says, "All it takes is one." Thus, Karen isn't ready to give up, especially since she still hasn't vindicated herself. She wants a war. She says, "That was just one boy. We vindicated Lisa, but what about all those women who will be fucked over or have been? We started a revolution, guys. We have to stay tough. All great leaders were tough." With her usual exaggeration, Karen compares their struggle to Gandhi's and Jefferson reminds her that he died for his cause. But Karen retorts, "What's life if it's not great? Gandhi lived a great life; he had a movie written about him." Like Lola, Karen exploits this historical figure in a display of ignorance. But while Lola does so playfully, Karen does so with attitude, ignorance, and (like, Lola) selfishness. But Karen is, ironically, following her own version of Gandhi—she's pursuing a "great life" and *The Smokers* is a movie written about her. She is the revolutionary martyr she wants to be, even if her revolution is ultimately shallow and misdirected.

The boys in this film represent a spectrum, giving all of the characters more layers. Each one reacts in different ways to the rumors of girls who rape guys at gunpoint. When David returns to the dorm after he's attacked, the boys want to hear about his escapades. But David tries to avoid sharing. When Dan pushes for details he's aroused to hear about these "three town chicks" with guns. But Dan is clearly shaken, and only Jeremy cares enough to inquire about whether he's all right. Dan also shows his lack of sensitivity when he shows up at a bar in a handmade shirt that reads, "Rape Me Too." While Dan's statement is hurtful in light of his friend's experience, and a major slap in the face to many women, it is also representative of the way he really feels. The thought of being raped turns him on, and as an extension of his male privilege, he's not afraid to share these feelings. "Dan," as Jefferson tells Karen, "just wants to have fun." But then again, so does Karen. However, because of the double standard and Karen's warped and misguided intelligence, she is forced to find her brand of fun in an unconventional way. Unfortunately, because Karen can't get past her feelings about Dan (she wants him and she wants to be him), she fails to realize that if anyone deserves to be punished on behalf of all women, it is Dan. Looking at his shirt, she says, "Be careful what you wish for big boy." He responds, "Don't tease me." Karen enters into a competition of lewdness. Him: "Suck this; make sure you swallow." Her: "Whip it out, baby. Whip it out." But even playing Dan's game fails to get her noticed by him, and she is turned down again when Dan leaves with a girl who doesn't care that he's wearing a shirt that says "Rape Me Too." And like all real or perceived scorns, Karen looks for someone to fill the void she feels.

Like the first bar scene when Karen picks up the stranger, she keeps her eyes open for a guy to occupy herself, especially since her friends are both busy with boys of their own. Unlike the previous scene, Karen has found power in this game—a phallic power despite her desire for real power. When Jeremy leaves, Karen follows him in Jefferson's coat and hat. She runs past him and, thinking Karen is Jefferson, he follows her into an abandoned building. Karen confronts Jeremy with the gun, as well as an onslaught of generalizations about guys. She tells him to "Munch the muffin, big boy." When he asks if she's kidding, she cocks the gun. But Jeremy is not easily intimidated; he says, "Karen, that is some fucked up shit." She tells him, "The whole thing is fucked up.... The minute I let you inside me, you have all the control. I'm sick of the man always having control." Jeremy figures out that she was the one who raped David (or as Karen says, "I prefer the word used"), and tries to talk some sense into her. She says, "Thanks for pretending to care, but my panties are already off." Karen can't believe that Jeremy doesn't want to have sex with her, and doesn't understand that he's trying to be her friend. "You could never understand," she says. "You could never know what it's like to have this gaping hole between your legs just waiting to be filled by the likes of you." Jeremy's sentimental response (after making a joke), "We all have a space we're waiting to fill," gets a "blow me" in response from Karen, though she decides to put the gun away and asks Jeremy not to tell anyone because she doesn't want Jefferson to get in trouble. Of course he complies.

Karen is a mix of insecurity, charisma, crudeness, and intelligence. She wants so desperately to be powerful, but fails to realize the power of personal empowerment. She'd rather pursue power through external, rather than internal means. The field hockey scene demonstrates some of Karen's personality. She charges down the field saying, "Take that you stupid frosty bitches!" When she scores all by herself and the team wins, she screams and hollers. But some of her teammates have issues. One girl says, "You're defense; that's your position." Karen responds from sitting on the ground with her legs spread wide open, "I don't really care about my position." Clearly, Karen cares very much about her position off the field, especially when that position mirrors the pose (or lack of pose) she takes against these girls. But Karen can handle girls with no problems. She doesn't play as a part of the team; she is the team, and the others can follow along like Lisa. As long as the team wins, there's no problem. If Karen thinks she can take control, she does. And this is what she tries to do to Jeremy. Once she realizes he won't submit to her phallic power, she figures she's already got him anyway. He was nice to her, so they must be dating. But despite the fact that her delusional relationship with Jeremy makes Jefferson jealous, she freaks out when she realizes that he is no longer in the group. Karen tells him, "I'm not dating you if you're not in the group." But Jeremy is unsure where Karen got the idea that they were ever dating in the first place, and she freaks out even more when she thinks he's trying to dump her, especially when he calls Dan a "schmuck." "Remember, I dumped you," she says as she runs off, once again leaving Jeremy confused.

Karen and Jefferson are not the only ones who are confused. Refusing to recognize Jeremy as more than a friend, Jefferson pursues her own crush. But she's not having any luck with the singer at the bar that she drooled over all night (making Jeremy pine for her even more). Christopher, whose name is "cool" with Jefferson, is unlike the people and environment these girls are usually saturated with. He wears a cowboy hat and lives in a barn. When Jefferson takes a stroll through the country with him, stopping to pet a stray dog, and ends up back at his place, she turns him off with her aggressiveness. She flirts with him and thinks she's made a clever connection, so she lays by him in his bed and starts undoing his pants. He tells her to slow down, but she keeps pursuing until he finally tells her to stop and she leaves in embarrassment. Later, hanging out with the girls she ignores her earlier confused failure and, like a schoolgirl with a crush, she says, "I wish Christopher went to our school. I have so many outfits he hasn't seen yet." She wonders why he hasn't called and Karen asks why she doesn't just call him. "If you want something, Jefferson, go after it," Karen says. But in this case she is clearly not talking about a phone call. She's talking about the revolution.

When Jefferson confronts Christopher back at his place, he easily takes the gun from her. She is even more impotent with the gun than she was without it. She's shocked when another man comes in. She shrieks, "Oh my God. You have AIDS." In her ignorance she figures that if he's with a man, he must be gay, and if he's gay he must have AIDS, but the response from Christopher's friend shows her ignorance. "Why didn't you tell me?" she asks. His answer, "I hardly even know you," reveals the nuances of relationships that Jefferson has not yet learned how to read or handle. She wanted him so badly that it didn't matter that she barely knew him. She jumped into sex quickly because this is the only style she knows. And her only models, her friends, are no help.

When Jefferson returns she finds Karen preparing to meet "the limo guy," who called her since he was in town and figured they could get together. She's borrowing one of Jefferson's outfits, and also wants the gun. Jefferson tells her that he's a jerk, but Karen disagrees because he owns his own paper. Jefferson tells her that she's done with the whole thing, "with the gun, with the whole revolution," and of course Karen is irate. Jefferson's quick lie that she buried the gun can't hide the truth and Karen wrestles it away from her. Jefferson tells her it's a mistake and Karen says, "I don't take advice from people who aren't my friend." But nothing Jefferson can say talks any sense into Karen, and she leaves with a rift that isn't healed until it's too late.

Like Jefferson who is weaker with the gun than without, Karen has come to rely on the feeling of power the gun gives her. But this power is only a feeling. Her "date" tells her that they really don't have time for dinner, gives her a drink (which she sets aside), and starts taking off his pants. She tells him "there's plenty of time to work up to that," but he says he's "already worked up," and starts to climb on top of her. She says, "not like this," but he doesn't listen. He just says, "Tough, girl; you said you like it like this." So, she pulls out the gun. But this guy isn't afraid, and continues. She fires four empty shots and he only gets more aggressive. Karen opens the door and escapes in vain. They are the only car on the road, and he steps out of the car, bends her over the hood and rapes her while she begs him, pleads with him not to.

Since Karen has alienated Jefferson, she knocks on Lisa's door. Meanwhile Lisa has been dealing with different sex problems. David is not doing anything to pleasure her in bed. He has his way, gets off of her, and turns over and pretends to sleep. Lisa gets up, gets dressed, gets back in bed, and kicks him out of it and her room while he asks why. Little by little these girls are learning to navigate sex, but none of them seem to be able to really grasp onto anything. Lisa ousting David from her bed is a big step for her, but she fails to communicate to him why she's kicking him out. She also continues to let Karen drag her around. Karen blames the boys for tearing apart their friendship. But Lisa knows that "they haven't done it to us, we've done it to ourselves." She wonders why Karen can't just make up with Jefferson, and they can all go on with their lives. But Karen, in her infinite wisdom, tells Lisa that "sometimes you're so naive."

While everything around Karen and Lisa is falling apart, Jefferson is getting herself back together. She is, after all, the protagonist and the narrator. She dumps all of her opera CDs into a bag and takes them over to Jeremy. She tells him he should have them because she's sick of them. This leads to the two of them walking and talking, and this is a key difference between Jefferson and the two other girls. Karen doesn't listen to anyone and Lisa doesn't communicate much with anyone. But with Jeremy, Jefferson has the opportunity to do both. The two of them talk everything out. This doesn't take just one conversation, but several. The first time they talk about how Jefferson, and other girls, always fall for musicians and how they may sing about love, but it's just to sell records. After a few cheesy lines, Jeremy tries to kiss her and Jefferson asks, "What about Karen?... Don't you like her?" Jeremy's response, that he never liked Karen, sets Jefferson off. She misunderstands and makes Karen's generalization, "You guys are all the same." Jeremy calls after her, "What am I doing wrong?" She stomps away saying, "Everything." The next time the two talk things go a little better. Perhaps because they're jogging they lack the energy to get really worked up. At the prom the two soon find their way outside to talk and finally get to the real issues. When she tries to kiss him and he doesn't immediately respond she wonders, "Are you gay too?" When he tells her no, she says, "I thought you liked me." Like Christopher, Jeremy is a thinker, and he's been thinking about all the gun business. Jefferson explains, "We were sick of being weak; I was sick of being weak." When Jeremy demands to know why she had to "fuck all the guys," Jefferson slowly admits that she's never had sex with anyone. She's been fronting. When he's relieved, she goes on the offensive. "Why is it okay for you, but it's not for me?" The entire conversation is messy, like good communication is, and by the end of it, the two are in a new stage of their relationship.

While Jefferson has matured through her experiences, by the prom the girls still haven't made up and Lisa and Karen go to the prom without Jefferson. When Jefferson confronts them, Karen and Jefferson play a tug-of-war with Lisa, who says she's going to the bathroom. Lisa discovers that Karen still has the gun; she hasn't taken it out of her purse since that night. She gives it to Lisa who later disappears with Dan. For once, Karen isn't thinking about herself. She asks David if he cares about Lisa because "when Dan's done with her she won't care about anyone, maybe not even herself." And of course Karen is right. Dan is using all of his regular sweet talk on Lisa, telling her how pretty she looks tonight, how long he's been waiting for this. Lisa asks if he has anything, and he responds, "Don't worry, I'll be careful," as if such a thing were possible and urges her to "just let it happen." With every one of Dan's lines Lisa looks a little bit uneasy, but not enough to stop him. He pushes her to bend her at the waist so he can take her from behind, but she turns around. All of the generalizations that Karen made about men and the boys at school are only true about the person she most wanted attention (and sex) from—Dan. Once Lisa lets him inside her, he has all the control. He stops kissing her, and hardly seems to notice that she's there. Finally something, maybe Karen's words, click, and Lisa tells him to stop. She screams and pulls out the gun. But Dan doesn't go impotent like David. He doesn't try to talk his way out of the situation like Jeremy. Dan is turned on. He asks, "Are you the rape me girl?" She doesn't need to respond because he's already getting off on the idea. Karen's four shots have ensured that the only bullet in the gun is the only shot that remains, and with this single shot Dan falls to the floor. Lisa smoothes her skirt and walks away.

Dan is discovered a few moments later and everyone is ordered back to the living rooms for attendance. Karen frantically tracks down Jefferson and Lisa arrives from stashing the gun in Karen's room (because "that's where we keep it"). The girls retrieve the gun and wipe it clean just in time to wait in the living room to be questioned. Oddly enough, Karen is the one who insists that they should come clean. "Easy for you to say," Lisa says, "you didn't pull the trigger." Finally remorseful, Karen says, "Yes, I did," though neither Lisa nor Jefferson knows that she means this literally, or what the outcome was. The girls decide to get rid of the gun while Lisa sets off the fire alarm. But just as she stands, she is called in for questioning, since she's already up. In the face of chaos, Karen finally has real, honest conversation. She asks Jefferson if she's ever been anyone's girlfriend. Neither have been. Karen asks her if she's ever wanted to be, and Jefferson answers, "Sometimes." Karen confirms, "Me too." Perhaps Karen's sudden depth and self-exposure are a bit hard to believe, or maybe she really has learned from her mistakes. Whatever the reasons or the effect, it doesn't matter. When Jefferson is setting off the fire alarm she slips and gets stuck as she starts a fire. When the alarm goes off Karen sneaks up to see where Jefferson is and finds her and her dress stuck in the flaming bathroom. Karen helps her pull free, but gets trapped herself. Jefferson frantically, hysterically, leaves her to get help, but it is too late. The bathroom, and everything in it, is destroyed.

While everything in *The Smokers*, from the pot smoking to the subject matter, seems to be antimainstream, and while the girls use inarticulate actions to try to remedy their situations, the ending is another version, a darker version, of mainstream romance. Only Karen pays the price while everyone else lives "happily," conventionally, ever after. She is an easy sacrifice both for the film, and for mainstream ideology. She was the poor one, the troublemaker, the instigator, the mentally unstable one. In death she takes the blame for Dan's death, even though Lisa tried to tell the truth. Jefferson's narration wraps things up for everyone. Lisa and David never made it past their freshman year; Jeremy went to California and became a winemaker in Napa; and her sister, Lincoln, who showed up for Jefferson's graduation, graduated from Lindenhurst four years later, moved to New York, and edits a liberal newspaper. As for Jefferson, she "had some business in California."

The Smokers is unique within the genre of girls' film because it deals with the underside of the upper classes rather than the surface images and privileges that come with money and status. The girls in this film, despite their money, or perhaps because of it, are ignorant about so many things. They can dress like adults and substitute "adult" behavior for their boredom, but their money cannot give them the knowledge or experience they need in order to become women. The girls' unsanctioned rites of passage are, ultimately, transformative for Jefferson, but only because she figures out their futility on her own, before and without her friends. Their acts are inarticulate partially because of their ignorance and partially because of their privilege. Jefferson starts to realize this, but Karen's death makes it easy to stop analyzing and in her final narration she still sounds like a child who is trying to please not her parents, but her audience. And despite this film's exposure of the upper classes, it still fails to critique the power and privilege that comes with money, and, not coincidentally, whiteness. But even films that deal with blackness often fail to critique whiteness, or the power structures that keep black subordinate to white. Instead, they often create their own spaces, spaces from which such critiques can grow—on and off the screen.

Negotiating Race

As I discussed in chapter one, and have illustrated throughout my analysis of girls' films, race is dealt with usually only superficially and incompletely in the mainstream. And while it is important to note the growing inclusion of visually identifiable minority characters like Rhonda in *A Cinderella Story*, Arita in *Ella Enchanted*, Kevin G in *Mean Girls* and the boys in *Crazy/Beautiful* and *Save the Last Dance*, these inclusions often cause more problems through their representations. Further, while films like *Mean Girls* deal a little bit with whiteness, it fails to provide the critique of white supremacy that *Shake, Rattle, and Rock!* provides, if also incomplete itself. Further, no film really challenges the concept of race. Its permanence is undercut by its very real effects. Thus, race is considered immutable, rather than negotiable. But despite the slow progress of racial and ethnic representation, some of the important gains made in this genre, and in teen film more generally, can be seen through a close examination of the ways in which *Shake, Rattle, and Rock!* adapted the original 1956 movie by the same title not only into a film that deals with race, but also into a girls' film.

The original film, *Shake, Rattle, and Rock*, not only does not feature any African American characters (besides an appearance by Fats Domino, as himself), but also does not focus on the female protagonist, who is young, but is not one of the kids. Instead, she is the fiancée of the TV host protagonist, and, thus, she is not fighting to pursue her passion for rock and roll, but to take her place in the realm of domestic bliss. She is still fighting against her overly moralistic aunt (not mother), who wouldn't approve of her plans to marry. But in all fights, she supplements her fiancé, the protagonist, focus, and hero of this film. Thus, this film is not about teens and it is not about girls. Instead, this film focused on the thoughts and actions of the adults. The kids in this film are mostly background characters and are the special project of the protagonist who sees rock and roll not as an element of moral disintegration, but as a tool to help get kids out of gang fighting and the slums. Unlike the modern version, the original deals more with the perceived social problem of youth run amok, rather than with youth trying to find a space of their own. And the adult characters are posed in bad-guy and good-guy roles from the older, moral guardians who see rock and roll as a disgusting culture form, to the older gang member who sees rock and roll as a bad influence that brainwashes kids into being good, to the protagonist and his fiancée who see rock and roll as something perfectly within the realm of civilized entertainment. But the biggest differences in these two versions come through in the character of Susan, the focus on youth, and the film's attempts to deal with racism. This difference is symbolized through the exclamation point that ends the title for the '90s version.

In the original version, racism is not as overt as it is in the '90s version. While Susan's mother and her cohort are almost constantly judging rock and roll based upon its connections to African American culture, and while the butcher represents overt racism (that Carol counters), the moral guardians in the past film bring up these issues less frequently, using different, but similar, language, noting rock and roll's "savage rhythms" and cannibalistic, ritualistic nature. In fact, during the trial in the first film, the prosecution plays footage of "savage" Africans in order to illustrate these points. However, despite this similar criticism, African Americans are not characters in the film, exposing the racism of the '50s in different, more subtle and covert ways than the '90s version which, despite its weaknesses, attempts to deal with racism and racialization more directly. This difference, perhaps, accounts for some of the other differences in these two films, namely the ending. At the end of the original, after a much longer, and more artfully constructed defense, rock and roll is victorious. However, in the '90s version, a version more conscious not only of the problems of race and racism, but also of generation, gender and, to a lesser extent, class inequalities, there is no room for a happy ending, only Carol's rebellion and escape. In fact, while the original film proceeds at a leisurely pace, the '90s version is much more intense and filled with the various representations of the angst of misunderstood youth. The dancing is more frenzied and sexualized, Carol's father much more spineless, and her mother, and her clique, much more controlling and powerful. The '50s could offer a film that didn't have to tackle issues like racism, but, in the '90s, because we are more aware of the ways in which racism affected culture and society—in the past, if not the present—*Shake,*

Rattle, and Rock! cannot avoid these issues. And, perhaps some of the limitations in the racial critique of the remake have to do with its nostalgic negotiation of continuing, growing, and evolving problems.

While few films contest the central position of whiteness in teen films, outside of the mainstream there are more films that represent the interest of girls who are at the margins of the mainstream due to their race, ethnicity, sexuality, and socioeconomic class. Thus, all of these films must deal with the tensions between stereotypes and realities and all of these films must maneuver within the confines of the social construction of race. The films that do this the best are often lower-budget films without big stars, such as *Just Another Girl on the I.R.T.*, *The Incredibly True Adventures of Two Girls in Love*, *Belly Fruit*, *Nikita Blues*, and *Stranger Inside*. But while these films locate their stories within radically charged spaces, the concept of race is not always dealt with, let alone contested. Further, the films that do deal with race often also include other issues like pregnancy (to be discussed in more depth in the next chapter), drug use, or prison, detracting from issues of race, and its social construction. Thus, while *The Incredibly True Adventures of Two Girls in Love* includes an African American character, it does little to confront issues of race, despite the interracial sexual relationship between Evie and Randy Dean. Evie, it seems, has more privilege than Randy Dean due to her higher socioeconomic status. Thus, in this film, race is superseded by sexuality.

Belly Fruit, on the other hand, complicates issues of race and ethnicity with issues of socioeconomic status and both *Nikita Blues* and *Stranger Inside* provide foundational alternative films about young African American women. Conversely, films like *Mi Vida Loca* rely upon stereotypes and exploit romanticized mainstream obsessions with gang life, even as they deal with important issues. In this HBO film, Echo Park is used as the important, self-contained geographical location for several stories about Mexican American gang members. While this film illustrates the importance of Echo Park in its residents' lives, it also portrays Echo Park as if it were solely the home to gang members. In fact, Echo Park is infamous for gang activity and in Mary Pardo's study of this, and another Mexican American community in L.A., real Echo Park community members describe the way in which filmmakers want to use this reputation to create "authentic" gang culture and often create the look they want by adding graffiti and trash to spaces that don't look "authentic" enough. This misuse of space and power is not difficult to believe as the writer-director and producer comment about their desire to portray "the culture" of "the subculture" of "these kids." And while they may capture some of this culture, in the DVD commentary they talk about culture as if they were anthropologists. This patronizing attitude comes across in several aspects of this film, but especially in the DVD commentary, made 10 years after the film. In this case, and countless others, well-meaning white folk assume the authority to make an "authentic" and compelling story without problematizing this authority, power, or access. This film is especially problematic when we consider that it is one of the few mainstream (HBO) films that deals specifically with Mexican American girls, and does so without their creative input or work. An alternative to this mainstream (if marginally mainstream) film is offered in a book by Marie "Keta" Miranda as she records the experiences of Chicano and Chicana youth as they contest popular representations like *Mi Vida Loca* by creating their own alternative documentary film—"It's a Homie Thang!"

Likewise, *Belly Fruit*, a film that was made from donations and the vision of two social workers, walks the line between an anthropological approach and an "authentic" story. As Keri Lee Green states in the film's mission statement, they made this film so that "both teens and adults will have a deeper understanding of the reasons behind and the consequences of ... kids having kids." Thus, this film, like many others, does not do as much to critique mainstream structures and definitions, but, rather, provides a space for stories that the mainstream doesn't often want to deal with seriously. But despite some of its more problematic aspects, the girls in this film, while falling into the stereotype of the pregnant teen in, perhaps, unavoidable ways, also shatter these stereotypes by presenting multifaceted, intelligent girls who, despite their mistakes and the forces working against them, struggle through and survive. While this is a powerful film, it is also somewhat problematic in that it is a film "inspired by real-life accounts" of "teen mothers from Hollywood, South Central and East L.A." And although this film cuts across these locations and shatters stereotypes, it is also bound by these stereotypes. For instance, while this film is inspired by stories across these three locations, each story is stereotypically identifiable by geographic location. From South Central we find a young African American girl who has been in over 20 group homes since she and her sister were taken from their mother. Her sister is adopted because she is younger and Shanika floats around the system. In East L.A. a young Latina struggles to raise her child with her boyfriend against the wishes of her parents. Her boyfriend, Carlos, can't find a steady job as he freelances with other Latinos, and ends up falling into crime under the pressure of needing to provide for his son. In Hollywood, Christina, the 14-year-old daughter of a single mother who had her when she was 16, has a relationship with her mother that more closely resembles two sisters. All three of these stories walk the line between stereotype and truth, and perhaps this is one of the reasons why they are so powerful.

The anthropological attitude found in *Belly Fruit* and *Mi Vida Loca* largely disappears when women of color are allowed to tell their own stories. *Just Another Girl on the I.R.T.* is a film written and directed by Leslie Harris, a black woman who uses this film to confront mainstream conceptions of and stereotypes of race, but also to provide an alternative space for Chantel's narrative. In this film Chantel invokes Africa in a much different manner than Cady does in *Mean Girls*. For Chantel, the case of Africa's representation on maps symbolizes the way in which African Americans are treated in the U.S. The Eurocentric way in which history is taught is challenged by Chantel and her teacher sees her as a troublemaker. Chantel, despite her lack of knowledge about her pregnancy and her options for the future, struggles to get the education she deserves. She knows enough to know that the education she has received thus far has been Eurocentric, though the other manifestations of this Eurocentric education can been seen throughout her life and education. Before she has her baby, she's fighting to graduate early so that she can go on to college early. When her principal tells her he thinks that she's not mature enough to graduate early she gets angry. And after she has her baby she is still struggling to get an education, the only education that is available to her—at the community college. Thus, this film shows how girls can, and do, succeed without totally selling out. They survive despite the demands of a racist, white supremacist system.

This theme of survival is inherent in many teen films that deal with issues of race, particularly in *Nikita Blues* and *Stranger Inside*, two films that tackle race by making it the invisible focus of the film while dealing with a plethora of issues that are related to race, but often subsumed and consumed within the category of race. This can be seen in the categorization of *Nikita Blues* as an urban comedy, with "urban" acting as code for "black" and "comedy" acting to buffer the more serious issues that are revealed as the film progresses. However, unlike many of the films described in chapter one, *Nikita Blues* and *Stranger Inside* offer complex, black female protagonists and a variety of African American characters that do not fall so easily into mainstream characterizations. Thus, *Nikita Blues* offers what can be considered an alternative to the institutionalization of whiteness in film. For the first seven eighths of this film, Nikita represents a strong, young black woman who sticks up for herself and goes after what she wants, which is, in this case, her teacher, Mr. Jackson. In addition to her quest for Mr. Jackson, Nikita is also enterprising economically as she steals clothes from the store where she works and sells them to girls at school to make extra cash. She sees this as a way of making ends meet, especially since her father died. And while her actions have negative repercussions within the film's narrative, Nikita's actions could be seen from another point of view as a way of getting even with "the man," since her boss, and most likely the store's owner, are white. However, despite this focus on Nikita, and despite her strength of character, her coming of age in this film is more like a slap back into childhood than a transition into womanhood. In the end, a different form of the mainstream reigns in the important issues this film deals with through its characterization and plot lines.

The racial composition and the characterization of both white and black characters in this film also challenges film as a white institution. Opposite to the usual racial representation in film, the white characters are in the minority, acting as the big softy of a principal, Nikita's whiny boss, and the deranged pervert who obsesses over abducting and raping teen girls. Both the principal and the pervert are one-dimensional and stereotypical—the bland principal, and the crazy, racist, perverted white boy who takes the place often reserved for the black man in white films. However, he is over the top—saying things like, "just like I like them—out cold," and constantly sniffing the panties he tore from Tangy. He is countered with his less deranged (African American) partner-in-crime, Jerome (or J-Smooth) who wants to get out of the business and join his brother in Detroit who owns a detailing shop. The white boy chastises him about washing cars for the rest of his life and provokes him by thoughtlessly calling him a "nigga." Jerome erupts, offering one of the glimpses of black empowerment throughout the film. Jerome tells him that they're not that close to be calling him a "nigga" and the white boy counters with a typical reaction—"I'm a motherfucking Polack!" Besides, he argues, it's not like you haven't been called one before. Jerome answers, "I'm just tired of hearing it." Despite Jerome's frustration with his situation, the "perverted ass white boy" lures him back with promises and visions of going to Puerto Rico or Hawaii after their next big score, inadvertently showing another side of race relations—in these neocolonial spaces "perverts" and "criminals" can hide in luxury (or so they think), just like any other first-world tourist in the third world. In the end, Jerome wants to quit and plans to quit after their last job. And as he quits the police have them surrounded. Thus, Jerome also symbolizes the lack of options available to young black men, especially those who want to change or improve their lives. Their "luck" eventually runs out.

Beyond J-Smooth, this film provides a variety of male and female African American characters beyond the stock, stereotypical characters often seen in film. Mr. Jackson is intelligent, thoughtful, committed, responsible, athletic, community-minded, and sexy. He is a committed teacher who takes his job, and its responsibilities, seriously. Ms. Fox, Mr. Jackson's fiancée, and perhaps one of the more stereotypical characters, is the assistant principal who enjoys the power and prestige of her position and who, as Nikita narrates, fits her name. She also enjoys the excitement of making out with her fiancé in the teacher's lounge, where they get caught by the (forgiving) principal. While Ms. Fox may represent a number of stereotypes—controlling, bad with money, and over sexualized— she is not one-dimensional and she shows a variety of emotions, including vulnerability and compassion. Mr. Jackson's best friend, Coach Casey, offers support and advice based upon his experiences and at one point the two go to a barbershop, at Mr. Jackson's request and against the coach's will, where they get haircuts, but also have a space to discuss the issues affecting them on their own terms. This scene offers a brief departure into a space traditionally seen as crucial to the black community as opposed to the club where the coach wants to go and get his "groove on." Thus, Coach Casey represents an older version of Mr. Jackson, a black man who has been whittled down by the system so that he no longer thinks about his community, but only himself.

The teen boys in this film also offer a range of characters beyond the stereotypical thug or the overachiever. A few of the boys in this film harass the girls, though in a less threatening manner than the perverts in the van. The girls can brush these guys off since the best they have to offer, the girls joke, is McDonald's and their daddy's car. They are not a threat since they are part of the community. Within this community, *Nikita Blues* also offers the minor character of Tyrone, Nikita's friend since childhood, who warns her against stealing and against pursuing Mr. Jackson, but is also always there to support her when needed. This friend, and a few other characters, offer small glimpses into the dynamics of wealth and poverty as Tyrone, in particular, begins to develop an oppositional consciousness. In one scene another boy touts his academic achievements and future accomplishments in front of two boys he identifies as doomed for failure because they don't go to class and don't seem to have any ambitions beyond sneaking peeks up girls' dresses. However, Tyrone is educating himself outside the boundaries of school, reading Octavia Butler, which he says to Nikita is about "how the rich and poor struggle to survive," a book that Nikita jokes is beyond his comprehension. However, he shows that it is not beyond him when he argues that she isn't poor and shouldn't need to steal, to which Nikita remarks that she's not rich either. This character not only represents a strong, young, intellectual black man, but also introduces insight into some of the connections between race and class. He provides some of the theory behind the situations of Nikita and J-Smooth. And Nikita even provides some of this analysis herself as she remarks that high school can be tough regardless of your color or whether you have money. However, she amends this by stating that money does, in fact, matter since popularity is intimately connected to money or other resources.

While the men in this film have more diverse and varied roles, Nikita's best friend Tangy also offers a nonstereotypical black female character. Tangy, who lives with her sister, not only cautions Nikita that she is going too far with Mr. Jackson, but also fights off the perverts in the van (punching one and biting the other), just like she has been fighting off all the men in her life—brothers, uncles, cousins—throughout her life, she tells Nikita. Tangy lacks the attitude that Nikita has, but lacks neither strength nor strength of character. She goes with the flow and does what is asked of her, and in cases like when Nikita's mom has asked her to pass out fliers for a youth revival at church, Tangy also does what Nikita has been asked to do. Both Tangy and Nikita are sensible young women when it comes to sex, though a "normal" course of sexuality is never really presented within the narrative for either of these girls. Nikita aggressively pursues her teacher while Tangy fights off perverts, and only when Nikita gets the number of Jason, the cute youth counselor at her mom's church, is there a hint of a future with conventional adolescence and sexuality for Nikita, if not for Tangy.

Nikita's mother also represents a strong, committed, community-minded, and sometimes overbearing black woman. At many points in the film Nikita is rebelling against her mother, consciously or unconsciously. This rebellion is partially due to her mother's heavy-handed parenting techniques—such as getting in her face and yelling at her to get off the phone. After this scene, Nikita comes into the kitchen, hugs her mom and asks if the cake is done. As she ices the cake she asks her mother questions about her relationship with Nikita's father that are directly related to the potential relationship she sees with Mr. Jackson, though her mother dismisses her questions without suspicion. She has no reason, at this point, to worry about her daughter. However, Nikita's relationship with her mother takes on even more tension when Mr. Jackson comes to confront her mother about his suspicions of Nikita. Her mother defends Nikita and kicks Mr. Jackson out before going to do her own investigating. And when Nikita's mother takes her daughter's future and punishment into her own hands, the confrontation heats up and Nikita's mother decides to call the police. When Nikita flees she runs head on into Mr. Jackson and "Miss Thang's" car.

This accident not only softens Nikita's punishment; it also voids the problems and complaints she had, particularly those complaints about her mother's lack of time for Nikita and concern about her reputation over Nikita's well-being. With this event, the tensions in the relationship with her mother seem to dissolve. And Nikita's accusations that her mother is not there for her because she spends all her time at church and that she is more concerned about her reputation than Nikita's well-being also disappear. Thus these issues, as well as the issues of sexuality, are subsumed into the moralistic ending. Instead of letting Nikita figure out how to turn things around on her own, which she does just before she gets caught, her life is taken back under her mother's control, a control that is transferred to Nikita's pursuit of Jesus. Nikita shrinks back into a member of the status quo, even if this is a status quo determined by her mother, and by extension, her community.

When I read this film's ending, it seems strange and abrupt. Nikita seems empty and soulless, especially compared to her attitude and strength throughout the film. The implication is that this attitude was her downfall. But perhaps to other viewers Nikita has finally found the right path, the only way to a real life. The video cover gives the impression that Nikita will be triumphant in her quest and in her narrative—"what Mr. Jackson doesn't know is what Nikita wants, Nikita gets!" But the strengths that Nikita has throughout the film are washed away in her final narration and in the final scenes of the film. Not only does Nikita not get what Nikita wants, but her final narration strips her of everything that has made her a strong character throughout the narrative. She says, "I just needed attention, a man like Mr. Jackson to hold me or something. I don't know. Look, I'm just a teenager. I guess stuff just happens and then you die. Right?" Nikita says this "right" weakly and the screen turns from black to a decontextualized tribute "In loving memory" to Darryl A. Rogers and Darryl Solomon. She continues, "Mama always said I needed Jesus in my life. Well I guess she was right." The film purposely gives the audience the impression that this is the end of the film and that Nikita has died as a result of her bad decisions. However, the black screen turns back to light and she claims that she "don't know much about that Jesus stuff, but [she is] gonna try and find out."

Thus, through the film's resolution and Nikita's final narration, this film becomes about the loss of her father and about her searching (in vain) for him in Mr. Jackson, which turns into her finding him, post narrative, in Jesus. The larger issues are drowned in the simplicity of finding Jesus, and the larger patriarchal structures in both family and religion, are reinforced. For instance, this film is saturated in a variety of sexual tensions that underrun adolescence and life from the coach who screwed up his career by getting involved with an 18-year-old soccer player when he was a 21-year-old assistant coach, to the advances that Nikita puts on Mr. Jackson, to Tangy's defense against the advances of the perverts that surround her, to the predatory sex of the perverts in the van, to Ms. Fox's need for a little excitement, to the boys' lame attempts to get into Nikita's pants by taking her to McDonald's. These tensions are balanced between serious and comedic, but are ultimately drowned out by the film's moralistic ending, an ending that fails to capture the complexities and strengths in this film.

And the end of the film, which we could assume represents Nikita's strength and survival, is also fatalistic as she says in the last of the film, as the camera freezes on her smiling face, "Because of Curtis I got my job back, thank God." The class issues that this film touched upon are reinscribed with this final line, as we realize how important Nikita's job is to her survival. But the techniques and tactics that Nikita has in her arsenal have all been proven ineffective, despite their potential. The film implies that she will take her place in her community, that she will find herself when she finds Jesus, that she will calm down and become a "good girl." For these reasons, I find the film problematic. However, there is also safety in this ending and the implication that, within the black community, Nikita won't need those tactics of attitude, voice, and awareness. However, why is a critical consciousness, rooted in a black radical tradition, not available for Nikita when it is for Tyrone? Why doesn't she find Audre Lorde or bell hooks? Why doesn't she make plans for college or for something else? Now that Nikita has learned her lesson, but has not necessarily come of age, what does her future hold?

The future is also left open for Treasure in *Stranger Inside*, a film whose characters, like in *Nikita Blues*, are predominantly black, and unlike, *Nikita Blues*, is almost entirely focused on women. The women in this film represent a limited spectrum of women in prison from recovering addicts, to mothers, to prostitutes, to those trying to get out of the system, and those who have been stuck there all of their lives. Filmmaker Cheryl Dunne spent time with women in prison in an attempt to portray these women in a more humane and less stereotypical way. Thus, *Stranger Inside* is one of the few films that deals with women in prison without being a tribute to men's fantasies of what prison must be like. Rather than present stereotypes and sexy prison garb, this film shows a variety of women with a variety of problems. These women present individual stories as well as examples of structural problems, though these connections are both subtle and overt. For instance, when Treasure transfers, a white woman shares her cell (among several other women). This woman has her daughter working on her case, and when she disappears, it's clear that her daughter was successful. This example subtly illustrates white privilege, particularly since this woman's daughter had the resources to arrange for her mother's release. Further, when an Asian American woman arrives, stereotypes about the kinds of women in jail are shattered and the complex nature of race relations is exposed as this woman seems out of place and, perhaps, more sympathetic than the African American women who are in similar situations. Thus, this is also one of the few films that exposes some of the problems that arise with a rising jail population, an increase in women going to jail, and a corrupt prison industrial complex. This film not only exposes these structural problems, but also provides a fictional space for individual negotiation through Treasure. However, Treasure's story and *Stranger Inside*, as an HBO film, stray from some of these realities, particularly in the excessive use of violence, as a recent article in *Bitch Magazine* discusses.

When *Stranger Inside* begins, Treasure is being transferred from a juvenile detention center to state prison, where she hopes to be reunited with her mother. While Nikita lost a father, Treasure never had a father to lose. It was her mother that she lost to the system, and like many children whose parents go to jail, Treasure follows in her mother's path, not simply because she has no other option given her circumstances, but happily, because she hopes that someday, unlike many kids whose parents are in jail, she will be able to have a relationship with her mother, a relationship that neither one could have on the outside. Thus, metaphorically and literally she is searching for her mother. The circumstances that brought her to jail—dealing and prostitution—are circumstances similar to many of the other women in jail. However, Treasure differs in that she is on a quest of sorts; she is determined to find her mom, and once she's in the system she finds ways to achieve her quest. Thus, Treasure is not simply a character, she is a metaphor, representative of all of the shattered families that result from the massive, and growing, incarceration of African American, Latino, and Native American women and men. This is a particularly important film when we consider that women are the fastest growing population in prisons, which means that more and more families are being shattered and more and more children are being robbed of parents.

In some ways, Treasure's choice to be in jail is both a conscious acceptance of her place in society as well as a surrender to this expected place. Treasure knows the system—she's been there pretty much all of her life. In fact, at one point she says it is her life; it's all she knows. And she has few problems figuring out the new system after her transfer, partially due to her association with the "G Girls," a prison gang, and particularly due to her association with Brownie, the "lifer" whom Treasure thinks is her mother. Treasure's blood relationship has to compete with the family structure in prison, and despite the jealousy of Brownie's (white) "daughter," Kit, Treasure finds the long-lost family she wanted. However, this dream life turns out to be much more complicated. When she is confronted with Brownie's wrath she tries to distance herself, only to be pulled back in and told to kill Kit who has not only wronged Brownie, but has also taken up with the group of white supremacists, despite her earlier distress at being called a "cracker" by Treasure. When Treasure doesn't follow through and Kit severely injures Brownie, Treasure finds out the truth, appropriately, through blood. Treasure's mom became a victim of the system a long time ago when Brownie killed Treasure's mother and took her name. The Brownie that Treasure knew was not her long-lost mother, but her mother's long-lost murderer.

Perhaps because of Treasure's situation, there is no conventional happy ending to this film. As Treasure transfers to minimum security prison based on her testimony against Brownie and the prison guard she had been doing business with, there is no clue to whether Treasure might get out of jail soon or not. And if there were, what's she going to do when the only skills she has are those acquired after years in the system? When she sheds the name Treasure for the name Brownie, not only does she get as close to her mother as she can get, and not only does she strip Brownie of her right to the name and make her disappear, but she also takes on a totally new identity—one that has yet to be formed. Perhaps this new Brownie will be a criminal mastermind like the last Brownie, a victim of the system like the first Brownie, or maybe she will follow her friend Shadow's lead and find another way. Regardless, there is still a stranger inside of Treasure-Brownie.

This film, by combining harsh realities with fictional spaces of negotiation, brings up many issues that are usually buried in and by the mainstream. The mainstream likes to consider the prison population to be, simply, deserving criminals, people who are better locked up than on the streets, people who have done "their crime" and are now doing "their time." However, *Stranger Inside* reveals some of the problems with this conceptualization of prisoners by revealing some of the structural problems that contribute to a rising prison population, a population that is, not coincidentally, largely made up of people of color. Not only are there unsanitary conditions, inadequate medical treatment, rape and corruption, inadequate rehabilitation and educational opportunities, and other problems on "the inside," but the problems of institutionalized racism, growing unemployment, disappearing social services and drug rehabilitation programs, and other problems on "the outside" are directly related. To many there are only strangers inside, but these strangers are sisters, brothers, mothers, fathers, etc. And, most of all, they are human beings, with human rights. These are only some of the social problems that films like *Stranger Inside* expose. However, it is difficult for any film to push these issues past exposure and into change. Only by applying careful and conscious critiques to these films, and to their "real-life" counterparts (like Angela Davis and Critical Resistance), can we begin to change, or at least challenge, these problems.

The kinds of negotiations discussed in this chapter bring girls face to face with a variety of American systems and structures, myths and paradigms. I have tried to show the multifaceted ways in which girls in film have negotiated for space, identity, power, and empowerment. This is a complicated landscape of adolescence that requires critical, conscious, and compassionate negotiation and readings. Coming of age requires the same. Thus, in the final chapter I turn to negotiations of sex and sexuality, the most definitive marker and means toward coming of age. Because sexuality takes many forms, and because sexuality cannot be disconnected from other axes of identity, this chapter echoes themes, characters, and other examples from the previous chapters and builds upon these with further examples and interpretations.

FOUR

SEX AND SEXUALITY
Negotiating Structures,
Constructing Alternatives

Of all of the structures that girls negotiate, sexuality is often the most dangerous and the most transformative. Whether we wish to stand out or fit in, girls are searching for identity and engaging in thoughts and behaviors meant (consciously or unconsciously) to bring us closer to adulthood, and invariably, womanhood, both of which require a physical and mental negotiation of structures, sexuality, and personal identity, as well as the integration of all of these to acquire a sense of self and sexuality in relation to the micro and macro worlds around us. As I have shown, such negotiation is not easy in a culture that limits girls' options as well as their tools. Thus, a discovery, comprehension, and negotiation of culture, as well as of the self, is what comprise coming of age, and this is a process that is impossible without an understanding of sexuality, what Julia Cleaves Mosse describes as the "intricate and multiple ways in which our emotions, desires, and relationships are shaped by the society we live in" (55). Thus, empowering sexuality is an individual and structural negotiation, and a coming of age on multiple levels.

While popular culture has the power to present incomplete, decontextualized, fantastical, and dangerous conceptualizations of sex and sexuality uncritically and en masse, as we have seen throughout this book, it also has the power to offer more complex and nuanced representations of sexuality. And these nuances are further opened through the act of interpretation, negotiation, application, and internalization. Continuing many of the themes already discussed, this chapter focuses on the range of sexualities—from bodily development, to sexual experimentation, to violence, and to self-discovery—that protagonists in girls' film negotiate to come of age, to better understand their own sexuality, and to empower themselves sexually and socially. All of the negotiations discussed thus far are intricately connected to girls' negotiation of sex and sexuality, on and off screen.

Plunged Into the Abyss

Experience, age, peer pressure, and development are some of the factors that push a girl from childhood into adolescence. Crossing this line may be an inevitable and exciting transition, but many girls are forced into it before they are ready. Physical development is, perhaps, the greatest determinant because it makes the transition visible and, therefore, public. For instance, when *The Smokers* begins, the audience is immediately confronted with womanhood. Karen is lecturing Lisa about how to insert a tampon. While her directions are accurate, they are also lacking and Lisa mutters, "Why don't they teach you this instead of chemistry?" In a past era, Lisa might have been attending a school where they wouldn't be teaching about tampons, but they would be instructing the girls on how to be better wives to their future husbands, like the girls in *Where the Boys Are*. Instead, the girls are in an environment where sex, drugs, alcohol, and all of the other "glamorous" elements of adulthood are within easy reach. However, the girls find that sex, at least on their terms, is really just out of their reach, or at least just outside of their control. This all begins when Lisa is in bed with her boyfriend, David, the class president (although, as Jefferson reveals in her narration, he pays someone else to do his campaigning for him because he doesn't know how to do it), and they are about to have sex for the first time. She fusses about the lights being on, and then asks if he has a candle. He's frustrated that she's on her period, but that doesn't really get in the way. He asks her if she's ready and she nods just before Karen starts banging on his window and yelling for him to open up. Despite the distraction, David shoves it in before he gets up to let Karen in. As Karen is frantically trying to get Lisa out before they are discovered, Lisa is asking David, "Why did you do that?" He replies, "You said you were ready. I've already waited six months." But Lisa's response shows that she is not just another girl to be walked all over: "Well, I've waited 17 years." Lisa may be sweet and innocent, but she is not totally naive. This is the line that many girls walk as they are plunged into the adolescent abyss—a contradictory and demanding space, as we have seen.

Two movies deal specifically with girls who are plunged into the abyss by virtue of their bodies and are forced to deal with the stares and assumptions of those around them. In *Smooth Talk*, Connie's legs grow faster than anything else and she can wear clothes her friends can only stare at with envy. Connie enjoys the attention, even as she is unsure of what to do about it. In *Slums of Beverly Hills,* Vivian is plunged into womanhood by the development of her breasts and she cannot stand the way that everyone, including her brother, constantly stares at her chest or uses it as a topic of conversation. While these two movies share this theme, they are drastically different. *Smooth Talk* is a surrender to the confines of womanhood, while *Slums of Beverly Hills* is a celebration of one girl's strength and ability to define her own life.

Connie is playing childhood games with her friend when the movie begins, but she quickly dumps her less-developed friend and strikes forward into the world of men. When she and her new friend cross the highway to get to this other world—a hamburger place damp with testosterone—Connie is clearly not prepared for what awaits her on the other side of the highway. She flees one guy's car because she's "not used to feeling this excited." She runs away from these feelings, but she cannot hide for long. After a fight with her family, Connie is left at home, free from the responsibilities of a family barbecue, and left to the ennui of adolescence. She plays her music from every radio in the house. She sunbathes and makes bracelets. She is left to her own devices. A friend is the only intrusion that this day may bring. The friend who shows up may be A. Friend (Arnold Friend), but he is not her friend at all.

At first Connie is drawn to Arnold Friend, with his flashy car and his smooth talk. But his smooth talk quickly brings to surface what Connie is not prepared to deal with. A. Friend's smooth talk is not the romantic words, the benign flirting, found in similar scenes on and off the screen. Instead, it is threatening and manipulative, violent and sinister, and even criminal. It brings to the surface the subtext of any "innocent" smooth talk where the victim is unsuspecting of the intentions and consequences of words. But A. Friend's smooth talk is not merely threatening her virginity or her virtue; these things are farthest from Connie's mind. Instead, he is threatening her sanity, her power, her autonomy, and her right to make her own moves in the game of sex. A. Friend knows everything about Connie. He knows that her family went to a barbecue and that they won't be back for hours. He knows about the friends she's left behind and the men she's been exploring. He acts like he's doing her a favor, or he is about to do her a favor, but it is on his terms, not hers. His talk is the kind she has not heard; it is about experiences she has not had, but it is also talk she has not heard because, as she tells him tentatively, "no one talks like that." He becomes openly, terrifyingly sexual, calling himself Connie's lover and telling her he's going to "come, come deep inside where it's silent...." She has nowhere to run and nowhere to hide, and she is left having to confront sex, not on her terms, but on terms that compromise her self and her sexuality forever. Connie can no longer explore sex on her own terms; the terms have been set and now she is just along for the ride—a metaphor for dominant, mainstream control of girls' and women's sexuality.

Because he makes her feel as though she has no choice (and she has no choice as she is outnumbered two to one), Connie leaves her house and gets in A. Friend's car. Rather than being forced to witness the reality of A. Friend's words, the viewer sees a visual metaphor. The screen is nearly silent, but Arnold's car, the "vehicle" of his control, sits silently in the middle of an empty field. When Arnold drops Connie off back at home, she is the one with the last word—"I never want to see you again"—the most powerful words she can use.

Connie is reunited with her family, but she is hardly the same girl that she was when they left for the barbecue. She reaches out to her sister as she tries to remember the tactile feeling of youth. She makes a joke about being tainted as she convinces her sister to dance with her. She has silently accepted her sexuality and even though she told A. Friend off, she has lost all of her fighting words. She has silently accepted her place on bottom and she knows there is no turning back. Connie represents countless real girls who have their virginity (and thus control over their bodies and their sexuality) stolen from them by sexual predators far worse than A. Friend. But girls can learn from Connie's naive mistakes, and other celluloid girls have.

In *Slums of Beverly Hills*, Vivian also faces the point of no return, but for her this realization is not a surrender to the confines of womanhood, but a propulsion into waters that must be explored. At the beginning of the film, Vivian is faced with what she can no longer hide—her breasts, and thus, her sexuality. The film opens with Vivian being fitted for a bra and Vivian, in her bra, occupies most of the screen while her father and the saleswoman discuss her and her bra loudly in the background. Everyone in Vivian's family feels the need to make comments about her breasts, including the "building guy," Elliot, the guy Vivian uses to experiment with sex. One of the ways Vivian confronts this constant exposure is with her attitude—she talks back. When her brother makes a comment about her breasts (and he makes many), she snaps at him, "I don't go around talking about your morning wood, don't go around talking about my tits." Of course, he is hardly as sensitive about his show of masculinity as she is made to feel about her feminine exposure.

Vivian's visibility is only one of the ways that her burgeoning sexuality is brought into the gaze during the film; she is constantly confronted with stares, but she is also exposed. In more than one scene Vivian's sexuality, and its inopportune exposure, is painful comic relief. But she also handles each of these situations with her own weapons. In one scene her father makes her put a bra on underneath her halter top which draws the stares that its ridiculousness deserves. At a fancy dinner, she stains her father's potential companion's needlepoint seat cover with menstrual blood. The woman screams as if Vivian has just committed a mortal sin and Vivian leaves with an ancient menstrual belt and a box of pads so big that it cannot be missed. In an earlier scene, her cousin, Rita, applies depilatory cream to get rid of her mustache, and everyone has to comment about that as well. Also with her cousin, Vivian's father catches them dancing with a vibrator and Vivian can't turn it off despite her embarrassment. All of these situations force Vivian's development into the open and throughout the course of the film she deals with both the attention she receives and the situations her physical, emotional, and social development bring.

Instead of simply loving or hating the attention her breasts get, Vivian gazes at it from within, evaluates it, and appropriates it throughout the course of the narrative. At the start of the film, when Vivian is getting her first bra she stares at her viewers while she simultaneously stares at herself in the mirror. She sees her image and thinks she's deformed. She continues to think this until visiting the plastic surgeon forces her to come to terms with her body. She tells him, "I don't like them.... I don't want them." And when he agrees to consult with her, she looks in the mirror and sees her mother in her breasts (something both her father and Rita comment on earlier). She confronts her exposure by looking within herself and coming to terms with her body. But Vivian is also forced to gaze at herself (both literally and figuratively), an act necessary to the process of coming of age. Unlike Connie, Vivian has mastered a nonchalant attitude about sex. Nothing is going to let her feelings get away from her. When she makes out with Elliot in the laundry room, she controls the situation. When he immediately begins taking off his pants, Vivian is instantly on the defensive, saying, "I'm not gonna do it in the laundry room. I wasn't talking about that. Just breasts. Second base. That's it. Not all the way." Vivian does not spare him a word and he quickly complies to her lead. When the dryer buzzer goes off, Vivian calls off the make-out session and tells him not to tell anybody. Also unlike Connie, Vivian knows what she's getting into. When she dumps Elliot, she tells him what she told him from the beginning—it was just a building thing. She adds, "I just can't get attached. We're nomads." Vivian, in the midst of all of the other demanding factors in her life, has negotiated sex. She has learned that she is in control of her body and her pleasure. She has refused to take her place on bottom. She too knows that there is no going back to childhood. She also knows that she can continue to have self and autonomy despite whatever is thrown her way.

While Dawn, Nikita, and Connie all have factors pulling them backward toward childhood, Vivian has factors pulling her toward womanhood. In addition to the development of her breasts and her explorations with sex, Vivian has the responsibilities of a woman in a family that consists of her father and two brothers, and, at least temporarily, her cousin. She thinks there's something wrong with her family and she thinks there's something wrong with her body. When Vivian isn't looking at herself in the mirror—which brings disgust the first time she does it and closure the next—she is forced to look at her cousin, Rita, who, in almost every scene, somehow ends up naked or nearly naked. In her first scene, Rita needs a ride and she stops a trucker by throwing her robe open in the middle of the street. Then, when Vivian

Natasha Lyonne portrays Vivian, a smart, sassy, and sensitive girl, in Tamara Jenkin's *Slums of Beverly Hills*. Vivian negotiates the pressures of growing up a girl in Beverly Hills. However, Vivian's family is far from the popularly imagined Beverly Hills as they move from place to place, always staying inside the 90210 zip code. Within this unstable, and sometimes unsupportive, environment, Vivian discovers herself and her sexuality in her own ways. She also comes to accept her quirky family. (Copyright Fox Searchlight Pictures.)

first comes across Rita, she is in the shower and she is so ecstatic to see Vivian that when the two hug, Rita's towel falls off (and it falls off again later). Rita's constant exposure reminds Vivian of what she is becoming— a woman. But Rita does not offer the most empowering model of womanhood because she is still dealing with the same issues that adolescence introduces. Rita's primary role in Vivian's narrative is to remind Vivian that she is a woman and to help her with the little things that a father can't handle. But Rita can hardly handle her own life. Rita gives Vivian all sorts of guidance on the sexual and feminine fronts, but when it comes to life, Rita is not in a position to give advice. She joins the family after escaping, once again, from her drug treatment center, and it is clear that Rita has not kicked her drug habit. What Vivian finds out is that Rita is also pregnant. Rita puts up a front about the baby's father, trying to convince Vivian (and herself) that her situation is better than it actually is. She tells Vivian that she is "so ready to domesticate," and giggles like she is playing house. When Vivian shows concern, Rita tells her, "Don't worry Viv. I'm a grown-up; I've got it all under control." While Vivian knows that Rita does not have anything under control, this is a realization that must wait until the end of the film, when Vivian comes to terms with the weakness of adults, in general, and her father, specifically.

Despite Rita's lack of ability to help herself, she does help Vivian. She helps her to see what Vivian has not been able to accept about her father as well as the very things that Rita has yet to conquer herself. Rita helps Vivian come to terms with her self (and her body) shortly before Vivian watches Rita fall apart in front of Rita's father. As a role model, Rita may not provide the best vision of the future with her drug habit, her eating disorder, and her general lack of direction. But Vivian is not touched by her cousin's weaknesses. In her relationship with Rita, Vivian takes the good, the positive things that Rita has to offer and Vivian sees Rita's problems more clearly than Rita (even though Vivian's vision is also obscured). Vivian tries to help Rita, but Rita's problems are too big to be fixed by Vivian. At the end of the film, Rita is carted away by her father and everyone is back where they were when the film began, except for Vivian. During the course of the narrative, Vivian has come of age, but more importantly, she has come to terms with her life. She realizes that her family is a part of her self and her self is a part of her body just as much as her body is a part of her self. Just as she sees her mother in her breasts, she sees her family in her life. At the end of the film, Vivian narrates: "I used to think the good life was somewhere just outside the window of my father's car. But now I see it's on the inside. Sure we didn't know where we were going to live, but we knew where we were going.... A meal at Sizzler meant that we were halfway home." With these final words Vivian not only comes to terms with her family and their life as nomads, but she also comes to terms with her body. What's important is what's inside—both herself and her father's car. While in the beginning of the film she seems to be drifting away from her unsatisfactory family, in the end she pulls them back together. She is becoming a woman because she has begun to do the work of the woman. And there is always such "women's work" to be done.

As girls learn to negotiate the space between girl and woman, not all girls are lucky enough to have parental figures and role models like Vivian, or some of the other girls in this genre. In *Ripe*, Rosie's first few words of narration sum up the parents that she and her sister leave behind as the film begins: "Our dad was a real motherfucker. So when he bashed that deer, I dragged Violet from the burning car and watched mom and dad explode." The story that follows this explosion is one that could not take place with any kind of parents in the way, and Violet and Rosie are free to develop according to their own devices. As their names suggest, Rosie is only a blush while Violet is a deep purple. Rosie is not interested in sex; she is too concerned with (obsessed with) her sister. She says, "I'd do anything for Violet," and goes on to show this dedication throughout the movie. Violet, however, is beginning to become aware of sexuality and her body, but she has always been the one the boys liked, according to Rosie. Rosie is awkward, gangly; Violet is sexy. Rosie is annoyed by her sister's curiosity about sex, especially since she makes her promise, "no boys, just me and her forever." But this is a promise that Violet could not keep. She may be confused by her feelings as she begins to discover the power of her sexuality, but she's also sure about her path. After all, as the title implies, once a piece of fruit is ripe, it must be eaten, otherwise it will spoil. This is the same inevitability that drives the narrative of Rosie and Violet. Rosie and Violet may be fraternal twins, but they do not begin puberty at the same time. For two girls who are so close, puberty is a huge rift; it puts one girl in the midst of adolescent turmoil while the other continues to be content with childhood (or childish) games. But in the lives of these celluloid girls, who are without parents and without a "normal" social context, such a rift puts a lot more (in fact, everything) at stake.

The split between these two sisters is evident from the first few frames of the film. In glimpses of their childhood, a young Violet curiously looks at two bugs mating. She asks her sister if she can imagine what it would be like if they were those bugs. But the young Rosie prefers not to use her imagination; she hits the bugs with a stick, chanting "kill them." While this scene may seem like an innocent childhood game, in the scheme of the narrative, it foreshadows what is to come. A more developed version of the bug scene takes place when the girls are adolescents. The sisters see two rats mating and Rosie quickly smashes them with a shovel. Violet asks her, "Why do you always have to do that?" Rosie gives no answer, because she can't. The narrative to follow asks the same question, but has as much trouble answering the why. Why does Rosie stay rooted in the realm of childhood and platonic friends while Violet propels forward into the world of sex? The question cannot be answered, especially not by simple biological development, but the film explores the ripeness (and rancidness) of sexuality and the inevitable death of childhood. In fact, the entire narrative is saturated by sex, but a portion of the film juxtaposes childhood (innocence) with adulthood (sex) in a series of scenes. When the girls hide in Pete's truck because their picture dominates the front page of the paper, they find their ride is filled with pornography. Violet is especially interested as she reads from one of the magazines. Annoyed and disgusted, Rosie explores the other boxes and the two girls find all sorts of toys to enliven their imaginations and ignite their giggles, including the anal intruder. Like many of the scenes in *Ripe*, sex is exposed to Rosie and Violet. As they ride in the back of Pete's truck, even with boxes full of porn, they don't have the context to make sense of it all. The actual use of the "anal intruder" is clear enough to the girls, but the sexuality connected to it is something that is pushed just below the surface on the military base—a seething cauldron of testosterone and dirty sex mixed with discipline.

Pete innocently lets them stay the night and the girls continue to be pulled between the world of childhood and the steamy world of sex when they go exploring the next day. A group of military men begin a chant, "I don't want no beauty queen," but Ken, who later becomes a mentor to Rosie, squelches their chant before it can go much further. This scene cuts to Rosie and Violet mocking a military chant as they step in time. The girls chant their way right into a line of cat calls which Violet loves as she lingers to bask in the whistles and words that Rosie hates. They run right into a younger girl absorbed in her hula hoop. They scamper around her, mock her and try to mess up her count, but are shooed away by the girl's mother as if they are pests. The girls then encounter Pete and the lady who wants him to "sell her a vacuum cleaner" as she anxiously and obviously seduces him. They peer in through the window and burst into giggles at the sight. They run in opposite directions and agree to meet later. These scenes, juxtaposing childhood and sex, underline the themes of the narrative. When the girls explore alone, what they find is exactly what they need—freedom for Violet and discipline for Rosie.

When the two split, Violet encounters a building full of recycling and looks at a magazine with a picture of a naked man. She looks and then blushes as she puts the magazine down. Rosie comes across a bunker full of guns and ammunition. Searching for a gun and role-playing as secret agent 007, she is apprehended by Ken. Once he realizes the perpetrator is only a young girl, he pretends to give her a hard time, but lets her go, telling her, "You come see me. I'll show you a few things." While Ken's words could be interpreted sexually, this is far from what he and the film have in mind. He wants to set Rosie straight with discipline, the same thing that set him on the right path when he was a wayward youth. He, like Anna's art teacher, is a mentor. And with more opportunity to mentor, things might have been different for Rosie, but instead, she falls through the cracks, like so many other girls.

The girls meet back up again and Rosie is excited about a "really cool guy" she met who is going to teach them to "shoot and stuff," but Violet is bored and ready to move on to Kansas like they planned. Without money, the girls are temporarily stuck at the base and Rosie is able to pursue Ken's teaching. Violet even offers to work the coat-check at the Fourth of July dance so they can steal the money they need in order to leave the base and move on. But while the girls wait for their chance, Violet begins to discover autonomy through sexuality—the only thing of which her sister is not a part. While Rosie is discovering the phallic power of the gun, Violet gets her period. The only adult around to help Violet is Pete and he fumbles for the words to explain and reassure her. Instead he comes up with, "You're just so beautiful." Violet initiates a kiss and asks him not to tell Rosie. Meanwhile, excited by her ability to shoot a gun, Rosie exuberantly hugs Ken. The split between the two girls is evident in their reaction to these two different situations. Rosie calls for what she is most comfortable with—a platonic hug. Violet chooses not a platonic hug, or even a platonic kiss, but a kiss that responds to Pete's flattery, and initiates a sexual relationship with him. While Violet was curious about sex before, she begins to actively pursue it after she begins to menstruate. She returns to the bunker where she looked at porn earlier, but she doesn't just look. Alone, among the porn that others have thrown away, Violet masturbates. She is interrupted by Rosie as she busts in and tells her to freeze, while holding up her gun. Rosie laughs about the look on her face, not realizing that the look she has walked in on is not only one of surprise or fear, but also one of interrupted pleasure and potential exposure. Violet's interest in sex also leads her to become more interested in Pete not only romantically, but sexually as well, and Rosie's jealousy is obvious. The Fourth of July Dance becomes the pivotal moment in the movie, as well as in the relationship between the girls. The dance and the day are a kind of independence day for Violet, and what happens after the dance creates a permanent rift between the two girls. At the dance, Violet dances and enjoys herself despite Rosie's annoyance. Violet pretends that her plan to steal from the coat-check does not produce enough money for them to leave and Rosie is distraught. Not only are they still short on cash, but now she is losing Violet to a man. While Rosie pounds down shots at the bar to alleviate the pain of seeing her sister dancing with Pete, Violet leaves with him. As they walk out the door, Violet looks over at Rosie and the last shot as they leave is of Violet's look toward Rosie. She knows she is leaving her behind.

When Rosie realizes Violet has left with Pete she becomes frantic and runs back to Pete's. Rosie peers into Pete's bedroom window, and she is torn apart when she sees Violet in Pete's room. Rosie runs off and while her sister is losing her virginity, Rosie stumbles upon the military men and their strange, homoerotic mix of chanting, wrestling, and dancing. The scenes flash between the blue glow of Pete's bedroom and Violet's pained face, to Rosie's observation of men wrestling each other to the ground. When one man sees Rosie, she makes a run for it, and he chases her down. While Rosie runs as if trying to escape from his sexual advances, she changes her mind and surrenders to his drunken pursuit. She grabs him and kisses him. She takes off his belt and pants and pulls down her underwear. Just when Rosie has completely (and actively) surrendered, Ken comes along and threatens to kill the man if he doesn't get off her. Rosie flees, throws up, and returns to Pete's to find Violet waiting in their make-shift bed. The two have each been initiated into sex, but hardly in the same way. Despite Violet's physical pain, she continues to be interested in sex, and because of Rosie's emotional pain, she is only further disinterested and confused. While Violet's first sexual experience reflects the physical pain that more than one character in these films experiences, Rosie's first experience emulates similar circumstances that real girls are exposed to by being a part of their surrounding landscape. Because girls are often seen as being a part of the scenery, they are also acted upon like Rosie is (or in far more sinister ways involving sexual abuse, molestation, and other kinds of coercive and abusive sex). The sex the girls encounter at the base is not just sex, but the "real" side to sex—sex devoid of any kind of romantic preconceptions. This is the kind of sex that is hidden from the eyes of young girls, but often finds its way into their lives anyway, like it does for Tangy or Brenda. For Rosie and Violet it is impossible to ignore this sexuality because it is all around them, not hidden, but merely concealed. They begin to discover this side of sex in Pete's truck full of porn, but they don't fully realize what the chocolate sauce or the anal intruder are all about. Violet experiences one version of this side—painful sex. Rosie another—the display of latent sexuality and the link between sex and violence. Thus, violence becomes Rosie's way of getting back at Violet for betraying her even as she is also trying to secure Violet in her life.

Rosie cannot forgive Violet, but when Violet takes off for a ride on Pete's motorcycle and Rosie discovers Pete's money, she cooks up a plan that she thinks is sure to win back her sister and will enable them to move on with their journey to Kansas. While playing a game called "30 seconds in the closet," Rosie shoots Pete. Violet is shocked and calls the military police, but when Ken gets there and demands an answer, Violet protects her sister, telling him that Pete shot himself. Rosie thinks that it is all over, but when the girls return to collect their money, Rosie finds that Violet also has a plan. Violet pretends to play the game with Rosie that their father used to play. She pulls a gun on Rosie and tells her to hide. Rosie protests at first, telling Violet that she doesn't know how to use the gun. But Rosie quickly complies as Violet points the gun in her face and chants the words that their father used to chant: "Fe fi fo fum I smell the blood of a little one." Violet quickly disappears and the movie ends with the vision of a runway, Violet on a plane, and Rosie curled up on the floor of Pete's house, shooting a gun into her mouth. Violet opens her hand and she is holding the bullets.

We know that Rosie survives because the film begins with her narration. She tells of the long-haired guy with a broken-down motorcycle who will come between the two sisters. But it isn't simply the long-haired guy who comes between these girls. Rosie's love is platonic, but it is also obsessive and unhealthy. In her opening narration she could be describing a lover just as well as she is describing a sister. With Ken's mentoring, Rosie lights up and has confidence in herself. He is teaching her discipline, but she is not only gaining inner power, she is also learning to shoot and acquiring a power that is outside of herself. The discipline is inconsequential and the phallic power of the gun and the consequence of its use are more than she is prepared to handle, especially when she faces a future without Violet.

Is Rosie's decision to kill Pete ignorant, devious, or both? She killed Pete, but her intention was not only death, but also freedom for her and Violet. What results is freedom for Violet from her sister, the exact scenario that Rosie was afraid to face. With Rosie, Violet knows that she will never be autonomous and she will never be able to be free in her self or her sexuality. The split between these two girls is inevitable once sex, through puberty, has the chance to come between them. It is inevitable because Violet develops more quickly than Rosie, but eventually Rosie would mature and she and her sister may have become closer as women than they were as girls. But the split between Rosie and Violet is unavoidable not only because of Rosie's obsession with her sister, but more importantly, because Rosie's action makes reconciliation impossible. She has killed not only her sister's lover, but she has also denied Violet the choice to continue to mature, and in so doing, to make her own decisions about sex, life, and love. But there is also a freedom for Rosie. She no longer has to be obsessed with Violet and everything that Violet does. Rosie also has the opportunity to be autonomous to further develop her own sense of self, not a sense of self contingent upon Violet. Her narration of the film comes from somewhere beyond this obsession, and although the audience does not know how she got to this point, it is obvious that she got there without her sister.

Sex and Romance in the Margins

Perhaps the earliest girls' film is the 1944 film *National Velvet*, a film about an English girl whose love affair is with a horse, not with a man. Yet, both men and romance weigh heavily on Velvet's narrative. In fact, she dresses like a boy in order to compete in the Grand National horse race, not for her own fame (at least initially), but because she knows that her horse, Pie, can and will win. In fact, Velvet describes her love for Pie in the same words and physiological responses as her older sister uses to describe her own love interest. Pie makes her heart beat faster and she dreams about him all the time. She bounces around in her bed pretending like she's riding her horse. All she wants to do is ride. Of course, the sexual connotations of this film were probably, in its time, only innocent. But regardless, Velvet is so hot for her horse that she only cares about his happiness, his success, his well-being, and his achievement. And despite her mother's supportive role, Velvet's dream is, ultimately, perfect preparation for her future role as someone's wife, a timely message toward the end of World War II. After all, she may have briefly disrupted the gender barrier for jockeys, but this was her "one great chance at folly," as her mom puts it. But certainly, at the age that is now often considered "tween," Velvet could have more folly ahead.

The tween years are popular in family films and 15 is a popular age in many films that often use age 16 as a marker. The ages before 15 and 16 are less often portrayed in films, with the more recent exception of Mary Kate and Ashley Olsen's tween movies. But sometimes films in the tweens can offer an adolescent space like those family films discussed earlier. This romantic space is different at the margins of the mainstream where the tween years are some of the most difficult. Sometimes this space can be exploited and exploded. For instance, the film *Thirteen* can claim "authenticity," it can claim to be a wake-up call, but it's also an uncritical look at the "out of control" and "criminal" girls and the larger structures that contribute to the environments that produce these girls. Despite the publishing and cinematic epidemic of "mean girls," and the feel-good response of films like *Mean Girls*, Traci's problems and actions are blown out of proportion and context. And ultimately this film makes no attempt at romance; it is, according to the writer-producer, so real that it's almost like a documentary.

This tween representation is totally different from the dark, outsider comedy *Welcome to the Dollhouse*, which contests romance and popularity in its own ways. Romance, after all, doesn't always deliver the expectations that a girl hopes for. In *Welcome to the Dollhouse* the bare bones of adolescence are exposed through this biting representation of junior high, a space and time away from Velvet or Traci's world. Dawn is searching for popularity, attention, and acceptance and instead she is hit with all of the pain of junior high where she is an outcast. Dawn's little sister, Missy, who is always dressed in her pink ballet clothes, constantly prances around Dawn (literally and figuratively) and no one can stop talking about how cute she is. Missy, aside from being a constant nuisance, reminds Dawn not only of what she lacks as an awkward teen, but also of what she cannot go back to—childhood.

Dawn thinks the path to popularity is sex, though her concept of sex and flirtation is childishly naive. She lusts after Steve, the high school boy who is "the next Jim Morrison," the embodiment of sex with his long hair and soulful lyrics. But Dawn cannot mask her blundering naiveté with romantic notions. Instead, these romantic notions expose her lack of experience. For instance, after Dawn finds out that a girl she knows has been "finger-fucked" by Steve (a description that has Dawn staring at her hands for hours) she makes him fish sticks and Hawaiian punch, and plays the piano for him. Then she asks: "Want to see my fingers?" Her seduction is a mixture of ignorance and romance, two things junior high girls know plenty about. But the real world of junior high and the inescapable world of family still impose upon her romantic fantasy; she has to deal with boys her own age.

Dawn's relationship with Brandon begins with a threat that seems like a preadolescent version of the bully-teen comedy *Three O'clock High*. He tells her that he's going to rape her at three o'clock. Dawn really doesn't understand the concept of rape and decides to wait until the inevitable happens. It never does. Instead, they develop a friendship from their common state of being misunderstood. They have all of the same frustrations with their common enemies of school and parents, and they kiss in the clubhouse that Dawn's cruel family is tearing down the next day. But the romantic in Dawn cannot forget Steve. Torn, Dawn says, "I can't be your girlfriend," and she and Brandon play out a juvenile, melodramatic scene. Brandon becomes jealous and yells, "What's his name? Tell me his name!" Dawn tells him that she is in love with Steve Rogers. She says, "He's in high school. You don't know him," and Brandon calls her an asshole and storms away.

When Dawn tries to fight back against her reality—the boys who harass her and throw spitballs at her—she and her parents are called into the principal's office where she is further humiliated and misunderstood as the principal asks, "Are you having social problems?" Dawn's mother confirms that she is because she's a "loner" and she has no friends. (Her family hardly instills any confidence in her; if anything, they take her confidence away.) When Dawn tries to explain herself by saying that she was "fighting back," her mother asks, "Who ever told you to fight back?" Clearly Dawn is operating from a position where she has no power, not even the power to be listened to and certainly not the power to be understood. She is urged, like so many other real and celluloid girls, to be complacent, and not to stand up for herself. In this movie, Dawn's parents and principal represent all of the forces of institutionalized adult culture. Instead of being assured or helped by the powers that be, she is given a lecture about her "permanent record," as if something so inconsequential is of any concern to her while she deals with her "social problems." Instead, she invests her romantic dreams for the future in Steve and while Dawn isn't thinking about where Steve may take her, this unknown is far more comforting than the reality she lives with daily.

Most other teen and preteen girls are content to worship manufactured stars like the Backstreet Boys or *NSYNC, but for Dawn, who receives no positive (nonsexual or sexual) attention at home or at school, posters, like the kind found covering Lola's entire wall in *Confessions of a Teenage Drama Queen*, are only two-dimensional altars. She builds herself a three-dimensional one and she worships a star-in-the-making, rather than the packaged stars that other girls worship. His realness holds more possibility and she chants "Steve, Steve, Steve" over and over again in an adolescent séance. She says: "Steve, hear me. You will fall madly in love with me. You will make love to me. You will take me far away from this place." Of course, Dawn is as confused about making love as she is about rape; the key is that Steve has the potential ability to take her "far away from this place." In "this place" Dawn is dressed like a child and treated like a child. She can only look forward to the future or fantasy.

Dawn's lack of friends, coupled with a cruel and self-absorbed family, leaves her to navigate the sexual waters blindly, sexlessly, and powerlessly.

She can only wait for high school where her socially outcast brother assures her she'll at least have a niche where the harassment will lessen. While the future scenario is less than ideal, it is better than what she has now, and all she has now is a crush who understands that "junior high sucks." She clings to this commonality because Steve actually talks to Dawn, not to make fun of her and not because he likes her, but because he is indifferent to her. She is there and she listens to him, so he listens back. Dawn invents a relationship with Steve that is only destined to disappoint her. She identifies with his music as he sings to his "little girl" and says, "Welcome to the Dollhouse. I've got it all set up for you." In her mind and her fantasy, it's as if he is singing just to her. The only powerful act Dawn has is her crush on Steve; it is powerful because it is her own endeavor, her own creation, and her naiveté allows her some promise for the future, even if that future isn't with Steve. When she's done dealing with junior high, Dawn has a whole other world to survive before she can begin to breathe.

This film relies upon the same myths that films like *10 Things I Hate About You* and *Clueless* also rely upon, but *Welcome to the Dollhouse* subverts the myth of romance. Dawn represents the "real" Lolita—the Lolita that most films like *American Beauty* and *What a Girl Wants* sexualize. But Dawn cannot be sexualized because she is not a "Lolita" in the terms of dominant culture—she is a seventh-grader who is as torn by the Lolita paradox as any other real or celluloid teen girl, but she is not desirable according to the standards of dominant culture. She searches for sex because it is tied to the romance that allows her fantasies to make her life more livable, but she isn't prepared to deal with mainstream society's expectations of her or her sexuality. These expectations are cut from the same mold as those of the kids who make her life a living hell.

A different form of the romantic is seen in *The Incredibly True Adventures of Two Girls in Love.* When the movie begins, Randy Dean is ostracized because she is a lesbian. People yell "Dyke" at her from moving vehicles. Her only friends are a gay male friend, her female coworker at a gas station, and her older female lover (who totally controls their relationship). Evie, on the other hand, is a picture of perfection and is trapped by the expectations of such perfection and popularity. When the two meet, they begin to test the sexual waters not through sex, but through a close friendship, a friendship like neither has had before. Relationships, whether sexual or platonic, with peers or with adults, are important and integral to girls' coming of age but are underutilized in many girls' films like *10 Things I Hate About You* and *Virtual Sexuality* where friendship is often out of convenience. But many of the more marginalized girls' films explore girls' friendships like *Brokedown Palace*, *Bend It Like Beckham*, *All Over Me*, and *Thirteen*. Randy and Evie's relationship is a part of coming of age for the two, but in different ways. For Evie, it is a way of separating from her mother "which is a totally normal adolescent impulse, and in fact crucial to [her] adult development," as she reminds her mother in a quick tirade of words. It is also a way to "traverse [her] own landscape." For Randy it is a kind of coming out even though she is already "out." (At the end of the film when everyone is trying to get the girls out of the hotel room, one of Evie's friends tells Evie's mother that Randy is "already out." It is a joke that Evie's mother does not get.) The girls' relationship is one that lets Randy be happy with who she is. She may be shunned by the rest of school and society, but she is close to Evie, and the personal is more important than the public. But Evie also makes Randy deal with herself publicly rather than hide from view. Since she hasn't dealt with the harassment Randy has been subjected to, she doesn't understand how people can be so cruel. In both of their situations, their relationship—love (and coincidentally, lesbian sex)—is at first, a way of escaping who they are expected to be, and later, a way of making the world (their family and friends) deal with who they are.

The sex scene in this movie is not post narrative or off camera like many other romantic films; rather, the entire movie anticipates it. The girls cook and eat and smoke and drink together, pushing their way into adulthood by "playing house." Evie knows that her mother will be calling, but she doesn't pay any attention. When the phone rings the minute Evie turns 18, she has completely separated from the phone's umbilical chord. Instead of answering her mother's call, she doesn't even hear it. She is in the throes of passion. Since there is no penetration, no power struggle, this sex scene is unlike heterosexual sex scenes—there is no literal or figurative top and bottom, especially since both girls confess that they have never done *this* before. It doesn't matter if the girls are "virgins"; they aren't playing by the rules of that game. Thus, sex (unsanctioned by society) is the way that these two girls express their love, and sex is also the reason their relationship is forced to meet the eyes of the public. When Evie's mother comes home unexpectantly and finds them together in bed, she can't stop saying, "It's a girl!" Confronting her mom with a mess and a half-clothed girl is the only way that Evie can traverse her own landscape and make her mother deal with it (although this is not, of course, her immediate intention).

The two try to run, but there is no escaping. They end up surrounded by all of the players in their lives (and in the movie), standing outside, loudly waiting for the two to emerge, to surrender. Instead of ending the movie with the girls' surrender, the image of their embrace stands against the backdrop of confusion, anger, and nervousness that awaits them. And then there is silence and a cut to black, and the words, "For my first girlfriend. May our relationship finally rest in peace," appear. The film has achieved what the individual, alone, could not, and it is helped along by the strength of character in Evie and Randy Dean; however, neither Randy Dean nor Evie are playing for their lives like Brandon Teena in *Boys Don't Cry*. Thus, this film relies upon both realism and romance in various forms.

While romance can be an effective weapon and a means to acquire a sense of self and sexuality, it is also a plot device that compromises the development of female characters. When a character buys into romance, she is destined to follow a certain path. But one character, and her narrative, take issue with romance and convention and confront it head on. In *The Opposite of Sex*, Dedee refuses to be caught in the traps of her genre or her situation, and she reconstructs her average story—the blunderings of a pregnant and savvy, but savagely naive teen who has no satisfying alternative to her compromised situation—into a narrative structured, staged, interpreted, manipulated, subverted and delivered by her crude, confronting narration. This narration becomes her way out of her compromised situation, as well as a means toward her coming of age.

The majority of this narration focuses around Dedee's pregnancy (the sex act that happens before the narration begins and puts Dedee into her situation), but by the end of the film she seems more ambivalent about sex. She says: it "seems like everybody's having sex but me, not that I'm against sex." Dedee is obviously not against sex; she uses it to get what she wants. She tells us she's against "all of the attachment that goes along with it." She tries to convince us that she wants no attachments, but her argument is less than convincing. "Sex always ends in kids, or disease, or like, you know, relationships. That's exactly what I don't want. I want the opposite of all that. Because it's not worth it." But as she is reminded by her reflective introspection, what the viewer sees as flashbacks from the movie—"maybe it's not all shit." Without her plan, and without her narrative, Dedee would have nothing but shit. She has greater expectations for herself, even if these expectations are romantic, unrealistic, or unclear. Dedee has a fresh start, without a baby and without any other attachments that are going to drag her down. She is not detached, but disentangled, and that's the opposite of sex.

At the end of the movie Dedee does not have the same narrative control that she greeted us with in the beginning; she no longer knows the end of her own story. She says, "I thought the whole idea was I know what happens next." But like all other teen girls and women (and people in general), this is a power that she cannot be granted by anyone. Dedee's refusal to have a contrived ending is also a defiance. Despite the romantic narrative she has constructed, Dedee won't have anything forced upon her, not even a happy ending. In the closing narration she says, "I told you right off I don't grow a heart of gold and if I do, which is like so unlikely, gimme a break, and don't make me do it in front of you guys." She brought us, the viewers, into her life, but under qualified circumstances, on her terms. She wanted someone to talk to, but she doesn't want our advice. Dedee breaks the camera's gaze and demands that the camera "go, okay" finally leaving her alone. She asks, in the end, what all girls ask from the gaze of dominant culture—don't watch me grow up, "don't make me do it in front of you guys." It is quite a different experience of being viewed when Dedee knows her story. She controls and constructs what her viewer sees and hears. She redefines the gaze as she gazes at herself at the very same time we are gazing at her. When she doesn't know "what happens next," she pushes us away so that she can continue to have the power over her narrative. This power is one that other female teen narrators don't often have—the power to reconstruct her own story, to put her shattered life back together in a pattern that makes the most sense to her and allows her to be a person rather than an image. The end of the film leaves her in a similar situation to where she was in the beginning, but she has survived various rites of passage and she has determined her own narrative. She sits on the curb by herself, now completely autonomous—no baby, no lover, no plan. But she is also more connected to all of the people in her life. She is, in the end, unable to escape relationships altogether, just the ones that threaten to tangle an individual within herself. Thus, in this film romance, sex, and love are negotiated and redefined. This is also important with other sexual conventions like mainstream definitions of virginity which are negotiated in a variety of ways in girls' film.

Defining and Redefining Virginity

Losing virginity is a necessary step toward adulthood, particularly in most teen and girls' films. In fact, in girls' films protagonists actively pursue this loss, often hoping to "just get it over with." For Stacy, in *Fast Times at Ridgemont High*, losing her virginity is an anticipated and welcome relief (even though it "hurt like hell"), and the situation is the same for Anna in *Whatever*, and Violet in *Ripe* (who both also hurt like hell);

it is something that has to happen when leading, or in order to lead, a sexual life—to become a woman. It is the first step in negotiating another level of teenage life and life in general. It makes everything more complicated, and, in many ways, it is the only coming of age that our society allows or acknowledges both in teen culture and adult culture. The obsession that mainstream culture has with teen sex and sexuality, let alone with virginity, comes across in the male-centered virgin movies of the '80s and beyond. But is also seeps over into girls' film in several different ways. In fact, to girls like Cher in *Clueless*, being a virgin is somewhat equal to a social death. And to other girls, like Odie in *All I Wanna Do*, losing her virginity is both a right and a way of getting back at her parents for sending her to an all-girls' school just as she was about to "do the deed." Thus, since virginity is a concept created to protect girls' "virtue," girls' negotiation of this concept in girls' film is important to understanding negotiations of sex and sexuality.

This obsession with virginity is one reason why narratives that deal with same-sex relationships are so threatening, even when packaged within mainstream conceptualizations of couplehood. Virginity, the (male) mainstream's marker of sexual maturity, is irrelevant in these films. But despite any irrelevance and regardless of marginalized portrayals of sexuality, the concept of virginity is a convention in almost every teen film and many girls' films because it goes hand in hand with teenage sex. However, films that defy, or cleverly manipulate the constructed concept of virginity do the most to subvert its meaning and cultural importance. For instance, *Saved!* a parody of a Christian high school, contests not only the meaning and importance of virginity, but also the way in which some Christian dogmas construct this concept. When Mary finds herself confronted with her boyfriend's aberrant sexuality, she is convinced that she must save him. She opts for premarital sex as the only means through which she can save his soul, underscoring the fact that too many Christians believe that being gay is a far worse sin than premarital sex. In a different example, in *Slums of Beverly Hills* Vivian actively takes control of her sexuality, using a vibrator that she and her cousin, Rita, freely and playfully toss around and sing into like a microphone in an earlier scene, for her first sexual experience. She practices the safest, and, at least to girls in film, some of the most satisfying sex.

Vivian is also in control when she has sex for the first time, perhaps because she has already negotiated sex on her own, with the help of Rita's vibrator. (Unlike most other girls in these films, she experiences the "big O" before she has intercourse.) Elliot is teaching her how to drive (and she is, appropriately, in the driver's seat) in an empty parking lot and when the cops approach, he tries to get her to stuff his pot (he's a dealer like Ricky) in her panties because the cops can't search a girl. At first Vivian refuses, but she suddenly tells Elliot to kiss her, to put on a romantic show for the cops. The cops disappear, but the scene doesn't end. An overhead shot passes by the car and Vivian and Elliot are naked, side by side, in the backseat. Elliot's car is his pride and joy and this scene subverts the role of the backseat in common myths about teenage sex. While Vivian and Elliot "do it" in the backseat, their sex is not typical of the usual backseat scenario (which often involves coercion, date rape, or worse). Afterwards, when Elliot finds blood on his seat, he panics. He asks, "Are you telling me I popped your cherry?" Vivian replies, "I didn't say that." And she didn't say it, but *he* knows it is true because he defines it this way as he rants about the pressure involved in such a ceremony, even though the act has already been completed. Vivian explains that she "just wanted to do it with some guy to get it over with. No ceremonies." Despite Elliot's reaction, Vivian has emerged unscathed and in perfect control of her situation. She hasn't been taken in by the myth, but he has.

While some use virginity as a plot device, few films take issue with virginity as a term or as a concept. For instance, in *American Pie* Vicky has her first orgasm after Kevin gains some new techniques, but she is still technically a virgin and stresses the decision whether or not to go "all the way." In *Scream*, virginity is central to the plot, and is a device of horror films that *Scream* mocks and parodies; however, neither the definition of virginity, nor its importance (or lack of importance) in teen life, are dealt with. And since Sydney's loss of virginity plays right into the plot, even this challenge to convention is glossed over. And other films ignore the related issues, but not the topic, which makes a statement about virginity as well. For instance, in *Bring It On* the issues of virginity or sex never come up despite the developing relationship between Torrence and Cliff. Nor does the issue come up when Sarah and her boyfriend make love in *Save the Last Dance* or when Daphne's father tries to explain to her what a coming out ball is all about. "Coming out as what?" she wants to know. The absent or veiled role of virginity in many girls' films has to do with the romanticization of sex as well as the tendency to push sex off-screen or post narrative, as previously discussed. Thus, films that do deal with virginity also have to deal with a number of other issues and a few films like *American Virgin*, *Saved!* and *The Virgin Suicides* use this convention in ways that challenge mainstream definitions and limitations.

American Virgin is an interesting take on the concept of virginity and its treatment by the mainstream, especially since Katrina's virginity is the focus of the film. In this film, Mena Suvari plays the daughter of a porn king who decides, against her father's wishes, to sell her virginity. Her reasons for doing so are plentiful: for her own independence, to get the initial act over with, to spite her ex-boyfriend who she thinks cheated on her, to get even with her father, and to make some money. In the end, only Katrina owns her virginity, and rather than sell it, she shares it only with her boyfriend. While this film empowers Katrina through sex and beyond sex, other films that negotiate this myth do so by delving below the surface of virginity to connect with some of the larger issues.

The Virgin Suicides not only complicates the idea of virginity in teen and girls' film, but also complicates many other elements of these genres as well since it deals with both literal and figurative forms of virginity and acts as a magnifying glass to the obsession that the mainstream dominant culture has with girls' virginity, and, by extension, their bodies, their sexuality and sometimes minds and hearts. Part of this results from the film's adaptation from book to screen. Of course the film cannot capture every element of the book. It doesn't capture the cloying feeling of death, decay, and dying. It doesn't reflect the total lack of the girls' voices in the book. And it only partially reflects the relationship between the narrator, the collective "we" of boys, and the Lisbon girls. And instead of showing the relationship between the girls' lives and the larger culture they lived within, the film seems to focus more on the girls' lives under the rules of the oppressive mother. This focus undermines some of the larger issues, but it does not negate them. There are certain elements that would be nearly impossible to adhere to. For instance, in the book the girls' thoughts and actions, and sometimes even their words are pieced together (or nostalgically remembered) by the narrator. In the film the girls must talk but the book's spirit is maintained as they are often simply talking amongst themselves—meaningless chatter, sounds of camaraderie.

The translation from book to film cannot, of course, be disregarded; but at the same time, once a book becomes a film, the original text is lost in its re-presentation. The audience for the film is larger, or at the very least, different from the audience of readers, and the teens (and even the adults) who watch the film may not even realize that it's based on a book. In fact, many films, and many teen films, were originally books or short stories like *Ella Enchanted, 10 Things I Hate About You, Clueless, Lost and Delirious,* and *Foxfire.* By looking at some of the themes in *The Virgin Suicides,* and the way in which this film differs from the novel, not only do we gain a better understanding of what virginity means, but we also get a better understanding of the ways in which girls' sexuality, and girls' films, are often dictated by the demands of a masculine culture and society.

The Lisbon sisters' limited autonomy has to be controlled and revealed only through rare glimpses in *The Virgin Suicides*. Thus, director Sophia Coppola uses images like this one of Lux (Kirsten Dunst) to portray glimpses of the girls that reveal only some parts of the girls. In the book the girls' lives are constructed and reconstructed through the pieces the male narrators scavenge. However, Coppola's female perspective infuses this films with another level of understanding.

The Virgin Suicides offers a fictional representation of the obsession that researchers have with teenage sexuality, as the narrator and his friends stalk and catalog the lives (or lack of lives) of the five Lisbon girls. Throughout the book and film, the narrator is "we" as the boys collectively take part in their obsession. They watch the windows for signs of life and collect material objects that they hope may bring them closer to the secret life of the Lisbon girls. They live vicariously through these girls who, as Therese says in one of the few verbal interactions they have with one of the Lisbon sisters, "just want to live. If anyone would let us" (132). They are denied life until they take it upon themselves to end that (lack) of life. Thus, their deaths are *the* virgin suicides; they are their own special case. The title reaffirms the girls' lack of autonomy. They are plural in death as much as they were in life. Only Lux asserts her autonomy in the only way she can—through her sexuality (which is, coincidentally, co-opted by the boys for their own second-hand enjoyment). However, Lux is the only one who acts at all. Perhaps this is because her autonomy, because it is sexual, is the only autonomy the boys' gaze sees. While Lux is not a virgin, she is still a part of the virgin suicides. The rest of the Lisbon sisters are virgins not simply because they haven't had sex, but because they have yet to experience life. They have been denied any autonomy or control in their lives, and they never will (which is, arguably, why Lux takes such an active role in her sexuality). Rather than fight for autonomy, and rather then being led to freedom by their saviors, together, they choose death. They have been denied a coming of age, let alone a coming of age outside of the gaze of their "researchers" or their parents. They will never experience life because they have been robbed of their valuable youth and the title freezes the girls in this virginal frame.

This would explain the difference between the interpretation of Lux's sexuality in the film versus the book. In the book, the motivation behind Lux's rooftop escapades is only a matter of speculation, and, thus, it holds more complexity and ambiguity. The film makes them seem more like a desperate attempt at gaining back what Trip Fontaine stole from her the night of the Homecoming dance when the two wandered off and had sex on the football field, especially since this event was what led to the girls' further (permanent and terminal) imprisonment. But this inference undercuts the sexual enigma that Lux is to the boys.

The boys are most fascinated by Lux as they watch her with man after man on her roof—"the premises of her confinement" (146)—and collect testimonies from these men. The voyeurs' obsession with Lux's sexuality continues to define their sexuality more than it explains hers. "For our own part, we learned a great deal about the techniques of love.... Years later, when we lost our own virginities, we resorted in our panic to pantomiming Lux's gyrations on the roof so long ago; and even now, if we were to be honest with ourselves, we would have to admit that it is always that pale wraith we make love to" (146–47). These adaptations and obsessions reflect the dominant male's obsession with (especially teen) sexuality, but the dominant can't always handle this obsession, especially if the fantasy pushes acceptable boundaries. Even while these boys are fascinated by Lux's rooftop escapades they recognize that "it was crazy to make love on the roof at any time, but to make love on the roof in winter suggested derangement, desperation, self-destructiveness far in excess of any pleasure snatched beneath the dripping trees" (149–50). Even as they condemn her, her stalkers recognize that for Lux it is not about pleasure. It is about actively taking something she has been denied—life. She does so desperately—imitating and inattentive—"a sense of playacting permeated much of her behavior" and "she didn't seem to like it much" (148). But this lack of her enjoyment does not stifle her status as myth and obsession, which is also telling of male dominant culture's threshold for women's enjoyment.

Thus, metaphorically, the boys in this book are society, a position that echoes JD's claim in *Heathers* that people will conclude that the school had to be blown up because the school was society. They are the public that wants to know everything they possibly can about the very private, and incredibly secret lives of these, and all girls. And like society, they fail. "We'd like to tell you with authority what it was like inside the Lisbon house, or what the girls felt being imprisoned in it. Sometimes, drained by this investigation, we long for some shred of evidence, some Rosetta stone that would explain the girls at last" (170). There is no magical Rosetta stone. What we know about the Lisbon girls is only what the boys have found through years of biased observation and more years of collecting data. Because of the nature of their observation, they realize (or imagine) too late that "the girls had been trying to talk to us all along, to elicit our help, but we'd been too infatuated to listen." They miss the voices of the girls, the only part of them with any real substance, the only part that is not partially (or fully) fabricated by the investigators. "Our surveillance had been so focused we missed nothing but a simple returned gaze" (199). Their surveillance uncovers tons of meaningless "facts," which are really only details, but they concern themselves with what they can understand—the silence of a gaze, the same gaze they refined.

As we read, we participate in their voyeurism as these girls, and everything around them, slowly decays. By reading this book, we are inactively and automatically brought into their gaze despite the fact that we have no power to direct it. We gaze, but we rarely listen. Watching the film we are all allowed into the girls' world, but is this version of voyeurism the same as when reading? The gaze we are required to take on as a part of the novel's narrative is a "dominant male look" (Williams 83)—one that sexualizes and freezes the subject. They are determined to figure the girls out. In fact, it is a discovery essential to the boys' present, future, and past lives as they face their own midlife crises. The boys are not only desperate to know the Lisbon sisters, they also want to help them. They want to be their princes in shining armor even as they sit, old and bald, crowded into their childhood tree house, lamenting the suicides that echo the death-like existence of themselves and their neighborhood. They search for answers, but have nothing new to give them these answers, so they continue to construct girls' lives out of dust and dreams. What the gaze ignores is the part of girls' lives and voices that are not mediated, that cannot be easily cut and pasted coherently onto a screen. The gaze the film requires is not as complex. We feel bad for the girls, but perhaps we identify more with the plight of the boys. They are trying to help, after all. They are attempting to rescue the girls from their staunch, repressive mother and impotent father. What else can *they* do?

In many ways, all teenage girls are the Lisbon sisters. "Who had known they talked so much, held so many opinions, jabbed at the world's sights with so many fingers? Between our sporadic glimpses of the girls they had been continuously living, developing in ways we couldn't imagine...." (124). There are no Rosetta stones that can explain what the dominant male gaze cannot unravel. Thus, on a larger scale, girls continue to have control of their own lives, opinions, sexuality, and destiny. But there is no material evidence that can define the lost adolescence of the Lisbon sisters and there is no material evidence that can define the lost adolescence of countless other (real and fictional) girls. Like the boys' gaze determines our picture of the lives and essence of the Lisbon sisters, the "dominant male look" or hegemonic gaze determines the "picture" of girls. In the film Lux exemplifies this. She is subject to soft-porn montages, fantasy scenes. This gaze so often determines and defines many of the images and narratives that construct what we know of teenage girls. We make sense of ourselves through these very narratives—the visual and written texts that we read so this culture that pins girls with its gaze and attempts to confine them in a standardized definition succeeds to a large extent. But while the gaze has been concerned with its own constructions, its own representations of girls and women, girls have been "continuously living, developing in ways [the hegemon cannot] imagine."

Reconsidering the concept and trope of virginity in girls' films, particularly through *The Virgin Suicides*, it becomes clear that a girls' virginity does not have to be simply a sexual concept, but also a social and cultural concept as well. Girls' sexuality is often dictated, defined, and controlled through definitions of virginity, definitions that hold social and cultural weight and are controlled by mainstream conventions and expectations. But until girls contest these definitions in verbal and physical, social and spiritual ways, these definitions will continue to control girls' sexuality individually and collectively. The attitude, voice, and awareness that girls utilize are a few means, and confronting other stereotypes like those of whores and "bad girls," who are often juxtaposed to the virgins and the "good girls," is also important, as we shall see in the next section. But these definitions are also contested when girls actively pursue sex and sexuality, as we shall see in the final section of this chapter.

Reconsidering the Bad Girl

Throughout this book the trope and stereotype of the bad girl has been discussed in a variety of contexts. However, while the bad girl may be blonde or brunette, while she may be lower class or upper class, while she may be into the arts or into fashion, she is inevitably sexually active. Sometimes this sexual activity takes on classic stereotypes of the slut, and other times this sexual activity is assumed (by other characters) or from signs (clues planted for the viewer) of attitude or dress. Sometimes the bad girl, the slut, is victorious, like Suzie in *Wild Things* who plays the roles of both slut and victim as part of her master plan. She plays these roles because they are the roles expected of her; she sees this and uses it to her advantage. Other times, like in *Brokedown Palace*, the so-called bad girl sacrifices herself, showing that she wasn't really the bad one at all. And in the case of films like *Jawbreaker* or *Cruel Intentions*, the bad girls are stripped of their power and humiliated, a punishment that can, in the realm of teen culture, be more painful (at least metaphorically) than death.

Horror films are one genre that rely upon the conventions of virginity and promiscuity for their plots. Thus, these films also often rely upon the bad girl villain or victim. However, just because a horror or thriller film has a female protagonist, this does not necessarily mean that it is a girls' film or that it is a powerful or empowering narrative for girls, though they sometimes can be so. Instead, in these fantastic spaces many horror films focus their plots around teens, but few of these films offer power or autonomy for girls. Most often girls are the victims, being chased and frightened by the masculine presence of the killer. And eventually, if these girls "deserve" to be punished, they are killed. And even though some girls, the heroes of the film, or the sole survivors, are spared, their power and autonomy are still compromised in some way. For instance, Julie in *I Know What You Did Last Summer* is the moral character in the plot, the one who feels the most distraught about what happened last summer. She survives because she has this kind of character, but she is also subject to the constant and eternal harassment by what are, essentially, the demon or demons from her past. Likewise, while Sydney, in *Scream*, has many powerful moments, and complicates many conventions of horror films, she also falls victim to other conventions. For instance, she trusts her boyfriend and killer enough to finally move their relationship from "PG" to "R." This move is one trope of horror films that is subverted, but in the end, she needs help from her "enemy," Gail Weathers. Thus, while this film seems to subvert the catfight trope and a strong female protagonist emerges, it also follows the genre's expectations as Sydney's ghosts follow her to college and beyond.

But the bad girl is more often cited not strictly in horror films, but in thrillers like *Wicked*, *The Crush*, and other films that rely solely on the evilness of the bad girl and, in at least these two cases, an untamable sexuality focused on older men. In *The Crush*, the protagonist won't take no for an answer and attempts to ruin the object of her obsessive crush and his life and family as well. And in *Wicked*, Julia Stiles plays a selfish, self-absorbed girl who has all sorts of problems despite her comfy suburban life. When her mother is murdered, Ellie takes her place as the woman of the house in an eerie, chilling self-transformation. She transforms not from girl to woman, but from daughter to mother as well. When Ellie is finally defeated, her younger sister steps into her place, continuing this disturbing look at girls' obsessions with the adult world. Both of these films, and others, grant girls no power or authority despite their focus on a female protagonist. Instead, these protagonists are set up as being crazy in some way.

Other films like *The Glass House*, *Buffy the Vampire Slayer*, and *The Craft* provide a female protagonist who does not fall into good- or bad-girl traps and cannot be considered a slut, since her role is largely sexless. Instead, these girls are responsible for the safety of their families, towns, or the world. For instance, in *The Glass House*, Ruby, despite her tank top throughout all of the chase scenes, constructs this protagonist outside of her sexuality, in a familial, rather than sexual, role. In this film, Ruby not only has to save herself, but she also has to save her brother in the process of solving the mystery of what happened to her parents as well as the mystery of who her new parents are. And in *Buffy the Vampire Slayer*, its heavy theme is lightened through the comedy genre as the mall culture of the '80s and early '90s is overshadowed by the necessity to do "the right thing." Buffy cannot deny her calling, her responsibility, even though she might like the comparably cushy life of her peers. These films, and others, provide spaces within this otherwise oppressive genre where girls can have horrors without being whores. However, these films do not challenge the binary sexuality that they require.

The Craft also provides such an empowered, (mostly) sexless space as it focuses on four girls and the power they find, and use, and eventually misuse, together. In this film, the protagonist, Sarah, must use her powers, since she is the only one with real, natural powers, to put the other witches back into their place. While this film includes elements of feminist bonding rituals, female power, (stereotyped) alternative spiritualities, and other more progressive elements, it also relies upon the good versus evil dichotomy as Sarah faces off with Nancy. Good wins out over evil and the followers are returned to their bland status while Nancy is straitjacketed and shown writhing in an asylum. Sarah, on the other hand, holds a natural power that none of her friends had. Only through her were they able to make things happen. Only through her was Nancy able to fulfill the scary-bitch role that she was playing, proving that the only evil that exists in black magic is the evil in the heart of the witch. Thus, the importance of the exceptional individual is reinforced, which also makes this powerful, responsible, autonomous girl the exception rather than the rule. The implication is, unfortunately, that the average girl can't wield power or develop empowerment, at least not without outside help. And, like in *Mean Girls*, the evil power may have been destroyed, and there might be the illusion of peace, but Sarah, like Cady, is ready to demonstrate her power when need be.

This is almost the opposite of thrillers like *Ginger Snaps*, which take this genre beyond any of the previously mentioned films not only because its story is unique, but also because female rites of passage and sexuality are written into the plot elements. Thus, this film is infused with female power and empowerment as it reflects mainstream fears of sexuality within its narrative. For instance, when Ginger gets her period she simultaneously gains a kind of power and a kind of disadvantage as she shatters her ordinary life for the extraordinary, and inevitably tragic, qualities of the werewolf. This power transforms her in exhilarating and dangerous ways. She becomes a bad girl not only through her sexuality, but also through her animalistic and demonistic transformation. As her sister, Brigitte, fights to save Ginger's life, Ginger lets herself be taken over by this new power and enjoys the kind of sexually charged existence that her previous life lacked. She becomes sexy to the boys who had never before noticed her. But in this attraction there is also power, and this is something else that Ginger never had. She uses this power, as the werewolf must—voraciously. And she uses it to her advantage not only with the boys who ignored her, but also with the girls (the queen bees) who made her previous life miserable. And she also uses it in an attempt to escape her suburban hellhole.

Not only does this film contest mainstream expectations of girls' sex and sexuality, but it also infuses suburban angst with the not-so-ordinary elements of the thriller. Thus, this film is fantasy fused with fear and conflict, not only offering horror without whores, but also contesting this and other labels. In fact, Ginger's sister, Brigitte, becomes the protagonist of the film as she searches for a cure for her sister, even if only out of fear of being left alone in her suburban hellhole. And this process, which ultimately fails, is a coming of age for Brigitte. Not only does Ginger leave her alone, but Brigitte also breaks out of the boundaries of her previous existence as she tries to save Ginger. There is no happy ending here as Brigitte faces the future she always feared. However, the bad-girl persona is challenged here since Ginger's badness is not something inherent, like Nancy's badness, which is augmented through abuse of magic. Ginger's sexuality, power, and empowerment is what is augmented. And even though it leads to her undoing, this is more of a statement of the pressures put on young women than it is about the badness that comes with sexuality.

Ultimately, the kinds of sexuality found in the films described in this section, and the previous sections of this chapter, are connected to different issues and concerns than the films in the following section. While it is important to consider the ways in which romance and sex do and do not intersect, and to consider how definitions of virginity are contested, and how sexuality is negotiated in relatively safe environments, it is crucially important to consider the unsexy realities that girls face every day in life and less often in film, especially mainstream teens' and girls' films. Some of these unsexy realities, like STIs and HIV and AIDS are rarely, if ever, discussed, and are more often alluded to in veiled ways like in *10 Things I Hate About You* when Bianca assumes that teen pregnancy, and not disease, results from lack of using a condom, or when Jefferson ignorantly assumes that since Christopher is sleeping with another man he must be gay, and if he's gay he must have AIDS. Obviously the discussions surrounding sex and sexuality in the first half of this book partially reflect this lack. But what they don't reflect is the multiple ways in which unsexy realities are negotiated outside, and at the edges, of mainstream films.

Unsexy Realities: Negotiating the Consequences

Much of the negotiation of sexuality discussed thus far has focused on the portrayals and constructions of girls' sexuality and girls' negotiation of some of the myths surrounding girls' sexuality like the stud-slut dichotomy and mainstream definitions of virginity. However, sexuality is also negotiated through some of the consequences of sex and sexuality. These unsexy realities are some of the realities that lie behind the mainstream's shunning of pregnant teens and the mainstream's lack of adequate, unbiased discussions of sexually transmitted infections, particularly HIV and AIDS. Very few films deal with consequences of sex other than in its relation to a social stigma or pregnancy, which is why one independent teen film (tellingly not a girls' film) stands out from the others, not only because of its treatment of its subject manner, but also because of its focus on sex and the consequence of HIV and AIDS, a treatment many find to be problematic.

While *Kids* is not a mainstream film, it is certainly one that caught the attention of the mainstream because of its treatment of sex as well as the way in which *Kids* presents sex. According to one critic, "*Kids* pulls the rug out from under white-bread notions of what makes some teens tick—and exposes a world that is at once fascinating and deeply disturbing" (Steele). *Kids* is one of the most controversial of all teen films, so controversial that Blockbuster Video refuses to carry it and it was rated NC-17 for its theatrical release. Censoring this film is the worst way to deal with its controversial and realistic content. (It is, perhaps, so controversial because it is so realistic, or at least tries to be so.) It is this fascinating and disturbing world that does not subvert mainstream notions of teens, but simply reinforces them while hiding beneath the guise of a realistic and relevant film. While I don't think that *Kids* is realistic or relevant as a whole film, it does have points of relevance and it does deal with issues that few other films touch. Further, the world that *Kids* brings to light is not far from my experience as a teen or the other disturbing stories that are covered by the media like the Spur Posse or like "Frontline's" "The Lost Children of Conyers" which seems to be a suburban alternative to the New York City setting in *Kids*.

In *Kids*, Telly makes it his quest in life to deflower virgins—the younger, the better. Telly's commentary on virgins allows girls no room for negotiation and shrinks them to nothing more than objects—"No diseases. No loose-as-a-goose pussy. No skank. No nothing. Just pure pleasure." The film opens with Telly smooth-talking his current victim, a very young girl who is assured by his persuasive words. But one thing that is clear from Telly's words as much as from his sexual activity on screen, is that the "pure pleasure" is his alone. While this opening scene is immediately disturbing, it also reflects parts of similar scenes in other girls' films like *Ripe* and *Whatever*. And, while Telly is the protagonist, as well as the perpetrator, one of his victims is the center of the narrative.

After being tested for HIV, Jenny searches all over New York for Telly. She wants to tell him, but what Jenny doesn't know is that Telly is already on a quest for yet another victim. And when Jenny finally finds him, she is too late. She collapses on a nearby couch (under the influence of a mind-altering drug) and she is later raped by Telly's best friend (one of the few characters who will share Telly's fate because he forced it upon himself). In this film is yet another world where girls are consumed and disposed of and Jenny is powerless to change her fate or anyone else's. Because Telly has earned his fate, it is easy to dismiss him. But what about the lives of the girls? How many girls are literally or figuratively killed not only by the boys and men like Telly, but also by circumstances that they cannot escape? *Kids* deals with these questions as little as it deals with the realities and implications of HIV and AIDS. But few films deal with these issues at all, and only a few more deal with issues related to another consequence—pregnancy.

In the mainstream, pregnant girls are visually stigmatized as a statistic of a social problem, a social problem labeled as teenage pregnancy, despite the age of the father. This is yet another example of the ways in which the double standard holds girls responsible for behavior that the hegemon cannot control as girls are blamed for something done *to* them. In general, the pregnant girl, in and out of film, is a transgressor of the limits of cultural control by her visibility, which makes her sexuality blatantly visible as well. As Nathanson writes, "Pregnancy can be terminated by abortion, but there is no action that can eliminate the association of pregnancy with sexual activity" (5). But despite this treatment, pregnant girls also have support networks like the cheerleading squad in *Sugar and Spice*, a younger sister *Manny and Lo*, and friends like Cassandra and Roland in *Saved!*

The fact that very few teen films deal with the issue of pregnancy, and even fewer deal with it seriously, reinforces the mainstream's lack of acceptance for girls who become pregnant in their teens, despite their circumstances. However, there seems to be even less acceptance for pregnant girls when they are not white, considering that all of the mainstream films in this study that deal with pregnancy, and many of the alternative narratives as well, feature pregnant white teens (like *Fast Times*, *Sugar and Spice*, *The Opposite of Sex*, and *Saved!*) and white teens as mothers. Some of these mainstream films that deal with teen pregnancy, like *Where the Heart Is* and *Riding in Cars with Boys*, begin with protagonists in their teens, but the story quickly moves forward into the future to deal with their struggles as mothers who are no longer teens. Thus, the whole issue of teen pregnancy is avoided since the mothers in these films are only temporarily teens. This could be a powerful statement since it means that a mother's age is not as important as her circumstances; however, since teen pregnancy is such a hot topic politically, these films gloss over the important implications that teen pregnancy has within mainstream assumptions and discussions.

Saved! is one mainstream film that deals with teen pregnancy in more complicated ways than most mainstream teen films. As previously discussed, Mary thinks that having sex with her gay boyfriend will save him from the disease of gayness. But she does not save him, and after his

In *Saved!* Cassandra and Mary face off in the bathroom as Cassandra is the only one at Mary's school with the knowledge, and the interest or attention, to notice Mary's predicament. While in some films this "bad girl" might use Mary's secret to ruin her life and her reputation, Cassandra becomes one of Mary's true and supportive friends. She and Roland (Macaulay Culkin) provide the social framework that Mary's hypocritical Christian friends can't provide. In these ways, this film offers an important counter to stories about parents' banishment of pregnant daughters. And in the end, good will is contagious.

parents send him to Mercy House, a treatment center reminiscent of the one in *But I'm a Cheerleader*, Mary finds out that she is pregnant. Because she thinks that her mom won't be able to deal with it, and because she knows that her Christian high school will definitely not be able to deal with it, Mary conceals her pregnancy. And because teen pregnancy is as rare as Jews and atheists, no one, except Cassandra, the Jewish transfer student, realizes her secret. Not coincidentally, Cassandra, and her boyfriend, Roland (the cynical atheist), are the only ones who help Mary while also helping to keep her secret. Through this secret a friendship is formed along with a new conceptualization of family and Christianity. And, in the end, what Mary conceals becomes the blessing that unites them all.

While Mary's negotiation of her pregnancy stems from the specific factors surrounding her decisions, particularly her religion and her family, in many girls' films girls are given more room to negotiate the limits of their visual stigmatization as well as their inevitable parenthood. While abortion, adoption, and other reasonable strategies are also options in film, many films portray girls who find other options, some of which are viable, and others that are not as viable, but end up being transformative for the girl. The girls in films like *The Opposite of Sex, Just Another Girl on the I.R.T.*, and *Manny and Lo* find creative ways of dealing with their individual situations that subvert both the social problem notion and give the pregnant teenager options that she doesn't normally have in life. The characters don't get abortions not because of politics, but because pregnancy allows these films to explore the complications and tribulations that accompany childbirth and, more generally, coming of age. These celluloid girls' solutions may not work in real life, but they are still valid commentaries on a real problem; and they are solutions that don't undermine, expose, or attempt to define and confine the girl.

In *Just Another Girl on the I.R.T.* Chantel lets the viewer know immediately that she is going places, specifically to college and on to be a doctor. She says "my life is gonna be way different," but the title of the film assures us that her life will not be any different. Like her friend points out, "Lots of girls have babies in high school," but Chantel refuses to believe that she is like other high school girls. Chantel thinks she can avoid her parents' fate by having big dreams and going after those dreams with a vengeance. But her relentless pursuit of education as a means out of the projects only gets her so far. One reason Chantel has trouble coming to terms with her pregnancy is because if she admits that she is pregnant, she admits that she is just another girl and she seals her fate. She'll end up like her mother (and, thus, her family), stranded in the projects—the place Chantel wants most to escape. She'll be just another part of a structural problem that plagues girls in her social position, rather than having a personal problem which she can, hopefully, solve on her own. To cope, Chantel ignores her pregnancy because, at the time, it is the easiest thing to do.

At first she goes about "business as usual" (which includes having sex), saying directly to the camera, "Maybe I'm not pregnant. Maybe it's just a dream and it'll go away." Chantel tries to avoid her mother's suspicion by throwing away food (that way she'll just think I'm a pig and not pregnant) and buying two sizes of clothes (one in the size she used to be and one in the size she is now). She also hides her pregnancy from her best friend and she uses the money that her boyfriend, Ty, gives her for an abortion to go on a shopping spree. In many ways, this shows why the mall may not be the best place for a girl to remake herself. Chantel buys things to try to avoid the circumstances of her life, but the mall is not a substitute for the problems she faces. But since Chantel's problems are the problems of "just another girl," the easy solutions that the mall offers won't do any girl justice. But all of these attempts at denial are useless and she ends up screaming and writhing in premature labor when the inevitable finally happens.

Chantel is just as unprepared for the inevitable as her boyfriend is. Before and after she gets pregnant Chantel may be occupied by her dreams for the future, but these dreams don't deter her from the distractions of adolescence. Chantel dumps the boy who likes her for another one who has a car—he can, literally, take her places, and perhaps she hopes he can also figuratively take her places as well, or at least to the mall, or his place. In a conversation with her friend, it is clear that neither girl knows much (or anything) about contraception, and when Chantel discovers she's pregnant she goes to a counselor. However, she decides to ignore the counselor's advice and desire to help, until she can't ignore it anymore and she ends up delivering her baby in Ty's bed. Hysterical, Chantel tries to make Ty "take it away." She sees the baby as the end to her future and the beginning of her life stuck right where she is and right where her parents have always been. Ty takes it away, but by the time he returns, she has changed her mind. She ends up able to deal with the life she thought she could avoid by ignoring it. Like so many other girls, she ends up on a path she didn't think she'd be on. And at the end of the film she tells the camera how she and Ty are "getting their shit together." In many ways Chantel ends up "just another girl," but at the same time, she has ceased being a girl altogether. She's a mother and she's going to community college, building a life by carving it out of reality, not her dreams.

Other girls don't have the luxury of dreams in the first place. For instance, when *Manny and Lo* begins, both girls have been abandoned by their mother's death. While Lo is old enough to remember all of their mother's flaws, Manny can only try to remember her and she sprays the sheets with her mother's deodorant in an attempt (or an excuse) not to forget. Lo has kidnapped Manny from her foster home in an attempt (or under the guise) to find her good parents. But the two are running not from those who want to find them, as Lo pretends, but from those who don't even care to look. The two girls steal their food and other necessities from convenience stores and stay in model homes or in parks. As the two practice for Lo's modest, yet impractical, dream of becoming a flight attendant (which involves her holding a tray and balancing on Manny's back to experience the effects of turbulence), Manny is afraid to tell Lo why she doesn't want to participate anymore—she noticed Lo's weight gain. Of course Lo gets angry and tries to deny that her weight gain is anything to be alarmed about. But Lo knows that the plan has to change.

Rather than submit to the "normal" way to do things, Manny and Lo kidnap a baby authority—a woman (Elaine) who knows everything about babies. Elaine is, in many ways, the adult version of Manny and Lo. She has no children and her family hardly notices when she disappears. Elaine also has all of the good parent criteria that Lo is looking for, but since Lo is, as Manny explains, one of those people who "won't trust somebody unless that somebody's wearing a chain on their ankles," she makes Elaine prove her worth. And as much control as Lo has as a kidnapper, Elaine knows what Lo needs physically as well as emotionally. Part of Lo's coping strategy is the character she has made for herself. She is tough, impenetrable, a juvenile delinquent, and she is annoyed with anyone who shatters her illusions. Lo plays her part the way she thinks it should be played and she gets angry when Manny (and later, Elaine) won't play along. When the girls go to the store for supplies, Elaine escapes and starts a signal fire. The girls catch her just in time and Lo struggles with Elaine until Elaine stops at the sight of Lo's protruding belly. It is the visibility of Lo's situation that makes Elaine realize why she has been kidnapped, and also makes her stop trying to escape. And because Lo is "one of those people and ... Elaine knew it," Elaine plays along with Lo's kidnapper scenario so that Lo will let her help. To earn Lo's trust, Elaine pretends she is still trying to escape while she cooks dinner, tends to Lo's condition, and even takes a hostage of her own when the owner of the house they are hiding in comes home unexpectedly. But when Elaine's hostage escapes, Lo is angry (mostly because hostages aren't supposed to take hostages). The girls are forced to move on and Lo, still clinging to the little power she has, decides to leave Elaine behind. Despite Manny's disapproval, Lo abandons Elaine at the side of the road.

The two drive on, but Lo soon goes into labor. Lo stops the car and she and Manny sit in the middle of the road waiting for someone, anyone, to come to their rescue. When no one comes, Manny finally convinces Lo that no one is going to come and Manny drives the car back to where they dropped Elaine. Lucky for the girls, Elaine has been waiting for them and she knows exactly what to do. In the end, Manny and Lo find exactly what they were looking for even as they were trying to run away—family—as Elaine gets in the driver's seat and tells everyone to buckle up. Lo drives the car throughout the movie, but when Lo goes into labor, Manny has to take the wheel in order to get help for Lo and to get back to Elaine. When Elaine takes her place at the wheel, it is clear that Lo has let Elaine into her life in a more important role than hostage.

Thus, despite the girls' unconventional negotiation, this film undermines teens' ability to be mothers when it reasserts adult authority and restructures this family in a romantic resolution to a real issue. But Lo is also successful in that she was looking not only for a good parent for her sister, Manny, but also a future for herself and her unborn child. Elaine takes over this unconventional family with no judgments, only love.

Like Lo and Chantel, in *The Opposite of Sex* Dedee also has a plan to deal with her pregnancy, though she takes her plan further than either of these girls do, and tries to avoid romance in the process. Chantel and Lo both ignore their pregnancy for as long as they can; their plans change only when they have no other choice. But Dedee is calculating from the beginning, and her plan changes as she digs herself further in. She gets in over her head, but in all this calculating and maneuvering, she figures out some pieces of the bigger picture. This whole time she's only been thinking about what she can get out of her pregnancy, and she knows that she doesn't have enough to put into a child. But she also realizes that what's important isn't just her immediate needs, but the needs of those around her, and, ultimately, what's best for her child. This concern also comes through in *Belly Fruit*.

In general, independent films are less accessible than mainstream films. Hollywood Video is one mega-chain that stocks a line of independent films called First Rites. One film in this line is *Belly Fruit*, a film written, directed, and produced by women who work with pregnant teens. The film opens with a director's note where they explain why they made the film. Of all of the teen films regarding pregnancy, *Belly Fruit* is one of the most realistic and the most in touch with the problems that face girls from different backgrounds when they have the same problem in common. While there are some problematic aspects of the representations in this film (some of which are discussed in the previous section about race), *Belly Fruit*, for the most part, portrays typical scenarios without falling into stereotypes, and captures some of the subtleties of adolescence that other teen and girls' films don't. The narrative switches back and forth among the stories of three girls at different stags of their sexual, social, and personal development. All three of the girls are young and all three are working class, but each girl is racially and socially different from the others. Rather than hitting the viewer over the head with judgments about these girls, the way in which the stories develop, intertwined with one another, draws the viewers' attention to the larger issues while keeping these issues very much grounded in the real, albeit fictionalized, experiences of girls.

The ways in which these three stories complement each other and contradict each other are interesting. For instance, when 14-year-old Shanika learns of her pregnancy, she celebrates, thinking that this means that she and Damon can be together and that she can move out of the group home. When the doctor asks her if she knows who the father is, she says forcefully, "Yeah! I ain't no slut!" This shows that girls hold conceptions and misconceptions of who is and is not considered a slut, just as much as adults, and that sex only qualifies one as a slut in certain circumstances. And when Cely says that she and Oscar want to raise Angel right, she is automatically making the assumption that is made by the status quo—the best way to raise a child is with two parents—a man and a woman, one mother and one father. However, neither of these judgments overpower the film because each girl's situation is different, if not unique. This difference comes through in many ways, including the girls' stories and narration.

Each of the girls have small bits of narration when their voices come through at the end of the film, and each girl's experience teaches her a lesson, a rite of passage. From Christina's story we see that she has a supportive mother who is there for her in limited ways throughout the narrative, often more as a sister than as a mother. But however her mother may be lacking, she is more than Shanika has and is more accessible than Aracely's mother. And in the end, her mother is key in her story just as much as Shanika's lack of a mother is painfully obvious at the end of her story. From Aracely's story we see her strength as she chooses to be with her baby's father rather than remain a child, with her own child, under her father's watchful eye. Because her father refuses to accept her baby's father (Oscar) Aracely moves out, despite the fact they have trouble making ends meet, which puts a different kind of pressure on her (and Oscar) than her father does. In her final narration Cely reveals that now that she and Oscar are together "it's not all romantic all the time." They just "know that they want to be together and raise Angel right." Thus, Cely and Oscar have the only story which comes close to a conventional happy ending.

And as the film concludes, and the girls have said their piece, some of the issues revealed through the narrative are underscored by the statistics that are flashed on the screen.

- 489,211 births occurred to teenagers in the U.S. in 1998
- More than 50 percent of teen mothers are victims of sexual molestation or rape
- 66 percent of fathers are legal adults

These statistics not only underscore the themes in the narrative, but they also show that this problem of "teen" pregnancy is both an adult problem and a social problem as well. However, despite the victimization of Shanika and Christina, they remain cognizant of their situations. Christina realizes that she must be doing the right thing since everyone says she is, but she also realizes that she doesn't have the means or the resources to care for her child. And Shanika tries to displace the pity that the general public and the specific viewing audience might have for her, or for girls like her. She closes the film's narrative with the statement: "Everybody be looking at me all sorry and shit. But I'm like, you should respect me. I'm gonna be a mother." It is, ultimately, respect that is lacking from arguments about teen pregnancy, and about teens and teen girls more generally. And, ultimately, respect leads to self-respect, which can lead to empowered sexuality, and beyond.

Empowering Sexuality

The power of sexuality that is used as a tool to manipulate boys and girls in teen and girls' films, and the power and empowerment found through pregnancy for characters like Mary in *Saved!* are different from empowering sexuality. In mainstream popular culture the two are easily confused because one of the few powers that girls can find in this market is as a sexual object. And girls, like Britney Spears and Lindsay Lohan, are encouraged to grow up fast. Thus, the encouragement here breeds sexuality that is tightly controlled and highly marketable. But when sexuality is deviant or worse, autonomous or empowered, it is dangerous to the mainstream and the girl's sexuality becomes a threat to the larger structures of corporate capital and its connections. Thus, the dominant, the hegemon, the mainstream, controls girls' (and women's') sexuality through myths like virginity and the double standard, as well as individual and state violence, and other means.

To review, again and again, in mainstream teen and girls' films, the slut character, or a character with slutty characteristics, like behavior or dress, is punished and the virginal, in behavior or appearance, are rewarded. The classic slut character appears all throughout teen and girls' films, and she is recognized by boys and girls alike, but in different ways and for different reasons. For instance, in *10 Things I Hate About You*, Bianca makes it perfectly clear what kind of girls get pregnant and Shanika in *Belly Fruit* backs this assessment adamantly. And in *She's All That*, Zach's sister asks him who the "rebound skank" is when she hears that he broke up with Taylor. But in *Belly Fruit*, Christina is considered a slut because she sleeps with, it seems, any and all of the boys at her school.

In one scene, after throwing up in a bathroom stall, Christina is confronted with graffiti on another stall that proclaims Christina as the biggest slut in school. These are only a few of the ways that we participate in our own subjugation. Often the socially and culturally charged insult of slut is used to exact all kinds of violence, whether or not it fits. Rarely is this term critically contested. And never is the term considered as it is in books like *The Ethical Slut*. Instead, for instance, in *Jawbreaker*, Courtney, the villain and new queen bee after Liz's death, is into kink and bullies around her lover before she has sex with a dead man in order to defile the reputation of the friend she just accidentally murdered. This bad-girl attitude only goes so far since at the end of this teen flick, the student body jeers her off the stage after she has been crowned homecoming queen. It is made clear that she is just plain evil and her sexuality supposedly matches.

Despite these stereotypes of sexual girls and women, and the lack of mainstream space where these stereotypes are, or can be, contested, there are many ways in which the girls in film negotiate sexuality. This negotiation not only explodes these stereotypes, but also reworks old, tired, limited and limiting conceptualizations of female sexuality. For instance, in the movie *Wild Things,* a film that relies upon male fantasies like catfights and threesomes, the bad girl is the smartest and the strongest, and while she appears to be one of the victims, she turns out to be the victor when the entire plot unfolds. What seemed to be manipulative sex turns out to be the terms of her master plan. But Suzie's power and empowerment in this film are also not the same as empowering sexuality—a sexuality that allows girls to define and redefine the slut, to explore and pursue pleasure on their terms, to challenge the restrictions on sexuality from peers, adults, and the culture at large, and to redefine what constitutes sex and sexuality. This empowering of sexuality takes place in many girls' films like *Slums of Beverly Hills, Coming Soon, Virtual Sexuality, All Over Me, Show Me Love,* and even in boys' films like *American Pie.* While a variety of films include bits and pieces of empowering sexuality on girls' terms, whether or not these terms conflict with the mainstream, a few films focus strictly on empowering narratives focused on sexuality such as *Virtual Sexuality, Coming Soon,* and *Secretary.* And other films like *Lost and Delirious, All Over Me,* and *Show Me Love* push discussions of sexuality to the edge of the mainstream, and beyond, as they consider love and friendship between girls. Collectively, these films provide a sketch of ways we might begin to imagine what are currently very limited bounds of sexuality as well as ideology, particularly within mainstream America.

Sometimes such alternative coming-of-age narratives for girls are found in the unlikeliest of places—in narratives focused on boys. For instance, despite its resemblance to the "virgin movies" of the '80s, *American Pie* is worlds past its predecessors where girls were only allowed to be the pie, and not allowed to eat a piece for themselves. Women and girls are still portrayed in these stereotypical roles as sexual objects, but girls are also negotiating this status while simultaneously providing new sexual fronts where girls not only have power, but are also empowered, often in the process. Or, as in the case of *The Girl Next Door*, she empowers the male protagonist. In empowering Matthew, Danielle has to shatter some of the porn-star myths that get played out in typical boys' narratives. She doesn't play into his, or anyone else's, sexual fantasies, except as she is a recycled version of the "hooker with a heart of gold," like Julia Roberts in *Pretty Woman*. Thus, Danielle becomes yet another girl in need of rescue, and Matt steps up to play this role in *his* coming-of-age narrative.

In *American Pie*, the girls are not only allowed to talk about, think about, and initiate sex, but they are given an advantage on the playing field of the virgin landscape of four (somewhat clueless) high school boys. In this narrative that is clearly focused on the sexual pact of Kevin, Jim, Finch, and Chris (Oz) to lose their virginity before high school is over (last chance: prom night), the girls are hardly powerless. The boys desperately pursue dates and are humiliated again and again (and often by each other), but they all score in the end, despite their prior humiliation. But the girls aren't humiliated, at least not in the same ways, and they score as well, sometimes in a different game and on a different playing field.

Jim, the most sexually inexperienced of them all (he doesn't even know what third base *feels* like), has an appropriate end to his high school days; he is, to his pleasant surprise, used by Michelle, the girl with a thousand band camp stories. Though Jim is convinced all night that prom night is not going to be *the* night, he doesn't realize that the ball isn't in his court. Michelle's been waiting for sex the whole movie, and she is exactly what the bumbling Jim needs—a woman to take control and tell him what to do. In this way, Michelle is a male fantasy—a nerd who is also an aggressive sexpot. But Michelle also subverts this myth as she takes her sexuality into her own hands. The popular kids shun her from their parties, but when she has the opportunity, she wants a piece of the pie just as much as the boys do. While Jim has been searching for any pie and can only hope that Michelle might be the one he will score with, he fails to realize that he can just as easily be pie to Michelle. When Michelle is the user, the outcome of the scenario is "cool." The roles have been reversed, and Jim is on his back. Michelle even uses his prior embarrassment to dominate him, telling him to use two condoms so he won't come as quickly this time. He is powerless, but this is exactly what he needs—to slip into manhood rather than force his way through.

While *American Pie* focuses around Jim's inadequacies as he searches for the figurative "apple pie" and embarrasses himself with the literal pie, it also falls into some of the same male fantasies as movies from the past, like Finch's James Bond–like seduction of Stiffler's mom, or the eastern European girl, Nadia, who strips down in Jim's bedroom, walks around nearly naked, looks through his stuff, finds his porn, and proceeds to "go downstairs" as one of the many viewers of the Internet link puts it. In a movie like *Revenge of the Nerds*, such a viewing would be the source of profit, pleasure, or performance, but instead, in *American Pie*, it becomes premature ejaculation—twice—while nearly the entire student body watches. On this screen, the fantasy of the European sexpot produces the outcome destined for any overly horny, adolescent male who finds a nearly naked, masturbating girl in his bed—not the sexual adventures of fantasy and film, but premature ejaculation, the reality that *American Pie* mocks. Jim's sexual failure becomes the punch line to his joke of an adolescent life. To use his father's comedic euphemisms, Jim keeps "banging [that] tennis ball against a brick wall" instead of hitting it to a partner. But, in the end, the wall that Jim keeps hitting isn't as solid as it seemed to be. Although *American Pie* is the teenage boy's equivalent to a romance—they all score and fulfill this rite of passage—the girls in the film are the ones who are strong, empowered, and who come of age with or without the help of the boys. Vikki is introduced as she urges Kevin to open the envelope that holds her future. When he assures her that she got in, her response to the good news is telling Kevin that she loves him. Although she doesn't fully realize it, Vikki's whole relationship with Kevin is caught up in her plans for her future, as evidenced in her choice of when to say those important words. Her coming of age is subsumed by their sexual relationship because she thinks she can't go to college as a virgin. She might end up "doing it with some totally random guy who totally turns out to be a jerk ... and [she'll] wish [she] would have done it with Kevin." This is a fate Vikki imagines after Jessica confirms that "it" hurts. She says, "The first time you do it, you know, it hurts. But then you do it again, and again, and it starts to feel good, really good." So obviously, if Vikki ever hopes to enjoy sex in the future, she better do something in the present when she has a chance to take care of the preliminaries. Even these reasons aren't enough without Jessica's supportive words: "You're ready. You're a woman. Look at you. You're ready for sex." But, when it comes to the act, Vikki isn't totally ready until she hears "the words," which reveals the lack of romance these words can have.

Jessica is, perhaps, the most empowered and autonomous female (or male) character in this film. She is experienced, but she has not been obliterated by her experience; she has been made stronger. She has fallen prey to the talk and the act, but she is now free to keep her options open. At the prom, while everyone else is subject to the pitiful dronings of the band, Jessica walks around with headphones on—impervious to the cheesy cover band the rest of the crowd is forced to endure. She chooses her entertainment like she chooses everything—independently. Jessica's autonomy allows her to be advisor and confidante to all of the clueless boys and girls. She instructs Kevin on what he needs to do in order to get Vikki back—"the big L or the big O," the former being the way she "was duped"; the latter being what experience has taught her, and what she can pass on to Vikki. (Coincidentally, Jessica is played by the same actor as Vivian in the *Slums of Beverly Hills*. Her past film role has something to offer her latest character.) While Vikki is still unsure about sex, Jessica figures out why—Vikki has never, in the words of Jessica, "double-clicked [her] mouse." Jessica clues Kevin in, and with some help from big brother (and, coincidentally, a long line of tradition), Kevin figures out what to do. This is certainly a scene similar to the virgin movies of the '80s, but with a more enlightened purpose. Kevin consults his brother for advice on how to make Vikki have an orgasm, not simply on how to get laid. It is this fact alone that allows Kevin access to the sex book that came from Amsterdam, but has been added to by a select group of high school boys and kept in the library for future generations to consult and add to it. Vikki is initiated into this realm of sex while her parents are downstairs. This oral sex, which isn't sex at all according to dominant mainstream definitions (made popular by Bill Clinton), is what it takes for Vikki to learn that (again in Jessica's words), "It's not a space shuttle launch, it's sex." In many ways, Vikki has lost her virginity, but not in any way that society deems a rite of passage. She may have had an orgasm, but love and virginity are still unresolved and those issues, according to main-stream culture, are what sex (for girls) is all about.

While Vikki tries hard for the love that should accompany the sex, Heather is not actively looking for what she finds. Of all the "pact" girls in the movie Heather is the most intelligent, autonomous, and self-aware. Vikki is aware of her future, but Heather is aware of herself. She knows the effect of her choir girl reputation, but she's not necessarily looking to Chris to help her shed such an image. She asks Chris to the prom because she thinks he'll be "someone interesting to go with." But when she finds what she thinks is him making fun of her with his lacrosse friends, she dumps him and Chris has to learn the truth behind the words of the college girl who laughs in his face early in the movie—he can't fake it with Heather. The movie does not make it clear whether Heather is a virgin or not, but it is not an issue. It doesn't need to be because she is always in control of what she wants to do. She may be smitten by Chris, but she is not swept off her feet.

The sex scenes that complete *American Pie* may seem to be in the boys' favor, like they are in so many similar movies, but in this virginity narrative, the girls are just as involved in sex as the boys are. For Vikki, losing her virginity, especially, as Kevin calls it, "normal style," may seem like powerless sex as the camera sees the pain on Vikki's face and she asks Kevin to go slow. But Vikki knew what was in store for her, and despite the fact that she gets the words she was looking for, the act is no more romantic than it is in *Ripe, Whatever,* or *Slums of Beverly Hills.* Before, she pined for perfection, but afterward we find that she has learned, perhaps from the sex itself, that nothing is perfect. And after the long-awaited and agonized-over event actually happens, she knows for sure that Kevin is a piece of her past and not a part of her future. She breaks it off, but he hardly disagrees. (His moment, however, was much more perfect than hers.) Instead of being the first step into womanhood for Vikki, sex is the cementing act. It enables her to leave trivialities behind and enter the next stage of her life looking toward the future rather than to the past.

The romantic part of the plot belongs to Heather and Chris. At first choir was a scheme, but choir quickly becomes the playing ground where this man is made. Lacrosse couldn't do it, but singing does. Chris grows up more than any of the other boys as the angle he was going for in the pact—sensitive—becomes the person that he is in life. He realizes that Heather is the only place where he isn't going toward one of many goals. He pours out his soul to her on prom night, and this is what sets Chris apart from his friends. Heather has turned Chris inside himself and only these two are granted sex with romance *and* foreplay. Chris has matured so much that he doesn't even need to brag about his conquest (because it was no conquest at all). Instead, he says they just "had a really nice night together," and confesses that he thinks they're falling in love. Though Kevin, Jim, and Finch have now all crossed that line between virgin and nonvirgin, they can hardly comprehend what Chris is talking about (and not talking about). They may have broken the barrier, but they still have some growing up to do. And, consistent with its genre and mainstream demands, this growth veers from the first film's more progressive representations of girls' sex and sexuality.

The sequel to *American Pie* and the final film in the trilogy, *American Wedding,* rely upon the same old jokes and stereotypes as the first film.

The main girls from the first *American Pie* all appear in the sequel as well. While Vicky and Heather are weaker versions of their strong selves (and have much, much smaller parts), the girls who are most sexualized in the first film—Nadia (the European sexpot) and Michelle (the band camp geek sexpot)—are at least somewhat redeemed in the second film. (And in *American Wedding*, some could argue that Michelle is finally fully redeemed since she is the bride, thus taking her place in the adult world.) Throughout most of the second film Nadia remains a sexual fantasy yet to come true. She sends Jim postcards along her travels telling him how much she can't wait to see him. Jim, afraid that his inexperience and penchant for getting himself into sticky situations (figuratively and literally, in part two), seeks out Michelle, first to find out if he was any good (which she assures him he was not), and then to get some coaching and advice from her. She even poses as the girlfriend to stall Jim until his superglued penis can recover enough to fulfill his fantasy destiny. While Michelle keeps her cool, pretending to be just a friend, she is clearly falling for Jim and doesn't understand why Nadia is worth all this effort. Of course, Jim is also falling for her without realizing it. But eventually he does—before he and Nadia do the deed. Such a romantic plot line is followed by a romantic ending. Jim realizes that he's also a band geek even though he was never in band. And this is why, we find out later, Nadia wanted him in the first place. In some ways this makes Nadia an even bigger fantasy. She can hardly keep her hands off "The Shermanator," even after every other girl at the party has scoffed at his corny routine. And Jessica's advice, which was so pertinent and enlightening in part one, is overturned in part two when Nadia finally deflowers the Shermanator *because* he is such a geek.

Of course there are still plenty of girls for the boys' and the audience's fantasies. It turns out that Stiffler's mom has been pining for Finch as much as he has been pining for her. She even insists that he call her "Stiffler's mom" rather than her first name as they steam up her car windows and rock her car. The girls in the house the boys are painting (who fuck with them when they find them spying) may not be lesbians, but they are more than willing to hop in the sack with Stiffler, together. If anyone in the film does not deserve to be rewarded, especially with the ultimate male fantasy, that character is Stiffler. He is the only boy who remains static not only from the first film to the second, but also throughout the final film in the trilogy (when he is finally punished when he inadvertently has sex with Jim's grandmother). In fact, in the *American Pie* trilogy, none of the boys grow or change in the way that the girls from the original film change. In fact, they change so much, that there is no place for most of them in the sequels. Instead, they drop out of sight and the boys remain the focus in the two sequels. Thus, they remain static, relying on the same jokes and the same stereotypical treatment of women in general, and sex, specifically. Thus, these films are not, ultimately, an example of empowered sexuality for girls and women, unless we consider their near escape from the trilogy as empowering.

Empowering sexuality in the mainstream is difficult to come by, but one glaring blight on the pursuit of empowering sexuality in girls' film comes in relationship to girls of color. While this is partially because of the general lack of nonwhite protagonists and plots, as discussed earlier, few films allow nonwhite girls the same autonomy and pleasure that white girls pursue and secure for themselves. For instance, in *Nikita Blues*, Nikita is actively pursuing a sexual relationship with her teacher that never comes to fruition, and in other films that feature girls of color, sex is either absent, as in *Bring It On*, or it is only a side plot to bigger issues that affect these girls. And in *Belly Fruit*, Shanika may find a variety of sexual pleasure, but she finds this pleasure at her ultimate expense when she finds herself pregnant and abandoned. And like Shanika, most of Chantel's sexual pleasure seems to be in the status Ty brings her. Further, the topic of sexuality takes a back seat to more practical matters like discussion of birth control and abortion. For Evie in *The Incredibly True Adventures of Two Girls in Love*, she finds sexual empowerment only to be denied this empowerment by the larger forces of society embodied in the parents and guardians of Randy and Evie. But the issue here is not race—it is (homo)sexuality. *Stranger Inside* is the only film in this study where a woman of color pursues pleasure on her terms, but these terms are, of course, limited by her location and situation, both extensions of the larger societal forces that determine the patterns of Treasure's life.

Other girls' films offer far more compelling means of sexual empowerment for girls, and other kinds of growth and development often accompany these narratives. For instance, in the *Slums of Beverly Hills*, Vivian actively pursues her own means of pleasure through masturbation and then through her "building guy." When she's done with him, she moves on. And in *Ripe* and *Whatever*, Violet and Anna pursue their sexual interests despite the lack of physical pleasure they initially experience. But in the film *Coming Soon*, Stream's pursuit takes on a more desperate tone. In many ways, she is the equivalent of the male protagonists in "virgin films"; she wants to lose her virginity, but she, like Justine in *Virtual Sexuality*, doesn't have the means. However, both Stream and Justine, by virtue of their social location, have clear advantages in this pursuit. They don't have to deal with the slut labels and they have endless monetary resources when it comes to snagging a man, not that these resources work any better than other girls' resources. While Stream's class advantages over Vivian are clear, she does not have the same level of self-esteem and attitude as Vivian. She's more insecure, with far less confidence than most protagonists, particularly those pursuing sex, and she desperately tries to follow the lead of her friends who proclaim their sexual prowess, but have little evidence to back it up. Stream knows what she wants, even if she doesn't really know what it is that she wants. And in her sexual quest, she inadvertently (and then purposefully) has her first sexual experience in her friend's bathtub when she discovers a strategically placed jet. Since her friends' experience is mostly made-up, the jet is about as real as Stream can get.

Coming Soon has many elements in common with *Virtual Sexuality*, particularly the protagonists' obsessive desire to lose their virginity. In fact *Virtual Sexuality*, a British film, does not differ greatly from many mainstream U.S. films as it writes a girls' *Weird Science*–type narrative. In this film, Justine is totally preoccupied with herself and unhappy with her 17-year-old virgin status. She is desperate to find a guy, any guy, to do the deed with, despite the fact that she is naive about what sex actually entails, as we see throughout the film. Her friend, Fran, urges her not to pick just any guy since she doesn't want to look back with disgust, but nostalgia. Thus, Justine wishes that blokes just had barcodes so she could zap them and find out if they're the right choice. She, like Vikki in *American Pie*, and other girls, wants everything to be perfect and has high expectations. And like many other characters, Justine wants a lot of romance and has a very specific list of expectations. Further, she doesn't understand why the stock slut character, appropriately called "Hoover," is able to get any guy she wants, and she is dismayed when the boys she pursues are sucked in by Hoover. But despite this film's resemblance to typical and less empowering coming-of-age narratives, *Virtual Sexuality* offers a look at empowering sexuality that few other films provide.

In many ways Justine is the typical upper-class girl of teen films. She and her friend, Fran, do everything together and the two of them discuss Justine's hopes to find the right guy in typical female spaces and activities like doing crunches in an abs class, frying on the tanning beds, and buying perfume and makeup. In fact, Fran's friend is, in many ways, the stereotypical token black character described previously—she is light-skinned and economically privileged, and any traces of her racial or ethnic background are buried beneath her perfect clothes and hair. And Fran is an undeveloped character as we only see her when she is supporting and complementing Justine. The two of them shop, spy on boys, and try to deal with Justine's issues with her feet. Everything for Justine (and Fran) is about being a girly girl. After all, "gender-wise, being a girl is the best. No contest." But when a freak accident happens in a virtual reality booth at a fair, she is confronted with the most perfect man alive— the male equivalent of herself.

For much of the film, Justine is in a man's body, and this is where most of her coming of age happens. As female Justine, she continues to be selfish, shallow, and self-absorbed. But as male Jake she is forced to look at herself, and others, in a different way. While the protagonists in *Just One of the Guys* and *National Velvet* can only *dress* like a man, Justine has all of the anatomy as well, and she checks out the equipment even though she doesn't know how to use it. She's amazed when she gets an erection and asks her awkward male friend, Chaz, all sorts of uncomfortable questions about the size of his penis and what sex feels like. Of course this plot line provides plenty of fodder for sex jokes and references similar to those in films like *American Pie*, but in this context gender and sexuality are exposed. For instance, when Justine turns into Jake, she stays at Chaz's house and when they go to sleep, Chaz thinks Jake is masturbating although the sounds she's making are actually obsessive polishing of a silver frame that she thinks Chaz has not kept up well. She is assumed to be practicing a favorite male pastime when, in reality, she is being obsessive in her desired, stereotypically feminine task.

While Justine grows and matures as Jake, such growth is not so easy for Justine who is not only stuck in her single-gendered body, but who is also stuck in her conventional dreams of romance. She continues to believe in her barcode theory, and, of course, Jake registers a perfect score. As Justine pursues Jake, she stays focused on her romantic expectations of Mr. Right: magic carpet rides, moonlit serenades, and other romantic and unrealistic desires. And while Jake is getting to know the Chaz behind his geeky image, Justine continues to belittle and use Chaz, telling him that everyone's growing up so he should too. Even after Jake proves to Justine that they are the same person by presenting her with the most perfect romantic night she can think of, Justine refuses to believe that there is any guy out there who is better than Jake. When it comes time to delete the program and become herself again, Jake has to persuade Justine as she whines about finding the perfect bloke only to have to delete him. But Jake has learned Justine's lesson for her. "You still don't get it do you?" he asks Justine, telling her that there's "no such thing as the perfect guy" and she won't be right back where she started. "This time," Jake tells her, "you can be the Justine you want to be, not the Justine you think you need to be." With these words, Justine finally gives in, though it takes her some time afterward to get herself back together. And when she does, she is a bit less self-centered and a bit more practical. In fact, in her final narration she begins by telling Chaz's story. After Justine, he grew out of his awkwardness and had many other girlfriends. Thus, the narrative was also a coming of age for Chaz. And while this narrative seems to mirror many other girls' films, it offers some elements of sexuality that other films are not able to touch.

Unlike most teen films and girls' films, *Virtual Sexuality* mixes up the strict separation between genders, though it does so in a PG (or PG-13) kind of way. When Justine is first introduced to Jake's body, she laughs at the novelty of her penis, slapping it back and forth on her man-thighs. Shortly after, in the bathtub, Jake is looking at a magazine. On one side of the page is a man and the camera focuses on the bulge in his pants. On the other side of the page is a woman and the camera focuses on her wet T-shirt and hard nipples. Male Justine (Jake) goes back and forth between the two pictures, faster and faster until the bubbles rise in the tub—to Jake/Justine's amazement and confusion. As a woman in a man's body, the lines of homo and heterosexual attraction are blurred and male Justine is attracted, presumably, to both. And, as a man, Justine finds herself being aroused by women, particularly her former nemesis, Hoover. And while female and male Justine think Jake is hot—as male Justine proclaims, "If I met me and I wasn't me, I'd be like, yes!"—when Justine realizes that Jake is actually her, she is disgusted by the fact that she could have had sex with him or herself and proclaims that that would be "the worst sort of incest!" This proclamation puts a dent in this film's more progressive look at gender and sexuality since there would be no better way for Justine to learn about her own sexuality than to have sex with herself, if not literally, then figuratively, as other girls like Violet, Vivian and Stream do. However, Justine's coming of age integrally relies upon her experiences as a male body, so she is not whole without this part of herself and reunited she feels "stronger, different." As this stronger, different person, she is able to pursue her desires for sex without getting hung up on her romantic expectations. Thus, in the final narration she tells us that she did do it with Chaz, and it was okay. She "didn't find a mate for life or anything," but figures that this is okay since it "would have been a bit boring if [she] had." Instead, she is happy that she can look back on her first experience not with horror and embarrassment, but thinking, "Chaz, awww, what a sweetheart." Thus, this film avoids the happily ever after endings that so many romantic films rely upon.

Both *Virtual Sexuality* and *Coming Soon* offer different, and less controversial forms of sexual empowerment, than, for instance, *Secretary*, a highly controversial film in both mainstream and feminist circles, though, perhaps, for different reasons. In the mainstream this film has received awards as well as denunciations, and it has been praised and panned in various feminist critiques as well. However, despite the wide variation of reactions and interpretations, *Secretary* does subscribe to mainstream convention by confining Lee's sexuality to one particular, heterosexual, couple-centric sexuality. Thus this film about aberrant sexuality is also a quirky (and kinky) romance. Despite this film's challenges to conventional sexualities, it also relies upon stereotypical power relationships like boss and secretary and what becomes husband and wife. But at the very least *Secretary* offers a different version of the romantic. In fact, on the DVD cover, Manohla Dargis of the *Los Angeles Times* is quoted as describing the film as "a gently bent old-fashioned romance." This gentle bending is a start, but it's not enough to change the shape and consistency of the original shape.

Perhaps one of the most empowering realms of sex and sexuality outside of the mainstream comes in films that focus on friendships and sexual relationships between two girls. Thus, it is no surprise that several of these films like *Lost and Delirious* and *Show Me Love* are not U.S.-produced and those that are, like *All Over Me*, are written, produced, and directed by women. Within this frame of U.S. independent girls' films, same sex relationships are treated as a viable alternative sexuality, and not always in socially sanctioned ways. And often, a girl cannot come of age until she realizes this viability and the legitimacy of her whole self, including her sexuality. And at the edges of the mainstream there is more room for girls to explore and negotiate, to be and become

Despite the almost Hollywood happy ending of *But I'm a Cheerleader*, this film confronts many of the stereotypes about homosexuality, particularly through its parodic portrayal of reform programs. For instance, when trying to instill proper masculine and feminine behaviors and characteristics, these behaviors and characteristics become sexualized or stereotypically gay. Megan can't hide her sexuality, even if she doesn't realize that her preference for girls goes against the accepted norms of her friends and family. Her plea of "but I'm a cheerleader" is not so much an argument against accusations of deviant sexuality as it is a plea against her removal from her home and her need for rehabilitation. At this rehabilitation school, Megan, like the others in the program, does not undergo a transformation into heterosexuality as she, conversely, comes to consciousness of her sexuality (through love) and an acceptance of herself the way she is. Thus, this film shows, like *Saved!* that status quo attempts to "save" someone from a fate of marginalized sexuality are not only ineffectual, but also unwarranted and unwanted.

While *But I'm a Cheerleader* handles the topic with humor and parody, *Lost and Delirious* is all seriousness and reveals some of the difficulties and challenges of unconventional friendships. As this film shows, these challenges even exist in girls' spaces, like this upper-class boarding school. *Lost and Delirious* is mainstream in many ways, but it also takes more chances than the average mainstream film, perhaps because it is partially funded through and produced by Canadian sources. In this film the narrator is the roommate and friend of Victoria and Polly, two seniors who are also best friends and, as Mouse (Mary) later finds out, lovers. Mouse tries to understand the girls' relationship, but also tries to deal with the lack of acceptance that Victoria and Polly receive from their friends and family when they find out. Mouse sees the girls' relationship progress from platonic to sexual; and if it weren't for Mouse's knowledge that other people would think that their behavior is wrong, she seems to see this as a natural, or inevitable, development, despite her initial surprise. Thus, *Lost and Delirious* acts as a coming-of-age film for Mouse/Mary B more than it is for Victoria, who conforms to mainstream expectations, and Polly, who mentally and physically succumbs to these pressures, particularly in the absence of her best friend. But this film also shows the tragedy of a legacy of silence surrounding love between women. The headmistress and one of the teachers, we slowly realize, are long-time partners who keep up appearances and are subject to rumors. Because of the taboo of their relationship, the headmistress fails to act as an effective mentor, and Polly is the sacrifice in the film's dramatic and tragic ending. But while the ending is symbolic, it is also largely ineffectual in the other characters' lives as they seem to go on without being terribly (visibly) affected by Polly's passion and sacrifice.

While *Lost and Delirious* relies on sacrifice and the power of the mainstream to reject difference, *Show Me Love*, a Swedish film whose teens are Americanized in several ways, offers a different narrative than many other empowering girls' films. This film, which does not include any sex scenes like *The Incredibly True Adventures of Two Girls in Love*, *Lost and Delirious*, *All Over Me*, and *But I'm a Cheerleader*, offers an alternative to heterosexuality while at the same time downplaying the sex and augmenting the aspects of sexuality. Perhaps this film is able to do this by virtue of the fact that it is a tween film (Agnes, 15, and Elin, 14) that deals with the trials and tribulations of the teenage years, as well as with marginalized sexuality. *Show Me Love* also offers empowered sexuality because it engages with many of the stereotypical reactions to homosexuality that arise through characters in the film—like when the teens ostracize Agnes for her (mostly perceived) differences—while also confronting many other commonly related themes. For instance, Agnes's mom is perfectly accepting of homosexuals when her son asks about what this term means, but when she finds out that someone used this word to describe her daughter, she is greatly troubled and decides to read Agnes's diary. However, Agnes's father is supportive of her and assures her again and again that she will find friends and that things will get better, at least eventually. And while this advice isn't particularly helpful to Agnes at this stage in her life, or in her current conditions, her father clearly shows love and acceptance of his daughter regardless of who she is attracted to. But the biggest stereotype that this film tackles is the fact that sexuality is not as intimately connected to sex as is often assumed, particularly by the mainstream (or radical right) contingency.

In this film, Agnes knows she is gay mostly because she knows that she is in love with Elin. And Elin, who initially decides to be gay because she is bored and wants to be different (again, suburban angst, but in the form it takes in a small town in Sweden), never really embraces any labels to describe her sexuality. Instead, she avoids the issue until she cannot avoid it any longer and comes out when she literally comes out of the bathroom, holding hands with her girlfriend, Agnes, for their figurative coming out. This coming out is difficult because of the stifling environment of the girls' school, but it is also easy because their coming out is an expression of freedom beyond the labels that are put on them and other same-sex couples. And even though Agnes and Elin kiss, their relationship is much more based on their friendship, particularly as they distinguish themselves from their peers, not only sexually, but ideologically. And because this film ends, essentially, when their relationship begins there is no need.

The coming-out scene in this film is also an example of empowering sexuality because even though it seems that the terms of the girls' coming out will be dictated by the harassment of their peers, the girls take control over their coming out. Metaphorically, this scene is packed with meaning. The girls are locked in the bathroom together, initially because this is the only private space at school where Elin can confront and confirm her feelings for Agnes. But this locked door soon becomes a lock imposed on them as their peers surround the bathroom thinking that they have caught Elin making out with her new boyfriend. The girls have to decide how to deal with a situation where the inevitable result is the same—they have to come out. This scene underscores the anger that people often express when two girls get locked into such a situation, particularly since it is a situation that sets them apart from mainstream expectations. However, Agnes and Elin's plan involves holding their heads high and confronting the inevitable as they unlock the door. And Elin invokes a little bit of her attitude as she introduces her new girlfriend to the crowd of shocked faces. In the end, they don't have to come out of anything, instead they enter a whole new realm of possibilities, a realm that is open to them together in ways that were closed for them separately. But this is not merely a reinforcement of coupledom, rather, Agnes and Elin's relationship is also an empowering partnership. Together they are stronger than they were apart.

Like *Show Me Love, All Over Me* also complicates assumptions about same sex love, friendship, and the stereotypes that the mainstream wields against the sexually deviant. Also like *Show Me Love*, this film is subtle in its discussions and portrayals of sex and sexuality, which amplifies its other important themes and normalizes, but does not erase or reduce, homosexuality. From the beginning of this film, Claude is struggling just to get by, let alone to figure out who she really is. She works and, like Lola, dreams of being a star in her band, which, at present, is comprised of her and her best friend, Ellen. While the relationship between these two girls is not a sexual one, Claude clearly loves, cares for, and takes care of her friend, a character who acts in many of the same self-destructive ways as characters like Brenda in *Whatever* and Traci in *Thirteen*. Claude balances her jealousy over Ellen's boyfriends with her concern about her well-being. But when Ellen's self-destructive behavior starts to hurt Claude, she must make the decision to step back and stop getting hurt. To help, and complicate matters, Claude is also discovering that she's not the only person who is struggling with the realities of being gay. This is particularly pungent when one friend is killed by homophobic predators and when she learns that her friend from work is also gay.

But while this film shows the violent realities that many gay people face, when Claude's friend is killed, she refuses to compromise who she is for the false security of normalcy. She sees the pain that her (codependent) friend, a friend she loves deeply, puts upon herself. And she finds a girl who is not self-destructive. Through her, Claude not only pursues love and sex, but also a discovery of herself. The first time she gets together with her, Claude winds up in tears when listening to a Joan Armitage song and abruptly leaves. But this is less because she is confused by her feelings than it is because she is still hung up on Ellen. In the end, Claude finds herself and allows herself to explore friendship and beyond, leaving the future open.

Clearly, empowering sexuality is a complex and contradictory process. However, one thing is clear—negotiating sexuality requires the ability to reconsider, ignore, and play with conventional sexuality. In some cases, this is empowering, and in others this negotiation simply leads to reinscribed conventions. However, it is also important to note that labels are rarely given to these empowering relationships. And these labels are sometimes subverted or at least brought into dialog. For instance, Agnes knows she is lesbian, though she is only beginning to discover this sexually. A truly empowering vision of sexuality is complicated, which is one reason why it is so difficult to find truly empowering narratives surrounding sexuality in the mainstream. Certainly it is easier to determine what sexual representations are degrading or dangerous to women or both. However, even if films are not complete in their empowering qualities, which is, perhaps, impossible, this body of films reveals the possibilities for reenvisioning what is empowering. And as we determine ways to represent and interpret empowering sexualities, at the very least we also find solid alternatives to less empowering, even degrading narratives, images, and stereotypes. Thus, one of the most important qualities of empowering sexuality is friendships and relationships between and among women, girlfriends of all kinds. All of these films challenge the limits that the mainstream erects between friendships and sexual relationships and assert the importance of female spaces and girls' films. Perhaps the most empowering forms of sexuality are found when friendships open spaces—all kinds of spaces—including spaces to talk about, and explore, sex and sexuality, identity, and the expectations and alternatives to hegemonic sexualities.

CONCLUSION
An American Coming of Age

Coming-of-age narratives can be found all throughout popular culture. This book is a small, specific (but extensive) sampling of a story that holds varying types and degrees of significance in U.S. popular culture. The trends in the girls' film genre certainly compare to trends throughout the film industry and the popular culture industry more generally. And romance, convention, consumerism, multiculturalism, tokenism, sexism, heterosexism, classism, white supremacy, and other material and ideological conventions are rampant not only in teen and girls' film, but throughout U.S. culture and popular culture as well. Girls' film provides, at the very least, space, but perhaps it also provides history, context, negotiations, and subversions. Thus, recognizing these patterns and the ways in which girls negotiate these structural powers holds an important key to unlocking these processes and transforming them. In girls' film, all of the social vectors are negotiated and there is always more room for critical reflection and an emerging or developing consciousness, and conscious cultural production. In short, girls' film is empowering in myriad ways, not only for girls and women, but for anyone who recognizes a lack of fit between mainstream expectations and reality.

As we recognize these patterns, and negotiate structural powers, it is important to consider and embrace contradictions inherent in culture as well those contradictions among competing and complementary ideas about coming of age. Some of these contradictions are between the symbols, myths, characters, characterizations, plots, themes, issues, etc. of mainstream films and those of independent or less-well-known films, or between teen films and girls' film—or between these expectations we have for ourselves versus the expectations that others—parents, teachers, society—have for us. But these contradictions make the concept of coming of age richer, and potentially empowering, individually and collectively. As Annette Kuhn recognizes, "There is always space for contradiction or at least a 'lack of fit' between the various levels at which discourses are produced and circulated in society." Once a discourse is circulated, its meaning can be negotiated, and the more this discourse is circulated, the more its meaning can be, and is, negotiated. As Jon Lewis concludes from Ann Kaplan's work on MTV (and from Mills and Ewen's "lamentation"), "If we wade through the morass, we can find subversive forms and progressive strategies" (101).

These progressive strategies and subversive forms aren't simply waiting to be discovered in the morass; it takes an active pursuit in order to separate them from the masses of limiting and defining social discourses and available cultural reference points. Some, like Annette Kuhn, suggest negotiation by "reading against the grain" which offers "the pleasure of resistance, of saying 'no': not to 'unsophisticated' enjoyment, by ourselves and others, of culturally dominant images, but to the structures of power which ask us to consume them uncritically and in highly circumscribed ways" (98, 8). This suggests, as does Kathi Maio, that critical viewing, and not a complete denial of Hollywood films, or any form of mass media entertainment, is the best solution toward transforming and challenging ourselves and our media. Kuhn and Maio both suggest not a sacrifice of the pleasure of media entertainment, but an act of defiance. We can still watch and enjoy movies that do not have women's best interests in mind, as long as we don't buy into their limiting discourse. But however important such "active watching" is, these tactics do not address the larger structures that are invested in keeping us watching, and actively shopping, but not actively, or critically thinking.

Thus, while we learn to question and scrutinize mass-mediated films, we also need to seek out narratives at the edge of the morass, those less available and less recognizable to the masses. Further, as more and more girls and women are already doing, we need to not only negotiate the messages of the dominant, but we need to bypass them as well. We need to create our own "cultural artifacts" and "alternative messages," as the editors of *Growing Up Girls* point out, and like organizations like "Reel Grrls" promotes. And while we need to "encourage and educate girls to resist, deconstruct, and negotiate" cultural messages, we also need to give all girls the tools to learn how to do this both on their own and together. But we also need to recognize that there is privilege and power involved in all this resistance, deconstruction, and negotiation. We need to realize that many of the most recognized savvy young women of today are often raised by conscious or feminist women (whether they identify as such or not), and they often have an arsenal of accoutrements and other tools at their disposal. Thus it is often the girls and women pushed furthest to the margins who have the most skillful and conscious negotiation. They have the most practice, the longest history of negotiation, and the most to lose. It is also important to remember that the popular culture forms that are often considered to have positive messages or to have strong girl characters are often created by and for girls and women. Generations of feminists have made such popular culture more available, but have often paid a price for this production and have not always provided space for women of color to produce their stories. But, because positive images sell, the mainstream will continue to manufacture such representations as long as we are willing to purchase and consume them. And as industry controls the production, the representations are sacrificed in a variety of ways, some of which I have touched upon here. I have tried to expose some of the privileges that influence girls' film and popular culture more generally, and the questionable trends that these pop culture forms reinforce, sometimes unconsciously or semiconsciously. I have also tried to show the ways in which girls and women, in life and on film, have challenged, negotiated, subverted, and transformed mainstream constructions and assumptions about girls and American adolescence. And I have tried to expose some of the work that still needs to be done.

Negotiating these structures is not easy for anyone given the economic, and mythic, contours of the entertainment industry and market. However, the very existence of the body of films that comprise this study is proof that hegemony does not have as tight a hold as it sometimes seems. Thus I have tried to bring to the center the narratives within girls' film, and within teen films and popular culture more generally, that are most often inaccessible, silenced, or ignored. I have tried to provide a critical paradigm of American adolescence, one that can help to develop oppositional consciousness and create progressive, even radical, social and cultural change. As these girls show, there is space for negotiation if we know how to maneuver. And these celluloid girls' experiences are made real when our maneuvering is inspired by the collective experiences of American adolescence—the pictures of girlhood—the stories told and retold and ultimately reimagined in girls' film.

FILMOGRAPHY

All I Wanna Do (1999, U.S.)

Written by: Sarah Kernochan. *Produced by:* Ira Deutchman and Peter Newman. *Directed by:* Sarah Kernochan. *Production Companies:* Redeemable Features and Alliance Communications. *Studio:* Miramax. *Genre:* Comedy, Teen. *Rating:* PG-13. *Cast:* Kirsten Dunst (Verena "Trina" von Stefan), Gaby Hoffmann (Odette Sinclair), Lynn Redgrave (Miss McVane), Heather Matarazzo (Tweety Goldberg), Rachael Leigh Cook (Abby Sawyer) and Monica Keena (Tinka Parker).

All Over Me (1997, U.S.)

Written by: Sylvia Sichel. *Produced by:* Dolly Hall. *Directed by:* Alex Sichel. *Production Companies:* Medusa Pictures, and Slam and Baldini Pictures. *Studio:* Fine Line. *Genre:* Drama. *Rating:* R. *Cast:* Alison Folland (Claude), Wilson Cruz (Jesse), Tara Subkoff (Ellen), Cole Hauser (Mark), Ann Dowd (Claude's Mom) and Leisha Hailey (Lucy).

American Beauty (1999, U.S.)

Written by: Alan Ball. *Produced by:* Bruce Cohen and Dan Jinks. *Directed by:* Sam Mendes. *Production Company:* Jinks/ Cohen Company. *Studio:* Dreamworks SKG. *Genre:* Comedy, Drama. *Rating:* R. *Cast:* Kevin Spacey (Lester Burnham), Annette Bening (Carolyn Burnham), Thora Birch (Jane Burnham), Wes Bentley (Rick Fitts), Mena Suvari (Angela Hayes), Chris Cooper (Colonel Fitts) and Peter Gallagher (Buddy Kane).

American Pie (1999, U.S.)

Written by: Adam Herz. *Produced by:* Craig Perry, Warren Zide, Chris Moore and Chris Weitz. *Directed by:* Paul Weitz. *Production Companies:* Zide-Perry Films/ Zide Entertainment and Universal Pictures. *Studio:* Universal Pictures. *Genre:* Comedy. *Rating:* R. *Cast:* Jason Biggs (Jim), Jennifer Coolidge (Stiffler's mom), Shannon Elizabeth (Nadia), Alyson Hannigan (Michelle), Chris Klein (Oz) and Clyde Kusatsu (English teacher).

American Virgin (1999, U.S.)

Written by: Jean-Pierre Marois and Ira Israel. *Produced by:* Aissa Djabri, Farid Lahouassa and Manuel Munz. *Directed by:* Jean-Pierre Marois. *Production Companies:* M6 Films, TPS Cinema and Vertigo Films. *Studio:* Granite Releasing and Studio Home Entertainment. *Genre:* Comedy. *Rating:* R. *Cast:* Bob Hoskins (Joey Quinn), Robert Loggia (Ronny Bartolotti), Mena Suvari (Katrina), Sally Kellerman (Quaint McPerson), and Lamont Johnson (Nick).

Bellyfruit (1999, U.S.)

Written by: Kerri Green, Maria Bernhard, Susannah Blinkoff and Jannet Borrus. *Produced by:* Robert Bauer and

Bonnie Dickenson. *Directed by:* Kerri Green. *Production Companies:* Independent Women Artists and Standard Film Trust. *Studio:* Vanguard Films. *Genre:* Drama, Teen. *Rating:* NR. *Cast:* Tamara LaSeon Bass (Shanika), Tonatzin Mondragon (Aracely), Kelly Vint (Tina) and T.E. Russell (Damon).

Bend It Like Beckham (2003, U.K.)

Written by: Paul Mayeda Berges, Guljit Bindra and Gurinder Chadha. *Produced by:* Gurinder Chadha and Deepak Nayar. *Directed by:* Gurinder Chadha. *Production Companies:* Kintop Pictures, Bend It Films, Roc Media and Road Movies. *Studio:* Fox Searchlight. *Genre:* Sports, Comedy, British. *Rating:* PG-13. *Cast:* Parminder Nagra (Jess Bharma), Keira Knightley (Jules Paxton), Jonathan Rhys-Meyers (Joe), Anupam Kher (Mr. Bharma), Archie Panjabi (Pinky Bharma), and Shaznay Lewis (Mel).

Boys and Girls (2000, U.S.)

Written by: Andrew Lowery and Andrew Miller. *Produced by:* Murray Schisqual, Joy Cohen and Lee Gottsegen. *Directed by:* Robert Iscove. *Production Companies:* Punch 21 and Dimension. *Studio:* Miramax. *Genre:* Romance, Comedy. *Rating:* PG-13. *Cast:* Freddie Prinze Jr. (Ryan), Claire Forlani (Jennifer), Jason Biggs (Hunter), Heather Donahue (Megan), Alyson Hannigan (Betty), and Amanda Detmer (Amy).

Boys Don't Cry (1999, U.S.)

Written by: Kimberly Peirce and Andy Bienen. *Produced by:* John Hart, Christine Vachon, Jeffery Sharp and Eva Kolodner. *Directed by:* Kimberly Peirce. *Production Companies:* Killer Films, Hart-Sharp Entertainment and Independent Film Channel. *Studio:* Fox Searchlight. *Genre:* Drama. *Rating:* R. *Cast:* Hilary Swank (Brandon Teena), Chloe Sevigny (Lana), Peter Sarsgaard (John), Brendan Sexton III (Tom), Alison Folland (Kate), and Alicia Goranson (Candace).

Bring It On (2000, U.S.)

Written by: Jessica Bendlinger. *Produced by:* Marc Abraham, Thomas A. Bliss and John Ketcham. *Directed by:* Peyton Reed. *Production Company:* Beacon Pictures. *Studio:* Universal. *Genre:* Comedy. *Rating:* PG-13. *Cast:* Kirsten Dunst (Torance Shipman), Jesse Bradford (Cliff Pantone), Gabrielle Union (Isis) and Eliza Dushku (Missy Pantone).

Brokedown Palace (1999, U.S., Philippines)

Written by: Adam Fields and David Arata. *Produced by:* Adam Fields, A. Kitman Ho, Lope V. Juban Jr. *Directed by:* Jonathan Kaplan. *Production Companies:* 20th Century–Fox, Adam Fields Productions, Fox 2000 Pictures, Two Girls Productions. *Studio:* Twentieth Century–Fox Film Corp. *Genre:* Drama. *Rating:* PG-13. *Cast:* Claire Danes (Alice Marano), Kate Beckinsale (Darlene Davis), Bill Pullman (Yankee Hank Green), Jacqueline Kim (Yon Green), Lou Diamond Phillips (Roy Knox), Daniel Lapaine (Nick Parks).

Buffy the Vampire Slayer (1992, U.S.)

Written by: Joss Whedon. *Produced by:* Howard Rosenman and Kaz Kuzui. *Directed by:* Fran Rubel Kuzui. *Production Companies:* Buffy Films, Kuzui Enterprises and Sandollar Productions. *Studio:* Fox. *Genre:* Comedy, Horror. *Rating:* PG-13. *Cast:* Kristy Swanson (Buffy), Donald Sutherland (Merrick), Paul Reubens (Amilyn), Rutger Hauer (Lothos), Luke Perry (Pike) and Michele Abrams (Jennifer).

But I'm a Cheerleader (2000, U.S.)

Written by: Brian Wayne Peterson. *Produced by:* Andrea Sperling and Leanna Creel. *Directed by:* Jamie Babbit. *Production Companies:* Ignite and HKM. *Studio:*

Lions Gate Films. *Genre:* Comedy, Drama. *Rating:* R. *Cast:* Natasha Lyonne (Megan), Clea DuVal (Graham), Cathy Moriarty (Mary), Mink Stole (Megan's mom), RuPaul (Mike) and Eddie Cibrian (Rock).

Can't Hardly Wait (1998, U.S.)

Written by: Harry Elfont and Deborah Kaplan. *Produced by:* Betty Thomas, Jenno Topping and Warren Zide. *Directed by:* Harry Elfont and Deborah Kaplan. *Production Companies:* Zide Entertainment and Topping/Thomas Productions. *Studio:* Columbia TriStar. *Genre:* Romance, Comedy. *Rating:* PG-13. *Cast:* Jennifer Love Hewitt (Amanda Beckett), Ethan Embry (Preston Meyers), Peter Facinelli (Mike Dexter), Lauren Ambrose (Denise Fleming) and Seth Green (Kenny Fisher).

A Cinderella Story (2004, U.S.)

Written by: Leigh Dunlap. *Produced by:* Ilyssa Goodman, Hunt Lowry, Dylan Sellers, Clifford Werber. *Directed by:* Mark Rosman. *Production Companies:* Warner Bros., Gaylord Films, Clifford Werber Productions. *Studio:* Warner Bros. Pictures. *Genre:* Comedy, Romance. *Rating:* PG. *Cast:* Hilary Duff (Sam), Jennifer Coolidge (Fiona), Chad Michael Murray (Austin), Dan Byrd (Carter), Regina King (Rhonda).

Clueless (1995, U.S.)

Written by: Amy Heckerling. *Produced by:* Robert Lawrence and Scott Rudin. *Directed by:* Amy Heckerling. *Production Companies:* Robert Lawrence Productions and Paramount. *Studio:* Paramount. *Genre:* Comedy, Romance. *Rating:* PG-13. *Cast:* Alicia Silverstone (Cher Horowitz), Stacey Dash (Dionne), Brittany Murphy (Tai), Paul Rudd (Josh), Dan Hedaya (Mel Horowitz) and Donald Adeosun Faison (Murray).

Coming Soon (2000, U.S.)

Written by: Colette Burson and Kate Robin. *Produced by:* Beau Flynn, Stefan Simchowitz and Keven Duffy. *Directed by:* Colette Burson. *Production Companies:* Bandeira Entertainment and Key Entertainment. *Studio:* Unapix Films. *Genre:* Comedy. *Rating:* R. *Cast:* Tricia Vessey (Nell Kelher), Gaby Hoffmann (Jenny Simon), Bonnie Root (Stream Hodsell), Ryan Reynolds (Henry Lipschitz), Mia Farrow (Judy Hodsell) and James Roday (Chad).

Confessions of a Teenage Drama Queen (2004, U.S.)

Written by: Gail Parent. *Produced by:* Bob Shapiro and Jerry Leider. *Directed by:* Sara Sugarman. *Production Companies:* Buena Vista, Touchstone Pictures and Walt Disney Pictures. *Studio:* Touchstone. *Genre:* Comedy, Teen. *Rating:* PG. *Cast:* Lindsay Lohan (Lola), Adam Garcia (Stu), Glenne Headly (Karen), Alison Pill (Ella), Eli Marienthal (Sam) and Carol Kane (Miss Baggoli).

Coyote Ugly (2000, U.S.)

Written by: Gina Wendkos. *Produced by:* Jerry Bruckheimer. *Directed by:* David McNally. *Production Companies:* Jerry Bruckheimer Films, Touchstone Pictures. *Studio:* Buena Vista Pictures. *Genre:* Comedy, Drama. *Rating:* PG-13. *Cast:* Piper Perabo (Violet Sanford), Adam Garcia (Kevin O'Donnell), John Goodman (Bill Sanford), Maria Bello (Lil), Izabella Miko (Cammie), Tyra Banks (Zoe), Bridget Moynahan (Rachel).

The Craft (1996, U.S.)

Written by: Peter Filardi. *Produced by:* Douglas Wick. *Directed by:* Andrew Fleming. *Production Company:* Columbia Pictures Corporation. *Studio:* Columbia Pictures. *Genre:* Comedy, Drama, Horror. *Rating:* R. *Cast:* Robin Tunney (Sarah Bailey), Fairuza Balk (Nancy Downs), Neve Campbell (Bonnie), Rachel

True (Rochelle), Skeet Ulrich (Chris Hooker), Christine Taylor (Laura Lizzie), Breckin Meyer (Mitt).

Crazy/Beautiful (2001, U.S.)

Written by: Phil Hay and Matt Manfredi. *Produced by:* Harry J. Ufland, Mary Jane Ufland and Rachel Pfeffer. *Directed by:* John Stockwell. *Production Company:* Touchstone Pictures. *Studio:* Touchstone Pictures. *Genre:* Teen, Drama. *Rating:* PG-13. *Cast:* Kirsten Dunst (Nicole), Jay Hernandez (Carlos), Bruce Davison (Tom Oakley), Lucinda Jenney (Courtney), Herman Osorio (Luis) and Miguel Castro (Eddie).

Crossroads (2002, U.S.)

Written by: Shonda Rhimes. *Produced by:* Ann Carli. *Directed by:* Tamra Davis. *Production Companies:* MTV Networks, Paramount Pictures and Zomba Films. *Studio:* Paramount. *Genre:* Comedy, Drama. *Rating:* PG-13. *Cast:* Britney Spears (Lucy), Dan Aykroyd (Lucy's dad), Kim Cattrall (Lucy's mom), Zoe Saldana (Kit), Anson Mount (Ben) and Taryn Manning (Mimi).

Cruel Intentions (1999, U.S.)

Written by: Roger Kumble. *Produced by:* Neal H. Moritz. *Directed by:* Roger Kumble. *Production Companies:* Cruel Productions, Original Film, Newmarket Capital Group and Neal M. Mortiz Production. *Studio:* Sony Pictures. *Genre:* Comedy. *Rating:* R. *Cast:* Sarah Michelle Gellar (Kathryn Merteuil), Ryan Phillippe (Sebastian Valmont), Reese Witherspoon (Annette Hargrove), Selma Blair (Cecile Coldwell), Louise Fletcher (Helen Roesmond) and Joshua Jackson (Blaine Tuttle).

Dirty Dancing (1987, U.S.)

Written by: Eleanor Bergstein. *Produced by:* Linda Gottlieb. *Directed by:* Emile Ardolino. *Production Companies:* Great American Film Limited Partnership, Vestron Pictures Ltd. *Studio:* Vestron Pictures Ltd. *Genre:* Romance, Drama. *Rating:* PG-13. *Cast:* Jennifer Grey (Baby Houseman), Patrick Swayze (Johnny Castle), Jerry Orbach (Jake Houseman), Cynthia Rhodes (Penny Johnson), Jack Weston (Max Kellerman).

Drive Me Crazy (1999, U.S.)

Written by: Todd Strasser and Rob Thomas. *Produced by:* Amy Robinson. *Directed By:* John Schultz. *Production Companies:* Amy Robinson Productions, Grand March Productions. *Studio:* Twentieth Century–Fox Film Corp. *Genre:* Comedy, Drama. *Rating:* PG-13. *Cast:* Melissa Joan Hart (Nicole Maris), Adrian Grenier (Chase Hammond), Stephen Collins (Mr. Morris), Susan May Pratt (Alicia DeGasario).

Ella Enchanted (2004, U.S.)

Written by: Gail Carson Levine and Laurie Craig. *Produced by:* Jane Startz. *Directed by:* Tommy O'Haver. *Production Companies:* Blessington Film Productions, Jane Startz Productions, Miramax, Momentum Films. *Studio:* Miramax. *Genre:* Comedy, Fantasy, Romance. *Rating:* PG. *Cast:* Anne Hathaway (Ella), Hugh Dancy (Char), Cary Elwes (Edgar), Adrian McArdle (Slannon), Minnie Driver (Mandy), Vivica A. Fox (Lucinda).

Ever After (1998, U.S.)

Written by: Susannah Grant and Charles Perrault. *Produced by:* Mirielle Soria and Tracey Trench. *Directed by:* Andy Tennant. *Production Companies:* 20th Century–Fox. *Studio:* Twentieth Century–Fox Film Corp. *Genre:* Romance, Comedy, Drama. *Rating:* PG. *Cast:* Drew Barrymore (Danielle De Barbarac), Anjelica Huston (Baroness Rodmilla De Ghent), Dougray Scott (Prince Henry), Patrick Godfrey (Leonardo da Vinci).

Fast Times at Ridgemont High (1982, U.S.)

Written by: Cameron Crowe. *Produced by:* Irving Azoff and Art Linson. *Directed by:* Amy Heckerling. *Production Companies:*

Refugee Films, Universal Pictures. *Studio:* MCA/Universal Pictures. *Genre:* Comedy. *Rating:* R. *Cast:* Sean Penn (Jeff Spicoli), Jennifer Jason Leigh (Stacy Hamilton), Judge Reinhold (Brad Hamilton), Robert Romanus (Mike Damone), Brian Backer (Mark Ratner), Phoebe Cates (Linda Barrett).

Foxfire (1996, U.S.)

Written by: Elizabeth White (Based on the short story by Joyce Carol Oates). *Produced by:* Mike Figgis, Marc S. Fischer, Laura Friedman, Jeffrey Lurie, John Bard Manulis, John P. Marsh, and Paige Simpson. *Directed by:* Annette Haywood-Carter. *Production Companies:* Chestnut Hill and Red Mullet. *Studios:* Columbia-Tri Star and Samuel Goldwyn. *Genre:* Drama. *Rating:* R. *Cast:* Hedy Burress (Madeline "Maddy" Wirtz), Angelina Jolie (Margeret "Legs" Sadovsky), Jenny Lewis (Rita Faldes), Jenny Shimizu (Goldie Goldman), Sarah Rosenberg (Violet Kahn).

Freaky Friday (1976, U.S.)

Written by: Mary Rodgers. *Produced by:* Ron Miller. *Directed by:* Gary Nelson. *Production Company:* Walt Disney Productions. *Studio:* Buena Vista. *Genre:* Comedy. *Rating:* G. *Cast:* Barbara Harris (Ellen Andrews), Jodie Foster (Annabel Andrews), John Astin (Bill Andrews), Patsy Kelly (Mrs. Schmauss), Vicki Schreck (Virginia) and Dick Van Patten (Harold Jennings).

Freaky Friday (2003, U.S.)

Written by: Leslie Dixon and Heather Hach. *Produced by:* Andrew Gunn. *Directed by:* Mark S. Waters. *Production Companies:* GUNNFilms Productions and Walt Disney Pictures. *Studio:* Disney. *Genre:* Comedy, Teen, Remake. *Rating:* PG. *Cast:* Jamie Lee Curtis (Tess Coleman), Lindsay Lohan (Anna Coleman), Mark Harmon (Ryan), Harold Gould (Grandpa), Chad Michael Murray (Jake), Stephen Tobolowsky (Mr. Bates) and Christina Vidal (Maddie).

Get Over It (2001, U.S.)

Written by: R. Lee Fleming Jr. *Produced by:* Michael Burns, Marc Butan, Paul Feldsher. *Directed By:* Tommy O'Haver. *Production Companies:* Ignite Entertainment, Miramax. *Studio:* Miramax. *Genre:* Comedy, Romance. *Rating:* PG-13. *Cast:* Kirsten Dunst (Kelly Woods), Ben Foster (Berke Landers), Melissa Sagemiller (Allison), Sisqó (Dennis Wallace), Shane West (Striker), Colin Hanks (Felix Woods), Zoe Saldana (Maggie), Mila Kunis (Basin).

Ghost World (2001, U.S.)

Written by: Daniel Clowes and Terry Zwigoff. *Produced by:* John Malkovich, Russell Smith and Lianne Halfon. *Directed by:* Terry Zwigoff. *Production Companies:* Granada Film, Jersey Shore Films and United Artists Films. *Studio:* United Artists (MGM). *Genre:* Teen, Drama. *Rating:* R. *Cast:* Thora Birch (Enid), Scarlett Johansson (Rebecca), Steve Buscemi (Seymour), Illeana Douglas (Roberta) and Brad Renfro (Josh).

Ginger Snaps (2000, U.S., Canada)

Written by: Karen Walton. *Produced by:* Karen Lee Hall and Steve Hoban. *Directed by:* John Fawcett. *Production Companies:* Copper Heart Entertainment, Lions Gate Films, Oddbod Productions Inc., TVA International, The Movie Network, Telefilm Canada and Walter Pictures. *Studio:* TVA International. *Genre:* Horror. *Rating:* PG-13. *Cast:* Emily Perkins (Brigitte), Katharine Isabelle (Ginger), Kris Lemche (Sam), Mimi Rogers (Pamela), Jesse Moss (Jason) and Danielle Hampton (Trina).

Girl (1998, U.S.)

Written by: David E. Tolchinsky. *Produced by:* Chris hanley, Jeff Most and Brad Wyman. *Directed by:* Jonathan Kahn. *Production Companies:* HSX Films, Kushner-Locke Productions and Muse.

Studio: Columbia/Tristar Studios. *Genre:* Drama, Teen. *Rating:* R. *Cast:* Dominique Swain (Andrea Marr), Sean Patrick Flanery (Todd Sparrow), Summer Phoenix (Rebecca), Tara Reid (Cybil) and Selma Blair (Darcy).

Girls Town (1996, U.S.)

Written by: Jim Mckay, Denise Casano, Anna Grace, Bruklin Harris and Lili Taylor. *Produced by:* Lauren Zalaznick. *Directed by:* Jim Mckay. *Production Companies:* C-Hundred Film Corp. and Boomer Pictures. *Studio:* October Films. *Genre:* Drama. *Rating:* R. *Cast:* Lili Taylor (Patti), Bruklin Harris (Angela), Anna Grace (Emma), Aunjanue Ellis (Nikki), Guillermo Diaz (Dylan) and Michael Imperioli (Anthony).

The Glass House (2001, U.S.)

Written by: Wesley Strick. *Produced by:* Neal H. Moritz. *Directed by:* Daniel Sackheim. *Production Companies:* Columbia and Original Film. *Studio:* Columbia. *Genre:* Thriller. *Rating:* PG-13. *Cast:* Leelee Sobieski (Ruby), Diane Lane (Erin), Stellan Skarsgaard (Terry), Trevor Morgan (Rhett), Bruce Dern (Begleiter) and Rita Wilson (Grace Baker).

Go (1999, U.S.)

Written by: John August. *Produced by:* Matt Freeman, Mickey Liddell, Paul Rosenberg. *Directed by:* Doug Liman. *Production Companies:* Banner Entertainment, Saratoga Entertainment, TriStar Pictures. *Studio:* Columbia Pictures. *Genre:* Crime, Comedy. *Rating:* R. *Cast:* Katie Holmes (Claire Montgomery), Sarah Polley (Ronna Martin), Scott Wolf (Adam), Jay Mohr (Zack).

Heathers (1989, U.S.)

Written by: Daniel Waters. *Produced by:* Denise Di Novi. *Directed by:* Michael Lehmann. *Production Companies:* Cinemarque. *Studio:* New World. *Genre:* Comedy, Fantasy, Teen. *Rating:* R. *Cast:* Winona Ryder (Veronica Sawyer), Christian Slater (J.D.), Shannon Doherty (Heather Duke), Lisanne Falk (Heather McNamara) and Kim Walker (Heather Chandler).

I Know What You Did Last Summer (1997, U.S.)

Written by: Lois Duncan (based on book by) and Kevin Williamson. *Produced by:* Neal H. Moritz, Stokely Chaffin and Erik Feig. *Directed by:* Jim Gillespie. *Production Companies:* Mandalay Entertainment and Neal H. Moritz. *Studio:* Columbia Pictures. *Genre:* Horror, Mystery, Thriller. *Rating:* R. *Cast:* Jennifer Love Hewitt (Julie James), Sarah Michelle Gellar (Helen Shivers), Ryan Phillippe (Barry Cox), Freddie Prinze Jr. (Ray Bronson), Bridgette Wilson (Elsa Shivers), Johnny Galecki (Max) and Muse Watson (Benjamin Willis, Fisherman).

The Incredibly True Adventures of Two Girls in Love (1995, U.S.)

Written by: Maria Maggenti. *Produced by:* Dolly Hall. *Directed by:* Maria Maggenti. *Production Companies:* Fine Line Features, Smash Pictures. *Studio:* Fine Line Features. *Genre:* Drama. *Rating:* R. *Cast:* Laurel Holloman (Randy Dean), Nicole Ari Parker (Evi Roy), Maggie Moore (Wendy), Dale Dickey (Regina), Stephanie Berry (Evelyn Roy), Kate Stafford (Rebecca Dean).

Jawbreaker (1998, U.S.)

Written by: Darren Stein. *Produced by:* Lisa Tornell and Stacy Kramer. *Directed by:* Darren Stein. *Production Companies:* Crossroads Films and Sony Pictures. *Studio:* Columbia TriStar. *Genre:* Comedy, Teen. *Rating:* R. *Cast:* Rose McGowan (Courtney Shane), Rebecca Gayheart (Julie Freeman), Julie Benz (Marcie Fox), Judy Greer (Fern Mayo), Chad Christ (Zach Tartak) and Pam Grier (Detective Vera Cruz).

Josie and the Pussycats (2001, U.S.)

Written by: Deborah Kaplan and Harry Elfont. *Produced by:* Marc Platt, Tony DeRosa-Grund, Tracy E. Edmonds and Chuck Grimes. *Directed by:* Harry Elfont and Deborah Kaplan. *Production Companies:* Riverdale Productions, Marc Platt Productions and Universal. *Studio:* Universal. *Genre:* Comedy, Musical. *Rating:* PG-13. *Cast:* Rachael Leigh Cook (Josie McCoy), Tara Reid (Melody Valentine), Rosario Dawson (Valerie Brown), Parker Posey (Fiona) and Alan Cumming (Wyatt Frame).

Just Another Girl on the I.R.T. (1993, U.S.)

Written by: Leslie Harris. *Produced by:* Erwin Wilson. *Directed by:* Leslie Harris. *Production Company:* Truth 24 F.P.S. *Studio:* Miramax. *Genre:* Drama. *Rating:* R. *Cast:* Ariyan Johnson (Chantel Mitchell), Kevin Thigpen (Tyrone), Ebony Jerido (Natete), Chequita Jackson (Paula) and William Badget (Cedrick).

Kids (1995, U.S.)

Written by: Harmony Korine. *Produced by:* Cary Woods. *Directed by:* Larry Clark. *Production Companies:* Independent Pictures and The Guys Upstairs. *Studio:* Shining Excalibur Pictures. *Genre:* Drama. *Rating:* R. *Cast:* Leo Fitzpatrick (Telly), Justin Pierce (Casper), Chloe Sevigny (Jennie), Rosario Dawson (Ruby), Harold Hunter (Harold) and Yakira Pequero (Darcy).

Legally Blonde (2001, U.S.)

Written by: Karen McCullah Lutz and Kirsten Smith. *Produced by:* Marc Platt and Ric Kidney. *Directed by:* Robert Luketic. *Production Companies:* MGM and Marc Platt. *Studio:* United Artists (MGM). *Genre:* Comedy. *Rating:* PG-13. *Cast:* Reese Witherspoon (Elle Woods), Luke Wilson (Emmette), Selma Blair (Vivian), Matthew Davis (Warner) and Victor Garber (Professor Callahan).

Loser (2000, U.S.)

Written by: Amy Heckerling. *Produced by:* Amy Heckerling and Twink Caplan. *Directed by:* Amy Heckerling. *Production Company:* Columbia Pictures. *Studio:* Columbia. *Genre:* Comedy, Romance. *Rating:* PG-13. *Cast:* Jason Biggs (Paul Tannek), Mena Suvari (Dora Diamond), Greg Kinnear (Professor Edward Alcott), Zak Orth (Adam) and Tom Sadoski (Chris).

Lost and Delirious (2001, Canada)

Written by: Judith Thompson. *Produced by:* Greg Dummet, Lorraine Richard and Louis-Philippe Rochon. *Directed by:* Lea Pool. *Production Companies:* Seville Pictures, Cite-Amerique and Dummett Films. *Studio:* Lions Gate Films. *Genre:* Teen, Drama. *Rating:* R. *Cast:* Piper Perabo (Pauline Oster), Jessica Pare (Victoria Moller), Mischa Barton (Mary Bradford), Jackie Burroughs (Faye Vaughn) and Graham Greene (Joseph Menzies).

Love and Basketball (2000, U.S.)

Written by: Gina Prince-Bythewood. *Produced by:* Spike Lee, Andrew Z. Davis, Jay Stern, Sam Kitt, and Cynthia Guidry. *Directed by:* Gina Prince-Bythewood. *Production Companies:* 40 Acres and a Mule Filmworks. *Studio:* New Line Cinema. *Genre:* Drama, Romance, Sport. *Rating:* PG-13. *Cast:* Sanaa Lathan (Monica Wright), Omar Epps (Quincy McCall), Regina Hall (Lena Wright).

Manny & Lo (1996, U.S.)

Written by: Lisa Krueger. *Produced by:* Dean Silvers and Marlen Hecht. *Directed by:* Lisa Krueger. *Production Company:* Pope Entertainment Group. *Studio:* Sony Pictures Classics. *Genre:* Comedy, Drama. *Rating:* R. *Cast:* Mary Kay Place (Elaine) Scarlett Johansson (Amanda "Manny"), Aleska Palladino (Laurel "Lo"), Paul Guilfoyle (Mr. Humphreys) and Glenn Fitzgerald (Joey).

Mean Girls (2004, U.S.)

Written by: Tina Fey. *Produced by:* Lorne
Michaels. *Directed by:* Mark S. Waters.
Production Companies: M.G. Films,
Broadway Video and Paramount. *Studio:*
Paramount. *Genre:* Comedy, Teen.
Rating: PG-13. *Cast:* Lindsay Lohan
(Cady Heron), Rachel McAdams (Regina
George), Lacey Chabert (Gretchen
Wieners), Amanda Seyfried (Karen
Smith), Rajiv Surendra (Kevin Gnapoor),
Ky Pham (Trang Pak), Lizzy Caplan
(Janis) and Tina Fey (Ms. Norbury).

Mi Vida Loca (1993, U.S.)

Written by: Allison Anders. *Produced by:*
Carl Colpaert and David Hassid. *Directed
by:* Allison Anders. *Production Companies:*
HBO, Cineville Inc., Showcase Enter-
tainment. *Studio:* Sony Pictures Classics.
Genre: Drama. *Rating:* R. *Cast:* Angel
Aviles (Sad Girl), Seidy Lopez (Mousie),
Jacob Vargas (Ernesto), Devine (Devine).

National Velvet (1944, U.S.)

Written by: Theodore Reeves and Helen
Deutsch. *Produced by:* Pandro S. Berman.
Directed by: Clarence Brown. *Production
Company:* MGM. *Studio:* MGM. *Genre:*
Drama. *Rating:* NR. *Cast:* Mickey Rooney
(Mi Taylor), Donald Crisp (Mr. Brown),
Elizabeth Taylor (Velvet Brown), Anne
Revere (Mrs. Brown) and Angela Lans-
bury (Edwina Brown).

Never Been Kissed (1999, U.S.)

Written by: Abby Kohn, Marc Silverstein
and Jenny Bicks. *Produced by:* Drew Barrymore, Sandy Isaac and Nancy Juvonen.
Directed by: Raja Gosnell. *Production
Companies:* Fox 2000 and Flower Films.
Studio: 20th Century-Fox. *Genre:* Romance, Comedy. *Rating:* PG-13. *Cast:*
Drew Barrymore (Josie), David Arquette (Rob), Marley Shelton (Kristen)
and Michael Vartan (Mr. Coulson).

Nikita Blues (2000, U.S.)

Written by: Marc Cayce. *Produced by:*
Marc Cayce. *Directed by:* Marc Cayce.

Production Companies: York Entertainment. *Studio:* York Entertainment/Mav-
erick Entertainment. *Genre:* Drama,
Comedy, Teen. *Rating:* NR. *Cast:* Essence Atkins (Nikita), Roz Ryan (Nikita's mom), Kenny Lee (Mr. Jackson)
and William L. Johnson (J-Smooth).

Not Another Teen Movie (2001, U.S.)

Written by: Phil Beauman, Michael G.
Bender, Adam Jay Epstein, Andrew Ja-
cobson and Buddy Johnson. *Produced by:*
Neal H. Moritz. *Directed by:* Joel Gallen.
Production Companies: Neal H. Moritz
Productions and Original Film Produc-
tions. *Studio:* Columbia. *Genre:* Comedy,
Teen. *Rating:* R. *Cast:* Chyler Leigh
(Janey Briggs), Chris Evans (Jake Wy-
ler), Jamie Pressly (Priscilla), Eric Chris-
tian Olsen (Austin) and Mia Kirshner
(Catherine).

The Opposite of Sex (1998, U.S.)

Written by: Don Roos. *Produced by:*
David Kirkpatrick and Michael Besman.
Directed by: Don Roos. *Production Com-
panies:* Original Voices. *Studio:* Sony Pic-
tures Classics. *Genre:* Comedy, Drama.
Rating: R. *Cast:* Christina Ricci (Dedee
Truitt), Martin Donovan (Bill Truitt),
Lisa Kudrow (Lucia Dalury), Lyle
Lovett (Sheriff Carl Tippett) and
Johnny Galecki (Jason Bock).

Party Girl (1995, U.S.)

Written by: Daisy von Scherler Mayer
and Harry Brickmayer. *Produced by:*
Harry Brickmayer and Stephanie
Koules. *Directed by:* Daisy Von Scherler
Mayer. *Production Company:* Party
Pictures Inc. *Studio:* First Look Pic-
tures. *Genre:* Drama, Comedy. *Rating:*
R. *Cast:* Parker Posey (Mary), Guil-
lermo Diaz (Leo), Omar Townsend
(Mustafa), Sasha von Scherler (Judy
Lindendorf), and Anthony De Sando
(Derrick).

The Princess Diaries (2001, U.S.)

Written by: Gina Wendkos. *Produced by:* Whitney Houston, Mario Iscovich and Debra Martin Chase. *Directed by:* Garry Marshall. *Production Company:* Walt Disney Pictures. *Studio:* Walt Disney Pictures. *Genre:* Comedy. *Rating:* G. *Cast:* Julie Andrews (Clarisse Renaldi), Anne Hathaway (Mia Thermopolis), Hector Elizondo (Joseph), Heather Matarazzo (Lilly Moscovitz) and Lana Thomas (Mandy Moore).

The Princess Diaries 2: Royal Engagement (2004, U.S.)

Written by: Gina Wendkos and Shonda Rhimes. *Produced by:* Whitney Houston, Mario Iscovich and Debra Martin Chase. *Directed by:* Garry Marshall. *Production Companies:* Brownhouse Productions and Walt Disney Pictures. *Studio:* Walt Disney Pictures. *Genre:* Comedy, Family. *Rating:* G. *Cast:* Julie Andrews (Clarisse Renaldi), Anne Hathaway (Mia Thermopolis), Hector Elizondo (Joe), John Rhys-Davies (Viscount Mabrey) and Heather Matarazzo (Lilly Moscovitz).

Raise Your Voice (2004, U.S.)

Written by: Mitch Rotter and Sam Schreiber. *Produced by:* David Brookwell, A.J. Dix, Sean McNamara, Anthony Rhulen, Sara Risher, William Shivley. *Directed by:* Sean McNamara. *Production Companies:* Brookwell-McNamara Entertainment, ChickFlicks, FilmEngine. *Studio:* New Line Cinema. *Genre:* Drama, Music. *Rating:* PG. *Cast:* Hilary Duff (Terri Fletcher), Oliver James (Jay Corgan), David Keith (Simon Fletcher), Dana Davis (Denise Gilmore), Johnny Davis (Kiwi Wilson), Rita Wilson (Francis Fletcher).

Reality Bites (1994, U.S.)

Written by: Helen Childress. *Produced by:* Danny DeVito, Michael Shamberg. *Di-* *rected by:* Ben Stiller. *Production Companies:* Jersey Films, Universal Pictures. *Studio:* MCA/Universal Pictures. *Genre:* Comedy, Drama. *Rating:* PG-13. *Cast:* Winona Ryder (Leilana Pierce), Ethan Hawke (Troy Dyer), Janeane Garofalo (Vickie Miner), Steve Zahn (Sammy Gray), Ben Stiller (Michael Grates).

Rebel Without a Cause (1955, U.S.)

Written by: Stewart Stern. *Produced by:* David Weisbart. *Directed by:* Nicholas Ray. *Production Company:* Warner Bros. *Studio:* Warner Bros. *Genre:* Drama. *Rating:* NR. *Cast:* James Dean (Jim), Natalie Wood (Judy), Sal Mineo (Plato), Jim Backus (Jim's dad) and Ann Doran (Jim's mom).

Riding in Cars with Boys (2001, U.S.)

Written by: Morgan Upton Ward. *Produced by:* James L. Brooks, Laurence Mark, Sara Colleton, Richard Sakai and Julie Ansell. *Directed by:* Penny Marshall. *Production Company:* Gracie Films. *Studio:* Columbia Pictures. *Genre:* Drama. *Rating:* PG-13. *Cast:* Drew Barrymore (Beverly Donofrio), Steve Zahn (Ray Hasek), Brittany Murphy (Fay Forrester), Adam Garcia (Jason at the age of 20) and Lorraine Bracco (Mrs. Donofrio).

Ripe (1997, U.S.)

Written by: Mo Ogrodnik. *Produced by:* Suzy Landa and Tom Razzano. *Directed by:* Mo Ogrodnik. *Production Companies:* Ripe Productions and C&P Capitol. *Studio:* Trimark. *Genre:* Drama. *Rating:* R. *Cast:* Monica Keena (Violet), Daisy Eagan (Rosie), Gordon Currie (Pete), Ron Brice (Ken) and Vincent Laresca (Jimmy).

Save the Last Dance (2001, U.S.)

Written by: Duane Adler and Cheryl Edwards. *Produced by:* Robert W. Cort and

David Madden. *Directed by:* Thomas Carter. *Production Companies:* MTV Films, Cort/Madden Productions and Paramount. *Studio:* Paramount. *Genre:* Romance, Drama. *Rating:* PG-13. *Cast:* Julia Stiles (Sara Johnson), Sean Patrick Thomas (Derek), Kerry Washington (Chenille), Fredro Starr (Malakai), Terry Kinney (Roy) and Bianca Lawson (Nikki).

Saved! (2004, U.S.)

Written by: Brian Dannelly and Michael Urban. *Produced by:* Michael Ohoven, Sandy Stern, Michael Stipe, William Vince. *Directed by:* Brian Dannelly. *Production Companies:* Infinity International Entertainment, James Forsyth Casting Inc., Single Cell Pictures. *Studio:* Metro-Goldwyn-Mayer, United Artists. *Genre:* Comedy, Drama. *Rating:* PG-13. *Cast:* Mandy Moore (Hilary Faye), Jena Malone (Mary), Macaulay Culkin (Roland), Patrick Fugit (Patrick), Heather Matarazzo (Tia).

Scary Movie (2000, U.S.)

Written by: Phil Beauman, Jason Friedberg, Buddy Johnson, Aaron Seltzer, Keenen Ivory Wayans, Marlon Wayans and Shawn Wayans. *Produced by:* Keenen Ivory Wayans, Eric L. Gold and Lee R. Mayes. *Directed by:* Keenen Ivory Wayans. *Production Companies:* Brillstein-Grey Entertainment, Gold/Miller Productions and Dimension. *Studio:* Miramax. *Genre:* Comedy, Horror. *Rating:* R. *Cast:* Shawn Wayans (Ray), Marlon Wayans (Shorty), Cheri Oteri (Gail Hailstrom), Anna Faris (Cindy Campbell), Shannon Elizabeth (Buffy) and Carmen Electra (Drew Decker).

Scream (1996, U.S.)

Written by: Kevin Williamson. *Produced by:* Cathy Konrad and Cary Woods. *Directed by:* Wes Craven. *Production Companies:* Dimension Films and Miramax. *Studio:* Miramax. *Genre:* Horror, Comedy, Teen. *Rating:* R. *Cast:* Neve Campbell (Sidney Prescott), Courtney Cox Ar-

quette (Gale Weathers), David Arquette (Dewy Riley), Skeet Ulrich (Billy Loomis), Rose McGowan (Tatum Riley) and Jamie Kenney (Randy).

Secretary (2002, U.S.)

Written by: Erin Cressida Wilson, Mary Gaitskill. *Produced by:* Andrew Fierberg, Amy Hobby, Steven Shainberg. *Directed by:* Steven Shainberg. *Production Companies:* Slough Pond, TwoPoundBag Productions, Double A Films. *Studio:* Lions Gate Films. *Genre:* Drama. *Rating:* PG. *Cast:* Maggie Gyllenhaal (Lee Holloway), James Spader (E. Edward Grey), Jeremy Davies (Peter), Lesley Ann Warren (Joan Holloway).

Shake, Rattle and Rock (1994, U.S.)

Written by: Trish Soodik. *Produced by:* Lou Arkoff and Debra Hill. *Directed by:* Allan Arkush. *Production Company:* Miramax Films. *Studio:* Columbia Tristar. *Genre:* Musical, Comedy. *Rating:* PG-13. *Cast:* Renee Zellweger (Susan), Patricia Childress (Cookie), Max Perlich (Tony) and Latanyia Baldwin (Sireena).

She's All That (1999, U.S.)

Written by: R. Lee Fleming Jr. *Produced by:* Robert L. Levy, Peter Abrams and Richard N. Gladstein. *Directed by:* Robert Iscove. *Production Companies:* Tapestry Films, Miramax Films and FilmColony. *Studio:* Miramax. *Genre:* Romance, Comedy. *Rating:* PG-13. *Cast:* Freddie Prinze Jr. (Zack Siler), Rachael Leigh Cook (Laney Boggs), Matthew Lillard (Brock Hudson), Paul Walker (Dean Sampson), Gabrielle Union (Katie) and Jodi Lyn O'Keefe (Taylor Vaughan).

Show Me Love (1998, Sweden)

Written by: Lukas Moodysson. *Produced by:* Lars Jonsson. *Directed by:* Lukas Moodysson. *Production Companies:* Sveriges Television Drama Goteborg,

Memfis Film & Television, Swedish Film Institute, Danish Film Institute, Film i Vast and Zantropa Productions. *Studio:* Strand Releasing. *Genre:* Comedy, Romance. *Rating:* NR. *Cast:* Alexandra Dahlstrom (Elin), Rebecca Liljeberg (Agnes), Erica Carlson (Jessica), Mathias Rust (Johan) and Stefan Horberg (Markus).

Slums of Beverly Hills (1998, U.S.)

Written by: Tamara Jenkins. *Produced by:* Michael Nozik and Stan Wlodkowski. *Directed by:* Tamara Jenkins. *Production Companies:* South Fork Pictures and Fox Searchlight. *Studio:* Fox Searchlight. *Genre:* Comedy, Drama. *Rating:* R. *Cast:* Natasha Lyonne (Vivian), Alan Arkin (Murray), Marisa Tomei (Rita), Kevin Corrigan (Eliot) and Jessica Walter (Doris).

The Smokers (2000, U.S., Germany)

Written by: Christina Peters. *Produced by:* Quincy Jones. *Directed by:* Christina Peters. *Production Companies:* International Production Company. *Studio:* United Artists (MGM). *Genre:* Comedy, Teen. *Rating:* R. *Cast:* Dominique Swain (Jefferson), Busy Phillips (Karen) and Keri Lynn Pratt (Lisa).

Smooth Talk (1985, U.S.)

Written by: Tom Cole. *Produced by:* Martin Rosen. *Directed by:* Joyce Chopra. *Production Companies:* Nepenthe and American Playhouse. *Studio:* Spectafilm. *Genre:* Drama. *Rating:* PG-13. *Cast:* Treat Williams (Arnold Friend), Laura Dern (Connie), Mary Kay Place (Katherine), Elizabeth Berridge (June) and Levon Helm (Harry).

Splendor (1999, U.S.)

Written by: Gregg Araki. *Produced by:* Gregg Araki, Damian Jones and Graham Broadbent. *Directed by:* Gregg Araki. *Production Companies:* Newmarket Capital Group, Desperate Pictures and Dragon Pictures. *Studio:* Samuel Goldwyn. *Genre:* Romance, Comedy. *Rating:* R. *Cast:* Johnathon Schaech (Abel), Matt Keeslar (Zed), Kathleen Robertson (Veronica), Kelly Macdonald (Mike) and Eric Mabius (Ernest).

Splendor in the Grass (1961, U.S.)

Written by: William Inge. *Produced by:* Elia Kazan. *Directed by:* Elia Kazan. *Production Companies:* NBI and Newton. *Studio:* Warner Bros. *Genre:* Drama. *Rating:* NR. *Cast:* Natalie Wood (Wilma Dean Loomis), Warren Beatty (Bud Stamper), Pat Hingle (Ace Stamper), Audrey Christie (Mrs. Loomis) and Barbara Loden (Ginny Stamper).

Stranger Inside (2001, U.S.)

Written by: Catherine Crouch, Cheryl Dunye. *Produced by:* Effie Brown, Jim McKay, Michael Stipe. *Directed by:* Cheryl Dunye. *Production Companies:* C-Hundred Film Corporation, HBO Studios, Stranger Baby Productions. *Studio:* HBO Films. *Genre:* Drama. *Rating:* (TV). *Cast:* Yolanda Ross (Treasure), Davenia McFadden (Brownie), Rain Phoenix (Kit), Ella Joyce (Doodle Alderidge), Conchata Ferrell (Mama Cass).

10 Things I Hate About You (1999, U.S.)

Written by: Karen McCullah Lutz and Kirsten Smith. *Produced by:* Andrew Lazar. *Directed by:* Gil Junger. *Production Companies:* Mad Chance and Touchstone Pictures. *Studio:* Buena Vista and Touchstone Pictures. *Genre:* Romance, Comedy. *Rating:* PG-13. *Cast:* Julia Stiles (Kat Stratford), Heath Ledger (Patrick Verona), Joseph Gordon-Levitt (Cameron), Larisa Oleynik (Bianca Stratford), David Krumholtz (Michael Eckman), Gabrielle Union (Chastity) and Andrew Keegan (Joey Donner).

Thirteen (2003, U.S.)

Written by: Catherine Hardwicke, Nikki Reed. *Produced by:* Jeffrey Levy-Hinte, Michael London. *Directed by:* Catherine Harwicke. *Production Companies:* Michael London Productions, Antidote Films. *Studio:* Fox Searchlight Pictures. *Genre:* Drama. *Rating:* R. *Cast:* Holly Hunter (Melanie), Evan Rachel Wood (Tracy Louise), Nikki Reed (Evie), Jeremy Sisto (Brady).

13 Going on 30 (2004, U.S.)

Written by: Josh Goldsmith and Cathy Yuspa. *Produced by:* Susan Arnold and Allegra Clegg. *Directed by:* Gary Winick. *Production Companies:* Revolution Studios and Thirteen Productions, LLC. *Studio:* Sony Pictures Entertainment and Columbia Pictures. *Genre:* Comedy, Drama, Romance. *Rating:* PG-13. *Cast:* Jennifer Garner (Jenna Rink), Mark Ruffalo (Matt Flamhaff), Judy Greer (Lucy Wyman), Andy Serkis (Richard Kneeland), Kathy Baker (Bev Rink), Samuel Ball (Alex Carlson).

The Virgin Suicides (2000, U.S.)

Written by: Sofia Coppola. *Produced by:* Francis Ford Coppola, Chris Hanley, Dan Halsted and Julie Costanzo. *Directed by:* Sofia Coppola. *Production Companies:* American Zoetrope, Muse, Eternity and Illusion. *Studio:* Paramount Classics. *Genre:* Drama. *Rating:* R. *Cast:* James Woods (Mr. Lisbon), Kathleen Turner (Mrs. Lisbon), Kirsten Dunst (Lux), Josh Hartnett (Trip Fontaine) and Hanna Hall (Cecilia).

Virtual Sexuality (1999, U.S.)

Written by: Chloe Rayban, Nick Fisher. *Produced by:* Christopher Figg. *Directed by:* Nick Hurran. *Production Companies:* The Noel Gay Motion Picture Company. *Studio:* Columbia Pictures. *Genre:* Comedy, Drama. *Rating:* R. *Cast:* Laura Fraser (Justine), Rupert Penry-Jones (Jake),

Luke de Lacey (Chas), Kieran O'Brien (Alex), Laura Aikman (Lucy).

Welcome to the Dollhouse (1995, U.S.)

Written by: Todd Solondz. *Produced by:* Todd Solondz. *Directed by:* Todd Solondz. *Production Company:* Suburban Pictures. *Studio:* Sony Pictures Classics. *Genre:* Comedy, Drama. *Rating:* R. *Cast:* Heather Matarazzo (Dawn Wiener), Brendan Sexton III (Brandon McCarthy), Daria Kalinina (Missy Wiener), Mathew Faber (Mark Wiener) and Angela Pietropinto (Mrs. Wiener).

What a Girl Wants (2003, U.S.)

Written by: Jenny Bicks and Elizabeth Chandler. *Produced by:* Hunt Lowry, Bill Gerber and Denise Di Novi. *Directed by:* Dennie Gordon. *Production Companies:* Gaylord Films, Di Novi Pictures and Gerber Pictures. *Studio:* Warner Bros. *Genre:* Comedy, Romance, Family. *Rating:* PG. *Cast:* Amanda Bynes (Daphne), Colin Firth (Henry Dashwood), Kelly Preston (Libby Reynolds), Eileen Atkins (Jocelyn Dashwood) and Anna Chancellor (Glynnis).

Whatever (1998, U.S.)

Written by: Susan Skoog. *Produced by:* Michelle Yahn, Susan Skoog, Ellin Baumel and Kevin Segalla. *Directed by:* Susan Skoog. *Production Companies:* Circle/DuArt Films and Anyway Productions. *Studio:* Sony Pictures Classics. *Genre:* Drama. *Rating:* R. *Cast:* Liza Weil (Anna Stockyard), Chad Morgan (Brenda Talbot), Frederic Forrest (Mr. Chaminsky), Gary Wolf (Eddi) and Kathy Rossetter (Carol Stockyard).

Whatever It Takes (2000, U.S.)

Written by: Mark Schwahn. *Produced by:* Paul Schiff. *Directed by:* David Raynr. *Production Companies:* Paul Schiff, I'll Be

You and Phoenix Pictures. *Studio:* Sony Pictures. *Genre:* Romance, Comedy. *Rating:* PG-13. *Cast:* Jodi Lyn O'Keefe (Ashley Grant), Shane West (Ryan Woodman), Marla Sokoloff (Maggie), Manu Intiraymi (Dunleavy), Aaron Paul (Floyd) and James Franco (Chris Campbell).

Where the Boys Are (1960, U.S.)

Written by: George Wells. *Produced by:* Joe Pasternak. *Directed by:* Henry Levin. *Production Company:* Euterpe. *Studio:* MGM. *Genre:* Comedy. *Rating:* NR. *Cast:* Dolores Hart (Merrit Andrews), George Hamilton (Ryder Smith), Yvette Mimieux (Melanie Coleman), Jim Hutton (TV Thompson) and Barbara Nichols (Lola).

Where the Heart Is (2000, U.S.)

Written by: Lowell Ganz and Babaloo Mandel. *Produced by:* Patricia Whitcher, Matt Williams, David McFadzean and Susan Cartsonis. *Directed by:* Matt Williams. *Production Company:* Wind Dancer. *Studio:* 20th Century–Fox. *Genre:* Romance, Drama. *Rating:* PG-13. *Cast:* Natalie Portman (Novalee Nation), Ashley Judd (Lexie Coop), Stockard Channing ("Sister" Husband), Joan Cusack (Ruth Meyers) and James Frain (Forney Hall).

Wicked (1998, U.S.)

Written by: Eric Weiss. *Produced by:* Frank Beddor. *Directed by:* Michael Steinberg. *Production Company:* Frankstein Entertainment. *Studio:* Columbia, Tristar Studios. *Genre:* Thriller. *Rating:* R. *Cast:* Julia Stiles (Ellie Christianson), William R. Moses (Ben Christianson), Patrick Muldoon (Lawson Smith), Vanessa Zima (Inger Christianson) and Michael Parks (Detective Boland).

BIBLIOGRAPHY

Some of these are sources I have cited. Others are resources for readers who want to know more about girls' film, girls' culture, and popular culture generally.

Bernard, Jami. *Chick Flicks: A Movie Lovers Guide to the Movies Women Love*. Secaucus, NJ: Carol, 1996.
Bitch Magazine: Feminist Response to Pop Culture. www.bitchmagazine.com.
Breier, Helga. "Special Report: TeenScreen: SmartGirl Web site in the know about teenage girls." *Kidscreen*. April 1, 1998.
Brown, Lyn Mikel. *Raising Their Voices: The Politics of Girls' Anger*. Cambridge, MA: Harvard University Press, 1998.
Bundy, Clare, et al. *Girls on Film: The Highly Opinionated, Completely Subjective Guide to the Movies*. New York: Harper Perennial, 1999.
Davis, Angela Y. *Are Prisons Obsolete?* New York: Seven Stories Press, 2003.
Docherty, Neil, producer and director. "The Merchants of Cool." Produced by WGBH for *Frontline*. Boston: WGBH Educational Foundation. Distributed by PBS Video, 1999.
Douglas, Susan. *Where the Girls Are: Growing Up Female with the Mass Media*. New York: Random House, 1994.
Driscoll, Catherine. *Girls: Feminine Adolescence in Popular Culture and Cultural Theory*. New York: Columbia University Press, 2002.
Dunn, Jancee. "The Secret Life of Teenage Girls." *Rolling Stone*. November 11, 1999.
Easton, Dossie, and Catherine A. Liszt. *The Ethical Slut: A Guide to Infinite Sexual Possibilities*. San Francisco, CA: Greenery Press, 1998.
Ford, Elizabeth A., and Mitchell, Deborah C. *The Makeover in Movies: Before and After in Hollywood Films, 1941–2002*. Jefferson, NC: McFarland, 2001.
Genovese, Catrina. "The Secret Lives of Teens." *Life* Magazine, March 1999.
Giroux, Henry. *Channel Surfing: Racism, The Media, and the Destruction of Today's Youth*. New York: St. Martin's Griffin, 1997.
Haag, Pamela. *Voices of a Generation: Teenage Girls Report About Their Lives Today*. New York: Marlowe, 2000.
Hebdige, Dick. *Subculture and the Meaning of Style*. London and New York: Routledge, 1979.
Hersch, Patricia. *A Tribe Apart: A Journey Into the Heart of American Adolescence*. New York: Ballantine Books, 1998.
hooks, bell. "bell hooks: Cultural Criticism and Transformation." Produced and

directed by Sut Jhally. Northampton, MA: Media Education Foundation, 1997.

Inness, Sherrie A. *Delinquents and Debutantes: Twentieth-Century American Girls' Culture*. New York: New York University Press, 1998.

Jowett, Garth, and James M. Linton. *Movies as Mass Communication*. Beverly Hills: Sage, 1980.

Karlyn, Karen Rowe. "*Scream*, Popular Culture, and Feminism's Third Wave: 'I'm Not My Mother.'" Genders: Presenting innovative theories in art, literature, history, music, TV and film. Issue 38. 2003 http://www.genders.org.g38g38rowekarlyn.html

Kearney, Mary Celeste. "'Don't Need You': Rethinking Identity Politics and Separatism from a Grrrl Perspective." From *Youth Culture: Identity in a Postmodern World*, edited by Jonathon S. Epstein. Malden, MA: Blackwell, 1998. 148–9.

Kirberger, Kimberly. "Are Today's Teens Different?" *Life* Magazine, March 1999.

Koch, Patricia Barthalow, and David L. Weis. *Sexuality in America: Understanding Our Sexual Values and Behavior*. New York: Continuum, 1998.

Kuhn, Annette. *The Power of the Image: Essays on Representation and Sexuality*. London: Routledge & Kegan Paul, 1985.

Lewis, Jon. *The Road to Romance and Ruin: Teen Films and Youth Culture*. New York: Routledge, 1992.

Lipsitz, George. *A Possessive Investment in Whiteness: How White People Benefit from Identity Politics*. Philadelphia: Temple University Press, 1998.

Ma, Sheng-Mei. "Mulan Disney, It Like Re-Orients: Consuming China and Animating Teen Dreams." *The Emperor's Old Groove: Decolonizing Disney's Magic Kingdom*. Brenda Ayers, ed. New York: Peter Lang, 2003.

Mahdi, Louise Carus. Introduction. *Crossroads: The Quest for Contemporary Rites of Passage*. Louise Carus Mahdi, Nancy Geyer Christopher, Michael Meade, eds. Chicago: Open Court, 1996.

Maio, Kathi. *Feminist in the Dark: Reviewing the Movies*. Freedom, CA: The Crossing Press, 1988.

Males, Mike. *The Scapegoat Generation: America's War on Adolescents*. Monroe, ME: Common Courage Press, 1996.

Mann, Judy. *The Difference: Growing up Female in America*. New York: Warner Books, 1994.

Martin, Karin A. *Puberty, Sexuality, and the Self: Boys and Girls at Adolescence*. New York: Routledge, 1996.

Mazzarella, Sharon R., and Norma O. Pecora, eds. *Growing Up Girls: Popular Culture and the Construction of Identity*. Adolescent Cultures, School, and Society. New York: Peter Lang, 1999.

McKeever, William A. *Training the Girl*. New York: Macmillan, 1914.

McRobbie, Angela, and Jenny Garber. "Girls and Subcultures." *The Subcultural Reader*. Ken Gelder and Sarah Thornton, eds. New York: Routledge, 1997.

Miranda, Marie "Keta." *Home Girls in the Public Sphere*. Austin: University of Texas Press, 2003.

Modleski, Tania. *Loving with a Vengeance: Mass-Produced Fantasies for Women*. New York: Routledge, 1982.

Mosse, Julia Cleaves. *Half the World, Half a Chance*. UK and Ireland: Oxfam, 1993.

Nathanson, Constance A. *Dangerous Passage: The Social Control of Sexuality in Women's Adolescence*. Philadelphia: Temple University Press, 1991.

Odem, Mary E. *Delinquent Daughters: Protecting and Policing Adolescent Female Sexuality in the United States, 1885–1920*. Chapel Hill: University of North Carolina Press, 1995.

Palladino, Grace. *Teenagers: An American History*. New York: Basic Books, 1996.
Pardo, Mary S. *Mexican American Women Activists: Identity and Resistance in Two Los Angeles Communities*. Philadelphia: Temple University Press, 1998.
Peske, Nancy, and Beverly West. *Advanced Cinematherapy: The Girls' Guide to Finding Happiness One Movie at a Time*. New York: Dell, 2002.
Pipher, Mary. *Reviving Ophelia: Saving the Selves of Adolescent Girls*. New York: Ballantine, 1994.
Pribram, Deidre. *Female Spectators: Looking at Film and TV*. London: Verso, 1998.
Reel Grrls. www.911media.org/youth/reelgrrls.html
Rich, B. Ruby. *Chick Flicks: Theories and Memories of the Feminist Film Movement*. Durham, NC: Duke University Press, 1998.
Sandhu, Sabeen. "Instant Karma: The Commercialization of Asian Indian Culture." *Asian American Youth: Culture, Identity, and Ethnicity*. Jennifer Lee and Min Zhou, eds. New York: Routledge, 2004.
Sandoval, Chela. *Methodology of the Oppressed*. Minneapolis: University of Minnesota Press, 2000.
Screen. *The Sexual Subject: A Screen Reader in Sexuality*. New York: Routledge, 1992.
Shandler, Sara. *Ophelia Speaks: Adolescent Girls Write About Their Search for Self*. New York: Harper Collins, 1999.
Smith, Linda Tuhiwai. *Decolonizing Methodology: Research and Indigenous Peoples*. London and New York: Zed Books; Dunedin, N.Z.: University of Otago Press; New York: Distributed in the USA exclusively by St. Martin's Press, 1999.
Stanford, Gene, ed. *Generation Rap: An Anthology about Youth and the Establishment*. New York, Dell, 1971.
Starr, Oliver Jr. "Teen Girls are Easy Prey for Over-20 Predators." *New World Communications, Inc.* Insight on the News. May 3, 1999.
Tanenbaum, Leora. *Slut! Growing Up Female with a Bad Reputation*. New York: Seven Stories Press, 1999.
Williams, Linda. "When the Woman Looks," from *Re-Vision: Essays in Feminist Film Criticism*. Los Angeles: University Publications of America, 1984.
Wurtzel, Elizabeth. *Bitch: In Praise of Difficult Women*. New York, Doubleday, 1998.

INDEX